Writing the College Essay

A Handbook and Workbook in Composition, Research, and Grammar

Fourth Edition

W 92
42.0

■ **James D. Zamagias** ■

Allegany College of Maryland
Cumberland, Maryland

KENDALL/HUNT PUBLISHING COMPANY
4050 Westmark Drive   Dubuque, Iowa   52002

___■ Contents ■___

Part 2 A Concise Handbook of Grammar   215

___■ Preface ■___

To the instructor

After thirty years of teaching the English language to college freshmen and sophomores, I finally decided to write a text which addresses specific problems students confront each time they attempt to write a composition. I do not regard myself as the anointed one inspired by divine will in setting about such a task, for there are many fine textbooks on the market today that deal with writing. Nevertheless, it has been my experience that too many texts are lacking in some area, specifically, sufficient exercises that reinforce classroom instruction. For instance, I have yet to examine an English textbook that deals *in depth* (or even correctly) with the outline or with research paper topics. Too many texts present material which students generally find boring. Dull, insipid rhetorics and grammars are guaranteed to alienate students. Therefore, I have included essays written by *teachers and students,* essays and exercises which provide interest, humor, and wit. The selections in my revised edition are models of clarity and conciseness, qualities classroom teachers value and students understand.

Here are a few of the special features of the revised edition:

■ Content—ease of comprehension
■ Contemporary subject matter—essays that reflect student interest, for instance, MTV and Rock Music themes
■ Broader scope of essays—writing strategies which culminate in a successful research paper
■ Class discussion sections—designed to aid the instructor in improving the student's writing and speaking skills
■ Extended section on sentence combining—subordination, noun clause strategies, absolutes, appositives
■ Expanded section on etymology—designed to aid the instructor in improving the student's vocabulary
■ Updated material on MLA and APA forms
■ Updated information on documentation online

This revised edition should provide more effective and complete information to enable you to deal successfully with the problems of the beginning writer.

To the student

Since we spend most of our lives communicating, you need to be skillful in a complicated process that may determine your success in college or on the job—writing. Regardless of your role in life, people react to you according to the way in which you talk and write. This text is designed for the practical study of basic English skills to meet your needs. A broad selection of topics permits your instructor to select those of interest to you. The exercises and suggested activities are an important feature which will give you additional practice in mastering fundamental principles in grammar and in writing the essay. I have tried to make the study of English composition as painless as possible by presenting a revised text which you will find easy to comprehend, interesting, and practical. But my real concern is improving your writing ability to thereby insure your success in the classroom. Ultimately, that success, or failure, will affect your ability to communicate in the "real" world of business and industry, of the legal and medical fields, and in the arts.

Acknowledgments

This text is unique in several ways. All of the material is based on papers written by students and faculty at Allegany Community College. I am grateful to my colleagues in the English Department for their contributions: Colleen Buckley, Noreen Hayes, Norman Kelley, and Joe Madden. I thank Dr. Frank Hager, Professor of Psychology, for his contributions. I am also indebted to Ms. Nan Putnam for her exercises in library research and in writing the summary. Other members of the department who advised and encouraged me include Janet Cook, Carolyn Kershaw, and Jon Loff. My special thanks go to Dr. Jack Shreve, Professor of English and Spanish, who helped prepare the expanded sections on the Outline and Etymology. Professor Dudley Brown, a syndicated columnist, contributed many of his personal essays. I am indebted to Mr. Matt Marafino for his assistance in writing the chapter on Argument/Persuasion. I thank all of my colleagues for their assistance.

I thank Ms. Carolyn Bond for designing the cover of this text and previous editions. Her work is fantastic. Ms. Mona Clites, of the Allegany College library, basically wrote and re-wrote the chapter on library research and helped me greatly with the fast-moving computer reference section. I owe her a great deal for her invaluable assistance.

I also wish to acknowledge those students who contributed to the compilation of my book: Mark Armstrong, Jim Kerns, Chris McGreevey, Bill Ultis, Chris Thompson, Rhonda Loar, Shirley Pratt, Mary Repsher, Frances Robertson, Cindy Rotruck, and Sally Berkebile.

I dedicate this edition to my wife, Sally.

1

Writing the College Essay

- Physical Description
- Narration
- Characterization
- Process
- Comparison and Contrast
- Classification
- Definition
- Cause and Effect
- Outline
- Research
- Cover Letter
- Resume

Chapter 1

Writing as a Skill

There are, no doubt, hundreds of books on the market today that deal with writing: grammar texts, composition and rhetoric texts, technical writing texts, creative writing texts, manuals, ad infinitum. Many of these "how to write" books are valuable. Not only have educators recognized the need for such information on an academic level, but they have come to realize the increasing demands by the business, legal, and medical professions for employees who are literate and capable of writing clearly and intelligently.

Writing and re-writing

Yet, in spite of the need for such instruction, the only way a writer *learns* to write is *by* writing. Studying books on writing is valuable, necessary, and should be encouraged. But only by writing—and re-writing—does one learn the craft of writing. It has been said that there "is no such thing as good writing, only good re-writing." The point is that writing demands work, "hard" work, which is not so much the product of genius (which it may be), but more often the result of logical organization, careful attention to detail, and correct English usage. Writing is a calculated, deliberate intellectual effort, especially in a form called the essay, literally from the French *essais*, "to try."

Getting started

The appropriate question follows: "To try what?" A writer must clearly formulate in his mind the thesis (central idea, subject, topic, point, moral) of his essay before he dares to commit one word on paper. Even such archaic juvenile topics as "How I Spent My Summer Vacation" should have a focus or point of view. Was that vacation enjoyable, dreadful, or simply boring? But, in the final analysis, who really cares about

3

how that student spent his summer vacation? Insipid topics, clichés, and trite expressions reflect lazy, sloppy thinking. Too many students depend on such reliable crutches in attempting to express themselves in college compositions. The dismal results of such reflexive writing are mediocrity and, more often, failure. Novice writers, generally, are too anxious to employ tired phrases and ideas passed on to them through the formative years and for which they were patted on their collective heads as a reward.

Pre-writing: listing

Many essays are poorly planned because the writers do not take time to decide what to include and what to leave out. Often, they write whatever comes into their minds about the topic without deciding what is actually important enough to include. Faced with time pressure or a deadline, many students apparently feel they must actually be writing every minute or they will not finish. There seems to be a frantic psychological need that the empty page is covered with words; to some, any word will do.

In recent years, a number of "pre-writing" or "brainstorming" techniques have been introduced into textbooks to help students select what points to include and what to leave out. Most writers need to be aware of *selectivity*, the process of realizing that some points are worth including, and some not. Approximately half a dozen pre-writing methods force the student to think about his topic and to jot down some preliminary ideas before he starts writing. Some teachers have begun to set aside considerable pre-writing time, often a whole class period. Some teachers also require that the pre-writing be handed in with the essay. By looking at the pre-writing, the teacher can sometimes see how the essay came about.

Recently, several classes, totalling about 100 students, tried three methods of pre-writing and then voted on which method was most useful in writing their essays. The overwhelming favorite was also the simplest: *listing* . . . which takes little time and adds immensely to the content and order of the essay.

Listing can be done with or without a time limit. It can also be done individually or in cooperative groups of two or three students, who will work on each other's topics. The listing described here is the writer's next step after choosing his topic; but listing can also assist in choosing a topic. If the student has time, he might apply listing to two or three prospective topics to determine which one seems to be the most effective.

This writer will now demonstrate listing exactly as it is practiced. I will choose a topic and write down, as fast as I can, everything that comes into my head about that topic. While listing, I do not worry about order or importance—that comes later.

The topic is MTV. In four minutes, here is everything I can think about MTV:

1. Celebrated its fifth anniversary in 1986

2. Increased sales of many records

3. Repeats same videos too often

4. Accused of racism

5. Controversial videos—violence, sex, parental objection

6. Damages music? Helps music?

7. Personalities of veejays—imitating

8. Needs more experimentation and variety, too conservative

9. Necessary to watch MTV to be aware of trends

10. Needs to change

11. Declining ratings and influence in 1986

Four minutes have passed. I have numbered eleven thoughts about MTV. Now, all eleven would be far too much material to cover in one essay. In fact, it would be possible to base an entire essay on almost any one of the above points. Or a writer could combine several points into one essay, possibly making each point a paragraph. For example, it would be possible to dredge enough material from the list for a Pro-MTV essay or an Anti-MTV essay—although more of the points are negative than positive.

Choosing topics

1. Most teachers offer a list of topics to the student. Sometimes these topics may have been drawn from student suggestions on topic requests. Assuming that you do have a choice of topics, the best advice is the old saying, "Write what you know." It's unwise to try to second-guess the teacher by writing on what you think is the teacher's favorite topic, or by writing what he presumably wants to read. This strategy often backfires, especially if you do not know the subject well.

2. Some students are comfortable only when the topics pertain to themselves, preferring to write "personal" essays. Others, more protective of their privacy, would rather write on impersonal subjects, ones not about themselves, their feelings, and experi-

ences. Hence, one student would choose the topic, "How I Overcame Shyness" or "Fighting with My Mother," while the second student would choose "Causes of Sylvester Stallone's Popularity," "Comparing Two Colleges," or "Defining Peace"— all topics outside himself. Some teachers may encourage or discourage personal or impersonal writing according to their individual preferences, but, ideally, a student should learn to do both well. Thus, the writer who excels at personal essays should learn to do the impersonal kind, and vice versa.

3. Not only in matters of topic selection, but in various areas of style and language, teachers do have individual preferences and their own lists of what to do and what to avoid. Teachers do not always agree on these matters, nor should they, but what they should do is make their preferences clear to the class. Therefore, students may wish to ask questions concerning topic selection and content early in the semester. For instance, and depending on the nature of the course, some teachers prefer students to adhere to the facts, especially in technical writing. Other teachers may encourage the free use of student opinion, while some may penalize it as inappropriate. So you need to find out about such requirements and then to abide by them.

4. Many students mistakenly assume, or complain, that teachers will penalize them because the teachers disagree with the students' opinions. How often have you heard someone say (or said yourself) that "He failed me because he didn't agree with what I said"? Probably, the teacher was not grading the opinions in the essay, but rather the manner in which the student presented those opinions. Simply follow instructions.

5. Many teachers have rules against use of the first person ("I"). Still other teachers forbid writing in the second person ("You"), while others allow you to write in any person that you wish—as long as you are consistent within the essay.

6. Some teachers permit contractions *(don't, can't)*; others strictly forbid contractions. Some teachers limit the number of "to be" verbs *(is, are, was)* used in an essay. Other teachers have no such limit. Most teachers have their own limits of avoidable or undesirable words. Some teachers have rules about whether to skip lines, or write on both sides of the paper, or how and where your name should be written. Others do not care about these matters, but sometimes disobeying these rules may affect your grade. The more a student can learn about these idiosyncrasies, the better chance he/she has to do well.

7. One commonly held misconception may be summed up in a student's complaint: "I like the way I write, but Mr. X doesn't." Realistically, the teacher gives instructions (and examples) and then grades according to how they are followed. This necessitates separating his personal likes from the grading process. The teacher may dislike a paper which is correct enough to earn a "good" grade. And he may like or admire some aspects of an incorrect paper which must receive a low grade.

The beginning, the middle, and the end

Writing is a guaranteed intellectual exercise. Aristotle's common sense approach to writing as balanced form still holds true today, over two thousand years later. It is simple logic to say, "Every essay should have a beginning, a middle, and an end." The axiom seems almost too naive, perhaps too simplistic, because novice writers have deliberately avoided practicing it in classrooms for centuries. Not only have freshmen composition students painstakingly avoided doing so, but they seem to defy, elude, and scorn it with cheerful relish.

Nevertheless, Aristotle's fundamental truth is the foundation of every well written essay. A writer must spell out the purpose of his essay at the *beginning*, usually the first sentence (in technical writing), or, at the very least, within the first paragraph. Stating the thesis clearly, the writer must commit himself definitely to a controlling idea. Attitude or point of view regarding the subject is all important. The writer must ask himself what his subject will be, what limits he will draw concerning its scope, and what he intends to maintain, immediately, at the beginning. What a writer must understand is that his reader, generally, is indifferent, if not hostile, to his point of view. To avoid confusing or misleading the reader, a writer must state his purpose clearly at the outset and in such a way that the reader *will want to read* further.

1. *Develop your own style in writing.*
   Put simply, style is the way you write. It is the combination of all rhetorical elements: sentence form and type, punctuation, diction, and tone. The individuality of the writer is reflected in his handling of the language to suit his ideas and personality.

2. *Avoid ambiguity in writing*
   Be specific. Avoid abstract, vague words. Use concrete ideas and words in expressing those ideas. Instead of writing, "He is very tall," be precise and concise: "He is six feet, ten inches tall." Perhaps the most overused and abused word in the English lan-

guage is "very." Other abstractions are *ugly, beautiful, fat, skinny, magnificent, breathtaking, gorgeous, fantastic,* and so on. Don't insult the reader's intelligence with generalities that reveal nothing about your subject.

If, on the other hand, you write a topic sentence such as "Pete was the ugliest student in our high school class," you are committed to support this thesis with concrete examples and facts. The rest of your essay should prove that statement with appropriate physical details.

Your composition should be *your* ideas on a particular subject and not a piece of plagiarism.

3. *State the central idea clearly.*
   Have a definite attitude (point of view) concerning your subject. Focus on your thesis, making sure that you cover it well and coherently. Be as complete as possible.

4. *Be logical.*
   Avoid arguing about subjective matters. Never make a statement that cannot be supported by facts. In particular, avoid the emotional pitfalls of religion and politics.

Many introductions are too short and abrupt. A one-sentence introduction is probably not enough, although many students insist on writing such short beginnings. The introduction should usually be at least three or four sentences, but occasionally the writer gets so carried away in the first paragraph that it extends into half or more of the paper. This is disproportionate and shows a lack of concern for organization.

Many students write awkward introductions to announce their intentions: "In this essay I will compare. . . ." "It is my intention to show how. . . ." "My purpose is to prove. . . ." These first-person announcements are totally lacking in originality or interest.

A turnabout paragraph contradicts its opening statement, proving it wrong. The main (true) idea is in the middle, disproving or changing the (false) opening statement. The remainder of the paragraph then supports the middle. More samples:

I expected . . . but instead

My friends say . . . but they are wrong

I used to think . . . but I changed my mind

It seemed to be . . . but instead

You might expect . . . but

Main idea at the end: "Climactic paragraph"

Example 1

First, I overslept. The alarm didn't go off. I couldn't find one shoe. I left the house without my keys or an umbrella; then it started pouring. At school, I had an argument with my girlfriend; then I failed an unannounced quiz in English. On the way home, a policeman ticketed me for speeding. *Without a doubt, this was my worst birthday ever.* (Main idea)

Everything before the last sentence is a list of examples which lead up to the main idea.

Example 2

I read reviews in every available magazine. I study music history books. I seek out life stories and interviews with performers. I follow and sometimes memorize the charts. *From all this, I understand the music I buy and learn what to buy next.* (Main idea)

Example 3

He lied. He cheated. He stole. He wrecked my car and lost all of my tapes. He copied from me at school and got me in trouble—*and that's how my best friend turned out to be my worst enemy.*

Main idea strategies

Many students have been taught that the main idea of a paragraph should always appear at the beginning—with everything after supporting the main idea. NOT necessarily. Sometimes the main idea may be placed in the middle or at the end of the paragraph. Students should learn the appropriate times to use such alternatives—to create variety in their writing.

Why would anyone want to move the main idea? Sometimes the main idea is not a sentence but a question, as in this very example. Starting a paragraph with a question is known as an *interrogative paragraph.* The question should be one which the reader may not already know the answer, one which will arouse curiosity.

Main idea in the middle: "Turnabout paragraph"

Example 1:

I thought that I was going to hate English class. In high school, English was my least favorite—full of rules and grammar, diagrams, and technical terms. *Imagine my surprise to find how different it is in college!* (Main idea) In college, English is full of jokes and thought provoking discussions. We have freedom of choice with only a few rules, quite reasonable ones. What a surprise! (Well, maybe you don't agree, but you get the idea!)

Example 2:

My mother thinks country music is "corny, twangy," and all about drinking and cheating. She adheres to old stereotypes from the past. She grew up in the '60s and would rather listen to classic rock or even modern music. *But I don't agree!* (Main idea) I have learned how sophisticated and complex modern country music can be. I love the lyrics and the beautiful voices of today's country singers. With some luck and a few concerts, I'll convert Mom.

Comments: A "climactic" paragraph should create a little suspense through a list of examples. From the beginning, each sentence should give another example, causing the reader to wonder what the paragraph is leading up to. (I know. I just ended a sentence with a preposition.) *Climactic* may also be a list ending with *most of all* or *above all.*

The *middle* or *body* of the essay should support your thesis. Do not digress. Learn to discuss one point at a time, logically and smoothly. Your reader should be able to move with you, particularly if you use transitional devices effectively. Remember that a paragraph is a concrete block of thought, an entity in itself, but related to all the other paragraphs in the essay. All of your paragraphs should move in one direction—validating your point of view.

Freshmen students usually begin their essays well, but they seem to bog down in the body of their essay. If you hope to avoid the chaotic middle, formulate an outline before you venture beyond the thesis. There are several ways that you can help yourself in this regard.

1. The topic sentence for each paragraph may be included in the very first paragraph; thus, the outline for the entire essay is established.

2. You may follow a chronological order or pattern, stipulating the order of events according to the time each event or step occurs.

3. You may follow a spatial pattern, dealing with the geographical or locational situation of the items. For instance, in the physical description of a room, you may describe the objects in that room as they appear from right to left, or vice versa.

4. You may deal with items or processes according to their order of importance, with the least important preceding or building up to the most important, which is usually reserved for the next to the

last paragraph. In describing a bedroom, for instance, you would not begin your composition with a description of the bed, because it is usually the most important piece of furniture in the room (for several reasons).

5. The last paragraph is usually reserved for the conclusion or a summary.

A *conclusion*, like the introduction, should not be too brief and should seldom be only one sentence. Many novice writers have a short conclusion or none at all because they have "run out" of time. They conclude the body of the paper and then hand it in. The teacher sometimes feels that he has lost a page of the paper that seems to have no ending.

If the conclusion is approximately the same length as the introduction, the paper will seem to have a pleasing symmetry. But the conclusion will be dull and uninspired if, as too often, the writer merely repeats the introduction word for word. True, the conclusion often summarizes or restates the main idea, but the writer should vary the wording to keep the conclusion interesting.

In the conclusion (or anywhere else), the writer should avoid apologizing for his inadequacy or incompleteness: "I'm sorry I didn't have time to cover other aspects of this topic"; "I didn't have time to discuss . . ."; "As I look over this I'm afraid I tried to cover too much." Such flaws, if they exist, should be left for the teacher to discover and note. Similarly, writers should avoid introducing new topics (usually called "after-thoughts") in a conclusion. Sometimes new subjects are suddenly brought into the final sentence in a vain attempt to appear me complete.

Too often, therefore, freshmen writers fail to conclude their essays properly. The end or conclusion of an essay is almost as important as the beginning, for it is the final impression that the writer leaves with the reader. Remember that the last section of an essay or report may be one of two types: the conclusion or the summary. Your conclusion may be one of three types.

1. An aesthetic conclusion brings your essay to a graceful close. Too many writers hurriedly end their essays with a hasty phrase or scribbled sentence trailing off the page, such writers apparently feeling that their mission has been accomplished. Do not end your essay abruptly but with skill and grace.

2. Your conclusion may present the results of your study or analysis, particularly in such papers as cause and effect, deduction-induction, or an investigation of a problem or issue.

3. Your conclusion may reflect a decision regarding a future course of action or propose recommendations that should be considered or followed.

Your final paragraph may be a summary

1. A summary restates the most important elements of your essay in a concise and brief manner.

2. Being a recapitulation of your main ideas, a summary should *not* present any new ideas or concepts.

Since a conclusion/summary is the final statement dealing with your subject, make sure that your parting comments leave a positive effect upon your reader.

Topics for discussion

Beginning writers often choose topics which are too broad for themes. Which of the following topics would make a "good" theme? Which do you consider to be poor? Why?

1. My first Job
2. Prostitution Should Be Legalized
3. My High School
4. Why I Hate English
5. College Social Life
6. My Favorite Television Program
7. Nuclear War
8. Cumberland Is a Beautiful City
9. Gambling in Atlantic City
10. Why I Will Never Get Married
11. Why I Love My Dog
12. My Father Is a Tyrant
13. Racial Problems
14. My Mother's Great Cooking
15. The Cause of My First Auto Wreck

The audience problem

One difficulty which confronts every student writer, and which, if unsolved, can damage many papers, is the "audience problem," an uncertainty on the writer's part about exactly to whom the paper should be addressed. A writer is unsure whether to write essays as though meant for a friend, a stranger, a peer, a boss or authority figure, or even an individual or a crowd. The student's puzzlement can result in various types of awkwardness, as in these sentences: "I'd like to give the ladies of America some advice" (which sounds absurd since they will not be reading it); or "All you guys out there, listen to me." Even such an introductory statement as "I'd like to tell you about . . ." seems jarring, and one student recently introduced himself by closing with, "That's all I can think of to say about this, so good-bye."

Usually, just one person (the teacher) will read the essay unless it is chosen to be reproduced for the class or even included as a textbook example. So it is unwise to write as though for a crowd or a group or even a gender (unless, of course, the assignment specifies it), nor is it necessary to address the reader directly with "tell you about" or salutations ("good-bye"). The writer should remember that, generally, he has one reader.

Another complication now arises due to teacher-student barriers. The writer's consciousness of the teacher (especially as judge, evaluator, grader) sometimes causes self-consciousness, an inability to relax. Most often, the result will be stiffly formal essays, filled with long or elaborate (and often mis-used words) which the student does not normally use. This "writing up" is an effort to rise to the teacher's perceived level, but it seldom succeeds or convinces. Thus, it is better when the student uses his everyday, if probably simpler vocabulary, occasionally enhanced by thesaurus usage. In other words, as nearly every textbook says, solve this part of the "audience problem" by writing naturally, not artificially.

But one can also write too naturally. To write naturally still requires being selective, since many of us are "naturally" given to slang and/or profanity which is inappropriate to college essay writing. Some teachers permit some slang; others none at all, and here it is best to find your teacher's policies and standards. Some teachers, for instance, would permit slang (and contractions like "don't" and "can't") only in humorous or informal essays, but not for more serious or formal essays and topics. However, few teachers will permit the use of profanity in any essay, and even fewer will accept obscenity. Yet it is surprising how many students think nothing of slipping the occasional "four-letter word" into an essay, and sometimes into otherwise dignified contexts.

Such matters as slang versus more formal language are frequently questions of *tone* or *mood.* An essay should sustain a consistent tone (feeling, emotional attitude). This means that, if you are writing a serious paper about death, illness, or religion, it would seem inappropriate to inject suddenly a joke or a slang word. Such lapses or changes of tone can be accomplished by experts and professionals, but few student writers are at that level of competence. Similarly, if you are writing a comical or even intentionally silly paper about a blind date or a wild party, it would startle the reader if you interrupted it with a few sentences of serious moralizing. Try to be consistent in mood. Consistency of mood requires a consistency of language levels, not a confused or changing mix of the formal versus the informal, the serious and the comical.

Some writers resort to childish or over-generalized language to express disapproval or approval, liking or disliking, or most judgments. For instance, some students put generic, meaningless, immature labels such as "garbage" or "stupid" on whatever they dislike. Sometimes a word like "garbage" or "stupid" turns up six times in the same paper, each time expressing dislike of something different. And other writers shower their papers with vaguely enthusiastic or overstated labels like "beautiful" or other empty superlatives which convey no specific quality.

A student once wrote this plaintive objection: "I don't see why we can't write the way we talk." This section has attempted to answer him and the many students who must have wondered why teachers are too "picky" about words. Most teachers (and editors and critics) are far more fussy about the written word than the spoken word; we may say things—with impunity—that we cannot write because writing has to be more "perfect." This is partly because, in speech, the words are not the only communication feature; in addition to the words themselves, the message is enhanced by body language, volume changes, expressions, and various kinds of emphasis. The words do not do all the work, as they must on paper. And we can ask a speaker to repeat or clarify a confusing point. The written word must be more perfect, more precisely and carefully chosen, more clear, because on paper the words do all of the work. And so, while we are ultimately urged to solve the "audience problem" by writing naturally, numerous reservations and cautions are still required.

Thinking critically

In order to convince the reader that your opinion is valid, or at least worth reading, you need to analyze your opinions. Similarly, in order to evaluate the validity of what you read (or hear), you must evaluate each point, which often means temporarily setting aside your own prejudices or emotions. This analytical ability is called *critical thinking*.

The discipline of critical thinking has, in recent years, become recognized as a major but hitherto neglected part of education. The subject is being introduced into many schools' curricula, and numerous textbooks have been written dealing exclusively with critical thinking as art, as discipline, as process, and so on. This rise to prominence of critical thinking may turn out to be one of the major educational developments of the eighties.

There are numerous obstacles which often prevent us from accurately evaluating our own writing, opinions, or those of others. A writer, or speaker, who wishes to be persuasive will learn to examine whatever he or she writes or says. Socrates (469-399 B.C.) said that "The unexamined life is not worth living." He meant that people must constantly question their lives, not live from day to day with no analysis. The same principle applies to writing, especially when the essay involves opinions. To paraphrase Socrates, "The unexamined opinion is not worth writing (or reading)."

Emotions: objectivity versus subjectivity

Emotions are one of the first barriers that a writer must hurdle. Few of us can help looking at issues subjectively (with our emotions) rather than objectively (rationally, unemotionally). Our likes, dislikes, prejudices, and other *feelings* often prevent us from reasonable analysis of what we write or read. Hence, we may reject someone else's writing which does not agree with our feelings or tastes. If we are "liberal," we reject any "conservative" statements. If we like MTV or favor capital punishment, we may immediately condemn an essay which is critical of MTV or capital punishment, however well written.

As it is necessary for teachers to set aside their biases and emotional attitudes in order to grade student essays fairly, it is equally necessary for students to overcome their own feelings to judge whether they are writing clearly. Sometimes this involves seeing both sides. The liberal writer must try to see the conservative point of view; the one who favors MTV or capital punishment must also consider arguments against it. If the writer plays the "Devil's Advocate" and tries to understand the opposing view, examining his own opinion with a hostile eye, he may perhaps arrange a more convincing case to support his beliefs.

Many of our emotions—destructive to convincing communication—are *ethnocentric:* characteristic feelings about our country, religion, race, town, school, team, or any other commitment or attachment to which we feel strong loyalty. If we dislike other races or religions, it is going to be difficult for us to write objectively or to read any essay which does not agree with our ethnocentrism. Therefore, the good writer, and the perceptive reader, must attempt the difficult mental feat of setting aside these long-held, sacred, but often unjustified, irrational feelings. The intellectual leap of getting past ethnocentrism is one of the most fundamental steps in *critical thinking.*

A. Discuss specific topics which may be difficult to write about because people may have strong emotions which will interfere with their writing objectively.

B. How many examples of ethnocentric thinking can the class name? Show how ethnocentrism could damage an essay in each instance.

Exercise

Make a list of subjects about which you might have trouble writing because of your own subjective feelings. For each subject, think of what the opposing view might say.

Individuality and critical thinking

Too often, instead of thinking out our own opinions, we passively accept those of others—parents, peers, or the media. Thus, we embrace stereotypes (often closely related to ethnocentrism), or new fashions and styles, or political views—not because we have examined such ideas, but because someone else wanted us to accept them. Then, our writing sometimes mindlessly parrots views which we did not question, but mimic unthinkingly from others. Critical thinking involves the ability to form and to defend our own views.

How many times have you "made fun" of someone that your friends think is odd or unusual—even if you privately thought that you might like the person? Often, the same type of conformity damages your writing: when we make a racist statement because we "inherited" racism from our parents; when we insult "punk" or country music because our friends don't like it; or when we write that the status quo is best because "We've always done it that way." Such thinking and writing constitute uncritical acceptance of others' views. How can we write a convincing essay when we are not convinced of the truth in what we say?

For class discussion

A. What are some of the ways students accept the thoughts of others? Discuss specifically how these examples can adversely affect writing.

B. How many ethnic, occupational, social, or other stereotypes can you name? In what ways can these stereotypes harm an essay? Do such stereotypes have many benefits for the writer?

C. Give examples of people you know who accept the status quo and reject the new. Discuss the pro's and con's of these attitudes. (Your examples might include parents, employers, friends. . . .)

Self-improvement exercise

Cite ways in which your attitudes/thinking have been influenced by others. How can you become more of an independent thinker?

Rationalization, honesty, and critical thinking

Sometimes we think, talk, and write with unconscious dishonesty, attempting to rationalize or justify some of our own limitations or tenuous, subjective opinions. A critical thinker is wary of essays in which the writer seems defensive, critical of others but not himself, finding scapegoats, or blaming someone else for whatever is "wrong." For instance, how often do parents blame each other (not themselves) whenever something goes wrong with the children? How many students always blame the teacher for a "bad" test whenever they get a low grade? How many drivers always seem to have an excuse for an accident? How many athletes are never to blame for losing the game? The honest writer will critically analyze situations, even if he may have to admit something disagreeable in the process. He avoids "face saving" or "passing the buck."

A particularly insidious form of rationalization occurs when we demean, mock, or otherwise malign a subject merely because we do not understand it or are secretly afraid it is beyond us. Most people who say (or write) that they do not like opera, Shakespeare, poetry, or ballet are actually people who know little or nothing about them, who perhaps fear them. Non-athletic people who criticize sports are guilty of the same hypocrisy. Ignorant criticism of such subjects is a form of intellectual dishonesty. If one feels uncomfortable with a subject, he should omit his prejudice in the essay. More profitably, he should try to get to understand his feelings and cope with motives regarding his prejudice.

For class discussion

What subjects or topics do you or your friends criticize or reject out of ignorance or fear? Why do so many people feel this way?

Choose one subject or topic which you "think" you dislike. Try to find out more about it. (If you dislike opera, listen to several, with help from someone who understands and appreciates opera. If you dislike Shakespeare, do the same. If you hate sports, get involved in a sports activity. What other subjects might apply?)

Either-or thinking

Another barrier to objective critical insight is a form of oversimplified reasoning sometimes called "Either-Or thinking" practiced by the person who sees issues in extreme "black and white." (Some people believe that life is actually "either-or" and the so-called "greys" are unnecessary complications.) Simple statements or questions as "Either you are honest or you're not," "Are you a good person or a bad person?" "America— love it or leave it," "Am I right or am I wrong?" "Either he is smart or dumb" are all examples of "either-or" thinking. In general, this person says, "Either you agree with me totally or you're all wrong." No compromise, no meeting half-way, no flexibility is permitted, though in each of the above examples the reality would be somewhere between, or a combination, or a degree halfway along the scale. "Either-or" statements sound naive and immature, generally speaking. Perhaps one of the more credible "either-or" statements is the irate father's angry ultimatum to his sobbing daughter: "Either you're pregnant or you're not!"

For discussion

Analyze each of the preceding "either-or" statements, discussing the various "in-between" possibilities. What other examples of "either-or" thinking can you name? Can you think of examples or cases when such thinking may be defended?

Opinions and facts

After seeing a movie, a young man and his girl leave the theater.
He says, "I loved that movie. Great!"
She says, "No, it was lousy."
He grumbles, "My opinion is just as good as yours, baby."
Is he right? Not necessarily. One of the most common misconceptions about opinions is that they are all equal. Perhaps his idea is encouraged by American ideas of democracy, equality, free speech. Many people like to feel that their opinions are equal to anyone else's.

In truth, some opinions are better than others: better in the sense of being more valid, more supportable.

Consider the two people who saw the movie. Suppose one of them knows a great deal about movies—has studied movie history, knows the background and credits of the director, the performers, and knows the context and genre history (type: comedy, western, musical) of the film. But the other person has no technical or historical knowledge whatsoever, and/or sees far fewer films than the other person.

The opinion of the first person will be "better," more valid, than the opinion of the second person. Why? Because a knowledgeable opinion by an informed person is preferable to a casual opinion by someone with no knowledge or background on the subject. That is only the first reason why all opinions are not equal. It is also one reason why people should write on what they know and avoid writing or talking about what they don't know—and risk exposing their ignorance. So, a person who knows a great deal about music is more qualified to express opinions than one who does not. The same principle applies in politics, religion, sports, or other topics. A useful personal philosophy, practiced by too few, might be to listen, to read, and to learn about subjects in which one is not versed. To paraphrase Montaigne, "I would have everyone write what he knows, and as much as he knows, but only what he knows."

Some people take pride in paying no attention to critics, such as film or music critics, or political analysts. The uninformed may ask, "What makes their opinions better than mine? What do they know?" This attitude shows no understanding of how opinions work: ideally, critics are informed experts, who know their subject far better than most of us do. A good critic is an expert at critical thinking.

Nevertheless, critics often disagree . . . on television programs, on radio, in the print media. Yet they are approximately equally well informed, and their opinions, even in conflict, are both valid and supportable. Opinions may be valid, but not right or wrong: facts are "right," and opinions are not facts.

Another serious misconception about opinions is the idea that "I don't need a reason for my opinion. I just feel that way." Or, "I liked it, but I don't know why." Such opinions are worthless and represent mental laziness—the non-thinking person who wants the freedom to have an opinion, but does not want to bother supporting it. Here we return to the central idea of this chapter: the unexamined idea (opinion) is not worth stating, writing, or reading.

The writer should always be aware of the difference between opinions (valid opinions are feelings supported by knowledge) and facts (which are provable, not feelings). He should not make the mistake of stating opinions as though they are facts, or of writing that he "knows" something which is not knowledge, but simply an opinion.

Summary

- Opinions are not true or right (or untrue or false) since opinions are judgements, not facts, and cannot be proven.
- However, there are "better" or "worse" opinions (best referred to as "valid" and "invalid").
- Opinions must be supported. Validity depends on the quality of support, examples, reasons, evidence. Teachers grade essays on this support, not on the opinions themselves.
- A valid opinion is well supported and informed.
- An invalid opinion contains inaccurate, inferior, or false support, or none at all.

Hence, experts may have opposing and contradictory opinions which will still be valid.

For class discussion

Have the students give several opinions which they feel are valid (informed, supportable). What opposite/contradictory opinions to these might also be valid? Can the class give examples of some invalid, uninformed opinions?

Mental exercise

On what topics are you sufficiently well informed to have a valid opinion? Which subjects are you unqualified to discuss? Do you ever attempt to discuss them anyway?

Some problems in critical thinking

A. Phrases to avoid
   Certain phrases are obvious signals of poor critical thinking. When a writer or speaker uses one of the following, the reader or listener suspects that an example of muddled reason will follow:

   1. "It's a simple matter . . ."
   2. "It's only common sense that . . ."
   3. "Only a fool would deny . . ."
   4. "Everyone knows" or "Everyone agrees . . ."
   5. "There's no doubt that . . ."
   6. "How dare you say . . ."
   7. "I don't care what you say, I still think . . ."

For discussion

Explain what is wrong with the examples listed above. Can you think of other examples?

B.   Critical thinking and the Bible

Well meaning, sincere persons often misquote or misinterpret the Bible by using citations out of context to support their views. Many people have a way of selecting only those sections of the Bible that support their particular views on morality or sexuality. An objective individual realizes that the Bible, written/translated by many men, contradicts itself on nearly every issue. Therefore, the Bible, properly used and understood, is actually a model of fair critical thinking because it presents both (or more) sides of most issues, but not in the same place. The Bible should never be used to support one narrow viewpoint.

C.   Critical thinking and letters to the editor

The Letters to the Editor column of almost any newspaper or magazine is usually a good place to study critical thinking. A minority of letters is well informed and fair, but most writers are too emotional, one-sided, biased, misinformed, and/or insulting to anyone who disagrees with them. If people sign their names to writing that appears in public, they should be prepared for any negative comments/letters that ensue, but they often fail to realize that they have made fools of themselves in public. Good thinkers and writers will therefore be careful in their letters and write only when informed and respectful of other sides of the issues.

Exercise

Collect "good" and "bad" letters. The latter are much easier to find. Class members could bring in the letters, share them, and discuss what is right or wrong with them, not only in terms of critical thinking but in grammar.

D.   Being fair

The most difficult part of critical thinking is overcoming one's prejudices or judgments. Ideally, a thinker can pass the difficult test of seeing what is wrong with whatever he/she likes—and what is right with whatever he/she does not. Thus, a good critical thinker who is a liberal should be able to see what is wrong with liberalism—and the positives of conservatism. Similarly, a conservative should be able to write a paragraph or essay that does not crucify liberals—or sanctify conservatives. Or, the country music fan can see what is positive about hard rock and vice versa (and how about classical music?).

Exercise:

Write balanced paragraphs showing both sides of issues about which you feel strongly without hostility to other views.

Discussion

Siskel and Ebert are two nationally known movie critics with their own television rating show. Statistically, they agree about two thirds of the time. What does it mean when these experts disagree? If they both like a movie, what are the odds of its not being a good one?

Other problems in critical thinking

At least four other obstacles can prevent us from clear, convincing writing: *generalizing, stereotyping, assuming, and "jumping" to conclusions.*

When we *generalize,* we might write or say, "Republicans are always conservative"; "Most alcoholics were abused children"; "Second marriages never work out"; "Delinquency is caused by a lack of religion in the home"; "Reading pornography leads to sexual violence," or similar generalizations. Most of these are carelessly stated opinions, seldom based on research or knowledge. Such statements need to be supported by specific evidence and data.

Stereotyping, a form of generalization (and usually ethnocentric), places labels on people or ideas. Ethnic and religious stereotypes are not the only kinds. We also stereotype occupationally, intellectually, socially, and in numerous other ways. How many stereotyped notions do people have about policemen, sanitation workers (garbage men), psychology majors, cheerleaders, Homecoming Queens, or people from another neighborhood or school? Writing such stereotypes, or trying to build a convincing argument around them, suggests immaturity in thinking.

Many people claim they have factual knowledge when, in fact, they are *assuming:* "I *know* she loves him!" (One doesn't know this; it is an assumption.) "I *know* the Orioles will win the Series!" "My car gets the best mileage." "Cats are smarter than dogs." Some of these statements may be true, but the writer has not done any research to find out, making such statements by assumption. This error is closely related to the confusion of fact versus opinion. (As you can see, many of the terms in this chapter overlap and sometimes combine.)

We "jump to conclusions" when we decide something or make a judgment on flimsy or inadequate evidence—sometimes as little as one example. It would be hasty to conclude that MTV is getting less popular only because your friends watch less of it. You need much more evidence. Too often we observe a trend or feeling in the people around us, and we conclude that people everywhere must share that same experience. This error also includes the attitude that what is true for us must be true for others.

Summary

Critical thinking is the ability to analyze one's thinking, speaking, or writing to find any errors which prevent our point from being made. An effective writer needs to recognize, in his work as well as in others' work, such problems as ethnocentrism, subjectivity, conformity, rationalization, either-or thinking, invalid or uninformed opinions, confusion of fact with opinions, generalizing, stereotyping, assuming, and "jumping" to conclusions.

A successful writer will learn to proofread his essay for all these errors, just as carefully as he should proofread it for grammar, punctuation, and spelling. Critical thinking is a key to effective content.

Exercise

Discuss which error is committed in the following situations, and/or how critical thinking would help to solve the problem.

1. Ginny, a vegetarian, keeps telling friends that people who don't eat meat are better than those who do. When she writes this in an essay, she gets a low grade and insists the instructor, not a vegetarian, penalized her for her beliefs. What parts of this chapter does she need to read?

2. John was buying Christmas albums by Merle Haggard, Stevie Wonder, Diana Ross, Willie Nelson, Dolly Parton, and Gladys Knight. John's friend said, "These albums can't possibly be any good. Christmas music wasn't meant to be sung that way. It only sounds right by Bing Crosby, Frank Sinatra, people like that." What are her critical thinking errors?

3. Garth comes home wearing one earring. His mother has a screaming tantrum and prepares to throw Garth out of the house. His father ignores that situation and watches television. Use critical thinking to show what should happen.

Discussion

How many similar situations can the class make up and analyze?

An exercise in critical thinking

A philosophy student presented his opinion on the nature of God in the syllogism:

> God is perfect and has a perfect plan. (major premise)
> Man is part of that perfect plan. (minor premise)
> Therefore, man is perfect. (conclusion)

God is defined as a being conceived as "the perfect, omnipotent, omniscient originator and ruler of the universe, the principal object of faith and worship in monotheistic religions; the single supreme agency postulated to explain the phenomena of the world, having a nature variously conceived in such terms as prime mover (Aristotle); Infinite Mind, Spirit, Soul, Life, Truth, Love *(Christian Science)."* *Perfect* is defined as "in a state of undiminished or highest excellence, without defect, flawless. . . ." (OED, 1933)

Since God is flawless, it would be inconceivable that He would deliberately create a flawed work. Therefore, his creation(s) would indeed be flawless. Since man is a creation of His work and His will, man is the flawless product of a flawless artisan (God). For a perfect artisan to create an imperfect product (being) would be irrational. Since God is Infinite Mind, Truth, Love . . . the creation of an imperfect being would be contradictory to the very essence of His nature.

> God is the perfect Craftsman.
> God's creations are perfectly crafted. (designed, implemented)
> Therefore, man is (one of) God's perfect creations.

To the student

Formulate a response to the philosophy student's arguments. Do you see any "loopholes" in his logic? Are you able to launch a sustained argument attacking his premises? Do so in four-hundred words or more. Try to be objective.

Another exercise in critical thinking

A sober philosophy student wrote the following syllogism:

It is a widely accepted fact that women are more sensitive than men.
If women are more sensitive than men, women must be more emotional.
Therefore, men must be more rational than women.

If men are less sensitive and less emotional than women, it must necessarily follow that men are more reasonable and more objective than women—generally. Do you agree with the conclusion that the philosophy student has drawn? Why? Why not? Write a four-hundred word essay defending or arguing against the generalization. Try to be objective.

■ Chapter 2 ■

Writing the Physical Description Paper

"Seeing" the subject through words

The most difficult task in writing is enabling the reader to "see" what we visualize in our mind's eye. Getting the reader to see the color, size, shape, weight, and texture of an object is a challenge which intimidates the best of writers. The most avid proponents of the so called "camera technique" in writing lived in a time appropriately called the Age of Realism. Great writers such as Flaubert, Dostoevsky, Tolstoy, and others dealt superbly in creating concrete images of their subjects. Scorning the abstract, they dealt with sensory perception skillfully, knowing that the things we hear, smell, taste, and feel are vital elements in the total writing effort. Today, although long passages of physical detail are not especially popular in contemporary fiction, the ability to describe something realistically is still an attribute greatly admired in writing.

The wealth of adjectives in the English language is abundant. The student who writes, "Rita has red hair," is not taking advantage of the resources available to him, for he could have done so much more with the color "red": crimson, ruby, scarlet, vermillion, cherry, blood red, copper, apricot pink, maroon, terra cotta, tangerine, Venetian pink, auburn, chestnut, rust-colored. . . . An after-thought also occurs: Have you ever seen someone with "red" hair? Remember that there are shades of red and pink and blue and green and, yes, even black. Make words work for you. *Do not let the word choose your meaning.*

On the other hand, the number of adjectives that modify the sensory perceptions of taste, smell, and touch are severely limited. The language used to convey images of the senses may, as a result of the dearth of multiple choices, be used to form images through similes, metaphors, and appropriate comparisons. A word of caution: since description is the

27

process of "seeing" or visualizing, the writer must use concrete language. Note the lack of imagination in the following sentence:

Pete was so hungry that he could have eaten a horse.

More realistically, without the hyperbolic dimensions of the above, the writer could have written in more appropriate and logical terms:

Pete was so hungry that he ate a ten-pound turkey, half a loaf of bread, two pounds of mashed potatoes, six sweet potatoes, a head of lettuce. . . .

Objectivity in writing the expository essay

Contrary to what many students think, imagination has little to do with the writing of a physical description paper. Objective analysis and matter-of-fact reporting have little to do with poetic inspiration." Describe an object as you see it, a person as you see him, and as you can truthfully convey that description to the reader. *Avoid the ambiguous and the subjective.*

My father is very tall, dark, and handsome. He dresses extremely well, is always neat and clean, even after a very hard day's work. On the other hand, my mother is quite short, light complexioned, and rather homely. She is untidy and sloppy, especially after cleaning the house or cooking supper. I often wonder why such extreme opposites were ever attracted to each other.

In the preceding paragraph, note the author's use of relative terms: *Tall, dark, handsome, quite short, rather homely, sloppy, neat.* Vague words frustrate the reader and increase his frustration with the author's work. Remember to interest the reader in your composition; do not use the abstract words which cloud the reader's vision. Select details realistically to make the reader see what you mean when you describe the subject. Writing is a defensive task. If you do not interest the reader in your material, you have failed. Readers are generally indifferent unless the writer excites them enough to want to continue reading.

Report accurately and concisely. Do not waste words. Study the following paragraph of *particular detail.*

The grey-haired man seemed like the terminal of a complex machine. Tubes led in and out of him into plastic bags supported by glistening metallic poles. A plastic catheter bag hung on the bottom iron rail of the bed, partially filled with a muddy liquid. The i.v. in his left arm trailed upward into a bag of normal saline solution supported by the i.v. pole at the head of the bed. The nasogastric rubber tube led to the intermittent suction machine; an oxygen nasal cannula of clear, hard plastic lay beside him on the bed, temporarily out of use until the necessary occasion arose.

Except for the simile in the first line of the preceding paragraph, the description is an accurate image of a seriously ill patient in a hospital room. There is no "poetic license," no romanticizing of illness. The writer is a reporter who gives the facts; no words are wasted; no sentiment distorts the accuracy of the image.

In the following paragraph, the writer takes more liberties in the use of similes and metaphors, but the vivid description is still an objective rendering of the scene. Connotative words—*grotesque, fickle, fantastic, seethes*—are trite, however.

> When the storm ended that morning, the valley seemed to hang in an eerie silence, smothered in a smokey-grey film. Patches of the Alleghany Mountains and the valley were completely lost in low-hanging ribbons of mist the color of pewter, hiding the vast sea of mud and rubble. It was about six A.M.
>
> Towering over the scene was a grotesque pyramid of stone and timbers, curtains and tires, shattered glass and pieces of furniture. A red Buick lay on its side at the foot of the grisly pyramid, like a toy an impatient child had tired of and discarded impulsively, flinging it angrily into the oozing muck which had no end. Telephone poles were leaning everywhere, some resting upon the myriad tangles of the wires for support. Others upon the sides and roofs of houses and cars. Several houses were apparently untouched by the fickle storm, while others seemed to be defying the law of gravity, tilted crazily on their foundations, shifted sideways into the streets and alleys. Cars were tossed about in fantastic positions atop each other, leaning upright against splintered telephone poles, some resting grimly in the rooms of shattered houses. Surging back and forth about the wreckage, the water, still about knee high, seethed with a yellow foam.
>
> Sloshing about in black hip boots, scores of people were atop the rubble and in the streets, already examining the debris and helping those too terror stricken and numb to help themselves. A grey-haired woman stared blankly out of a second-story window. Gazing ahead, unseeing, in paralyzed stoic expression, she seemed like a statue rooted to the ledge.

In technical writing, the more objective physical descriptive essay is recommended, as seen in the following description of the KMC 4000 Pocket Calculator.

The KMC 4000 is an electronic pocket calculator that is battery operated and economical. It is used by accountants, businessmen, housewives, and contractors to perform mathematical calculations that are too long or complex to be done by hand or to make sure that the calculations are correct.

It is approximately 2 ½" wide by 5" long. The depth of the calculator is 1" at the top sloping down to ½" at the base. The back half of the calculator is brown, and the front is an off-white. The basic body of the calculator is composed of a sturdy plastic. About 1 ½" from the top of the front side is a ⅜" by 1 ¾" screen, which is ¼" lower than the rest of the calculator. The lower 2 ½" squared section of the front has twenty-five ¼" brown plastic buttons, each of which performs a specific function. There is also a rectangular metal strip about ½" from the top on the right side that is 1" long and ½" wide. This metal strip contains the name of the calculator and the words "Auto Shut Off."

The back half of the calculator is different from the front. First, it has 1 ½" by 3" brown plastic piece that can be taken off to remove the batteries. Also, in the center of the back of the calculator is a metal strip that is ½" wide by 1 ½" long. This metal strip contains the size and voltage of the batteries and the place where the calculator was made. There is also a silver sticker about ⅛" wide by 1" long. Two silver screws, each ¼" in diameter and cross shaped, hold the calculator together. These screws are located one inch from the base on the back of the calculator.

The KMC 4000 calculator weighs only eight ounces, is carried easily, and is useful in performing many mathematical operations. Since it costs about eight or nine dollars, it is also economical.

Avoid using trite expressions, clichés, and personification in formal writing.

In freshman composition, students are generally discouraged from using so-called "poetic" language: similes, metaphors, hyperbole, and personification. Why? Unless a student is an unusually good or gifted writer, he will probably commit to paper the trite, worn-out expressions and phrases on which he has been weaned for years. Consequently, the writer's work suffers because it is suffused with stale comparisons and anemic expressions. It is good strategy to avoid using such brittle crutches in the essay.

All of the following phrases have been taken from student papers. Haven't you heard, read, or used them a hundred times?

Personification

Mother Nature
Father Time
Jack Frost
sighing breezes
whispering leaves
babbling brooks
angry storm
duty calls

Similes

fresh as a daisy
mad as hell
hot as hell
cold as hell
mad as a hatter
skin like peaches and cream
black as coal
white as snow
built like an athlete
built like a rock
crying like a baby
standing like sentinels
ugly as sin
pretty as a picture
clear as glass
sly as a fox
cute as a button
playful as a kitten
smooth as silk
dry as a bone
quick as a flash
quick as a wink
skin like leather
strong as a bull
red as a rose
sings like a bird

hungry as a bear
sharp as a tack
good as gold

Metaphors

eagle eyed
hawk eyed
sky-blue eyes
silver rivers
hour-glass figure
beer belly
bookworm
beady eyes
a sea of agony
a sea of despair
highway of life
life's hard road
crack of dawn
carpet of leaves
ruby lips
honeyed lips
poker face

Other trite expressions

home sweet home
stifled sobs
at that point in time
flickering love
ups and downs
torn asunder
a dream come true
clinging vine
towering oak
fame and fortune
everlasting love
tried and true

If you are to develop as a writer, free yourself from stale images and ancient, over-used expressions. Develop your own style. Express yourself in fresh ways. No one said it was easy!

Connotation and denotation

Connotation is the implied meaning of a word and its suggestive associations. Denotation is the opposite of connotation. Denotation is explicit, a specific reference, or the exact definition of a word or symbol. For instance, the connotative power of "home" suggests many subjective elements: family, good cooking, love, and security. "Home" cannot be measured objectively. On the other hand, "house" is a definite structure with explicit dimensions. Compare "Mother" to "Parent" and the reactions both intellectually and emotionally are almost antithetical. Connotative words may be used to great effect, but they are basically abstract and general. The student who wrote, "My father is a tyrant," relied upon the reader's negative reactions to the word "tyrant." But "tyrant" simply means, denotatively, someone who has absolute power. Perhaps the most widely used connotative words are *love, democracy, freedom, honor, justice*—all of which appeal directly to the emotions.

Remember that in expository writing (classification, process, definition) connotative words have little utilitarian value. When writing, make sure that you know what the words you use mean—if you are to use them for maximum effect.

In the following composition, notice how physical description and narration may be combined effectively. Scrutinize the writer's use of both denotative and connotative words.

Incident in a Pool Room

I walked out of the cool night air into the smoke-filled pool room. Loud cursing immediately greeted me. The musty atmosphere and smell were unpleasant. Uncovered piles of garbage stuffed in cardboard boxes and the pungent body odors were stifling. The foul stink of what was supposed to be a toilet formed a stagnant layer of dusty air.

I sat down in one of the wooden chairs. Two large lights illuminated the foggy pool room. The noisy players at both tables were black, but a skinny white boy, about sixteen, sat in one of the three chairs placed against the splintered walls. Next to a rotting stairway leading to the second floor, a chubby, bald-headed old man, snoring softly, slept on, serenely undisturbed by the heavy racket of shouting voices and the pounding of cue sticks.

Scars of neglect deformed the dismal hall. One small window was cut into the dirty walls, breaking the monotony of the cell-like structure. Only half of the little window was glass; the other half was a thick cardboard section taped to the frame of the window. Decorating the otherwise bare walls were obscene pictures and calendars of naked women who smiled teasingly down at the players. In the far corner of the flat walls a stringy spider web floated, the only carefully balanced structure in the place. Thick slits appeared in the ancient boards. The dusty walls were shabby with splinters and carelessly carved initials of the anonymous patrons. The cracks in and between the dirty boards provided a haven for platoons of cockroaches. At almost regular intervals, the roaches dared to crawl out of their wooden caves, dashed across a section of the grimy wall, and disappeared in another secret nook, like nervous shoppers scurrying from one bargain counter to another. The cue sticks were squeezed into a black rectangular rack which was nailed at a crooked angle on the wall.

Large, dusty holes pitted the surface of the stairway. Loose boards gave an antiquated dignity to the weak stairway which led to a shadowy platform at the top. The tarnished metal of the spittoons added to the dull appearance of the borders of the walls; the spittoons were favorite targets of the tobacco-chewing hustlers. Recently overturned, one spittoon had upset its contents on the floor. Saliva and tobacco had formed a slimy puddle around one of the wooden legs of a chair. Disregarded by the indifferent pool room citizenry, the ooze had become a small, stagnant pool. Scores of flies clustered around the newly formed morsel.

Annoying, buzzing insects infested the place. Hordes of flies and mosquitoes infiltrated the slime of the cuspidors and garbage. Crawling behind the metal protection of a spittoon, a large brown roach disappeared between the loose boards of the littered floor. A husky black man cursed as he swatted a persistent Kamikaze fly, but his gesture was useless. Chalk, white powder, broken cue sticks, and dead bugs were swept carelessly to one side of the floor. Colonies of roaches and flies thrived under the supports of the pool tables. Dead flies and mosquitoes lay scattered along the shabby green felt.

Clicking monotonously, the balls rolled dizzily over the thin, worn green of the tables. Frequently a familiar profane word was mumbled and a shower of laughter followed. Long, wide scars streaked the blood-red sides of the pool tables. A dead roach was stuffed at the bottom of one dusty pocket, its legs spread up to the ceiling.

The bathroom was a misnomer for the filthy stall barely large enough for two people to stand. The stench was so bad that a man usually sucked in a mouthful of air before he entered, not daring to breathe the foul odor that lay so heavily, like mist, in the place. The rusting water-closet was a breeding ground for the bugs which scampered and flew about as one entered. And the commode never seemed to flush consistently. The handle was broken. To flush the commode, one had to lift the top of the water-closet and pull the chain of the pumping element. Few took the trouble to do so even when there was water in the closet to flush. The commode was less of a utility for defecation than a receptacle for drunks to vomit in. More often than not, rather than use this horrid little cell, the patrons of the pool hall utilized the alley in the rear, especially at night, or they would use the bathroom of the tavern next door, depending on the urgency of their needs.

The pool hall was too dirty and discolored for one to discern its original color scheme. The walls seemed to be a deep brown with splotches of lighter shades appearing in large, undulating streaks. Shivering black shadows shaded the stairway where the light was least diffused. The door was painted black behind the scratched beer ads and posters pasted to it. Jet black appeared to be the favorite color in the hall. Only the ceiling was "clean" enough to see an ancient layer of yellow paint peeling beneath a thin coat of dust. The unsteady floor was colored with anything that fell upon its surface and had the misfortune of remaining there too long.

Pounding on the rickety old floor with their feet and cues, the bellowing players shouted the customary profanities at each other. Suddenly a dull restlessness quieted the noisy crowd. A slender young girl in a faded maroon bathrobe appeared at the top of the stairway. Two of the brawny pool shooters turned to look up. The white boy, who had been nervously sitting in one of the chairs, stepped meekly up the creaking stairway. After he had ascended a few stairs, the boy's timid smile broadened, exposing the whiteness of his teeth. Following the slender girl's subtle gestures, he disappeared into the room at the top of the dark staircase. The squeaking door closed. A brown spider crawled deftly along the door's hinges before settling into its web.

A man with a long scar across his cheek laughed as he leaned across the table to stroke the eight ball into the corner pocket.

Questions for discussion

1. Can you visualize the pool room? Why? Does the author convey a realistic description? Does the story disgust you? Why? Why not?

2. Does the author use any connotative words? Where are they? Are such words effective?

3. Does the author use any trite expressions?

4. What do you consider to be the most effective image in the narration?

5. Does the author use any symbols to convey his meaning?

From Up the Crick

. . . My sense of family grew in that big white frame house on Back Street. The stone walk that bordered the street, the silver-painted chain fence that enclosed the large front yard, the red brick garage walk fenced in with white rose bushes leading to the double-car red brick garage, the cherry tree and apple tree that canopied the back of the house, the sloping backyard that ended at an embankment of the crick, the orange-blossom bush in the bottom of the yard, the lilac and forsythia bushes on the other side, the tall cedar tree in front of the house, the four pine spreaders protecting the lattice work of the huge front porch, the cement walk that led from the front gate straight to the front porch and curved at the tall tree to lead to the back porch, the flower garden between the break in the cement walks, the wooden swing and glider covered with striped-cretonne cushions, the wicker rocking chair and ferneries— I loved it all.

My life was also church, Saint Joseph's Roman Catholic Church, which sat on one of the highest points in town. Church Hill began at Main Street, crossed over the cement crick bridge and the C&P Railroad tracks, and passed the white-frame Methodist Church, halfway up the hill. It then curved around the stone retaining wall until it reached the top of the hill, the macadam parking lot, the center of the complex that contained the rectory, the school, the convent, and the church, all cream-colored, green-trimmed frame buildings. A circular driveway, edged with tall pine trees, fronted the large, square rectory with its deep front porch. The trees protected the rectory from the weather and from the school children because its ground were off limits to us. The rectory, like the parish priest, was a thing set apart. I recognized its beauty and was awed by its mystery. One square building housing the first four grades sat at the back of the parking lot with only a narrow dirt road separating it from the hill of half-overgrown coalbanks. Directly across the parking lot was the convent-school-church complex. The convent jutting out to the side was surrounded on two sides by a pillared porch where I can still see the black and white garbed nuns silently sitting in green, latticed-back rocking chairs saying their rosaries or walking the distance of the porch intently reading their required daily "Divine Office." Connected to the side of the convent was the other school building with grades four through eight. These classrooms had windows on the one side that faced the coalbanks, but the other sides were the convent wall and the back of the church. . . .

The cross-topped bell tower reached one hundred feet into the valley's sky and held three bells. The inscription on St. Joseph's 2000-pound bell reads, "St. Joseph, deliver this church from lightning and storm." It was donated by Reverend Don Luigi Sartori, an Italian nobleman and first pastor of the church. The inscription on the blessed Virgin's 1000-pound bell reads, "Holy Mary, protect and defend this church from all evil," and St. Brigid's bell reads, "St. Brigid, pray for your Irish people." These bells rang out at 6 A.M., 12 Noon, and 6 P.M., signaling the time for the "Angelus," a prayer that we said, and even Mrs. Blake was known to stop scrubbing to kneel and pray when the deep-toned bells rang. They called us to weddings, to funerals, to happiness, to sorrow. They kept teaching me over and over the things I loved and the order that I needed and savored.

The church, an A-framed building with a stained-glass circle above the door of the main entrance, had a wide center aisle and narrow side aisles with pews between. Each family rented its pew, $6.00 per year, and ours was Number 24 on the left-center aisle. The main altar rested in an arched, recessed area, and on the wall above the recess was a stained-glass circle larger than but identical to the one at the front entrance. Marble angels knelt on either side of the top level of the marble altar, guarding the center tabernacle. The Blessed Virgin's altar was to the left and St. Joseph's altar was to the right. The golden sanctuary lamp dropped by a golden chain from the ceiling to the center of the sanctuary, burning constantly to remind us of the mysterious truth of the Divine presence, and an ornate, white communion rail separated the sanctuary from the body of the church.

Mary Colleen Buckley

Suggestions for writing the physical description paper

1. Write a four-hundred word essay describing in physical detail a person—your mother, your father, a friend, a classmate.

2. Choose a particular object—a watch, a class ring, a piece of furniture—and describe it in four hundred words. Make sure that the reader will be able to visualize it in terms of color, composition, texture, size, and shape.

3. Write a four hundred word essay describing a pet you own—a dog,

a cat, a bird.

4. Using "From Up the Crick" as an example, write an expository essay describing your home or school.

5. Describe in four hundred words an object or tool in your particular technical field.

Remember to limit your description to physical details, avoiding abstract qualities such as, "My boyfriend is really a nice guy," or "My mother always acts like a lady." Be specific. Make the reader visualize the qualities that you see in your mind's eye.

■ Chapter 3 ■

Writing the Narrative Paper

As an exercise in analysis, physical description tests the writer's ability in re-creating the images which he wants to share with the reader. In itself, description is a form of exposition. Another form of description closely allied to the physical description is narration, which produces the illusion of reality. Narration brings many other elements together: characterization, setting, plot, and dialogue. Physical description provides the necessary foundation, ideally, in the telling of a story and answers vital questions regarding the narrative: Where is the setting? What is the significance of the setting? Who and what are the characters? Are the characters described realistically, both in appearance and manner? Who is telling the story?

In writing a successful prose narration (either non-fiction or fiction), students need to follow conventional rules concerning plot, characterization, mood, setting, point of view, and dialogue.

Plot is usually defined as a plan of action aiming at a single effect. In devising a plot, the writer should ask the following questions: Is the plot interesting? Realistic? Suspenseful? Are there any unexplained or illogical gaps in the story? Details must be selected and arranged carefully if the writer hopes to arrive at a single effect and dramatic conclusion.

The writer should establish physical details, distinguishing characteristics and habits for the *characters*. Are the characters interesting, realistic, and important to the story? Do they fit the situation, the setting, and the mood of the story? Do they speak naturally and realistically for their types?

Mood refers to the feeling or tone of the story. The writer must decide on and maintain the overall mood that he/she wants to convey. Is the mood seen clearly in the character, description, and plot? Is the writer's attitude concerning his material consistent? Is the mood valuable to the story? Does it leave an impression on the reader?

Where does the action take place? Since the *setting* of any story is of paramount importance, the writer is obligated to render it realistically. Naturally, mood is determined by the portrayal of the setting.

The function of *physical detail* is to enrich the story. The writer must decide on how much detail he/she wishes to incorporate in the setting of the story and in the characters. Accuracy, naturalness, and effectiveness of detail are vitally important.

Does the story convey the illusion of *reality?* Even a fantasy or a science fiction story should appear to be logical, regardless of whether it could actually happen. The reader must be led to believe that the story is plausible if it is to be successful.

Who is telling the story? *Point of view* may be one of four approaches: the omniscient narrator, the limited omniscient narrator, the first person narrator, and the objective narrator. *Omniscient* means "all knowing"; the story is told in the third person by a narrator who is confined only by what he/she decides to tell the reader. In the limited omniscient point of view, a major or a minor character tells the story, generally in the third person; here, the narrator is limited to only one character. The first person point of view (I) combines the narrator and a character who reveals himself as the story progresses. The objective point of view (either first or third person) permits only observable action to be told, such as a reporter relates facts and figures, with no interior monologue by the character, with no examination of the characters' motives. The writer's task is choosing and maintaining the point of view that will most effectively contribute to the success of the story.

Dialogue makes a vital contribution to the illusion of reality. How a person speaks and what he says reveals his character, background, education, and personality. The writer must be careful to have his characters speak naturally and realistically for the types which they are supposed to reflect. Obviously few people speak "perfect" English; few people enunciate correctly all of the time. To be effective, the writer must avoid stilted/unnatural dialogue in the characters' speech patterns.

The culminating event, or the highest point of interest and excitement, is the *climax.* In drama, the climax is the decisive turning point of the action. In writing a short story or simple narration, the student should strive for an ending which the reader does not anticipate. Although the traditional "surprise ending" is an enviable feature in stories by the great writers such as Bret Harte, O. Henry, Edgar Allen Poe, and others, the novice writer should choose an ending which is appropriate within the context of the story — without violating logic or credibility.

Narration, as opposed to an incident, generally contains a theme or an idea which the writer wants to convey. What is the "moral" or "lesson" which the story brings to "enlighten" or "instruct" the reader? On the other hand, and for the sake of argument, does a story have to mean anything? May a story exist for its own sake, perhaps simply to entertain? The writer should resolve such questions in his own mind before he commits one word of his story on paper.

There are several types of narration. An *anecdote* is a short account of an interesting story or humorous incident.

> My wife Paula is an unwitting disciple of Mrs Malaprop. As we were lying in bed the other night, she mentioned that a mutual friend of ours had ignored her at the church picnic last Saturday. "That darn ol' Betty Wagner gave me the soft shoulder," she snorted. "The nerve of that woman!"
>
> I chuckled. "You mean she gave you the 'cold shoulder'!"
>
> Paula blushed. She always hated it when I dared to correct her English. "Well . . .," she hesitated, her pretty face pouting, "whatever you call it, she still snuffed me!"
>
> I laughed a little louder. "Snubbed! You mean she 'snubbed' you, my little darlin'!"
>
> The pink blush on her face deepened into an angry red. "You . . . don't have any symphony for me at all!"
>
> I dared not correct her again. I jammed the pillow over my head and only laughed harder.

An *anecdote* may be as short as one paragraph. Mr. Kelley's brief narrative has a beginning, a middle, an end, and, yes, even a moral:

> "The water certainly doesn't seem to be sudsy enough," I thought as I added a big squirt of liquid detergent. Just as I did, a woman behind me shouted, "That's *my* laundry!" And wouldn't you know the wash was on the rinse cycle? So I gave the woman four quarters along with my apologies. She was pleasant about it all, but I felt bad because she had to put that wash through another complete cycle, costing her time and me money. From now on, I'll *not* try to read the newspaper and do laundry at the same time, or, if I do, I'll look before I squirt.

An *allegory* is a story with symbolic implications illustrating a deeper sense than the apparent literal meaning. (Refer to Plato's "Allegory of the Cave" for an excellent literary example.) A "symbol" is something that represents something else. For instance, black is a symbol of evil in one context, but it may mean mourning in another. The white dove may be a symbol of peace for the United Nations, but if it flies over your newly waxed car it may symbolize something not so tranquil.

Discuss the following in terms of symbolic meaning: a tree in spring, that same tree in winter, a dog, a crucifix, a snake, a fat man, a woman wearing a white veil, a woman wearing a black veil.

An *analogy* is an *extended comparison* of two otherwise dissimilar things. To say that the heart is like a pump is *not* an analogy in itself, but simply a vague comparison, a simile. There are many types of pumps—water, gas, a low-cut shoe without fastenings, and so on. To form a proper analogy, the writer must prepare a more complete comparison, preferably with three or more similar characteristics of the objects under study.

The following example is an appropriate analogy.

The Human Heart and a Force Pump

Any type of pump has an energy source or force. The heart's energy source is electrical impulse; a force pump may use electricity, fluid pressure, or a variation of other stimulants. The heart uses a muscle which contracts in an upward and inward motion to force the blood through; the force pump works through a piston moving up and down in the pumping cylinder, which moves the fluid through the pump. The heart uses valves to control the flow of blood through them, the three valves helping in preventing the backflow of blood and allowing for the suction and pressure necessary for the pumping process. The pressure pump has two mechanical valves which act in the same way as the valves of the heart. Both the heart and the force pump are divided into chambers. The heart has two chambers on each side for pumping; the force pump is divided by the piston, which moves up and down, causing the necessary suction and force in each chamber. Both of these pumps have a chamber with valves to allow for the pumping action.

With the similar chamber structure, valve use, and pumping action, one can see the analogy between a human heart and a force pump.

A *narrative incident* is an occurrence of an action that is a separate unit dealing with an experience. The following episode, taken from Mary Colleen Buckley's "From Up the Crick," even contains a moral.

I revel in my memories of sliding down the coal bank on cardboard sleds at recess and hurrying home for my noon meal so I could hurry back to slide some more. I remember the stinging red ring of chapping around my calves caused by snow getting down in my rubber galoshes during too many trips up and down the bank. We rolled snowballs from the top of the playground to the edge of the hill and sent them smashing down through trees and bushes into the crick. We built igloos from hundreds of snowballs, and flopped backwards, with arms outstretched, into the snow, making angel wings. I can still see and smell the long, tan, cotton stockings and sopping wet woolen mittens and gloves drying on the radiators during the long afternoons of geography, art, "Evangeline," and penmanship. School was over at 3 p.m. unless it was our turn to wash the blackboards, always top to bottom, to clap the blackboard erasers out the window, to straighten the desks into a military line. Then, on home.

As soon as we got home from school, we grabbed a bite to eat, maybe sugar bread or syrup bread, or jelly bread and a glass of milk. We changed our school clothes for play clothes and headed for Squirrel Neck Hollow, a hill up behind the crick, to skate on the Frog Pond. If the Hollow were snow-covered, we put on our skates at home. If not, we'd sit on a log at the pond. I pretended to be Sonja Heine, but I was too cold to believe it, and besides, my snow-suit with its suspendered pants and hooded jacket bore little resemblance to her skating outfits. The pond was circular with a diameter of no more than ten feet, but a young child can enlarge and embellish anything. Bernadette Winner, who lived down Back Street, must have thought that it was quite huge. Without looking behind her, she put her one leg in the air and the edge of her blade gouged me in the right eyebrow. I hurriedly skated home, down the Hollow, up Back Street, around our walk, up the two steps to our back porch, and opened the back door, all the time blood running down my face. My daddy was seated at the supper table.

Mother looked at me, barked, "You're late for supper again."

The purest love is the most exacting and I had broken one of the rules: Be home on time. I lost nothing in my life by believing this. But I do have a scar—in my right eyebrow.

All narrative essays have one more requirement: a point, purpose, lesson, or moral—something to be learned. A story should teach the reader; otherwise, it is pointless, purposeless, and not worth telling.

Often the writer has learned a lesson from the story, especially if it happened to him; and whatever he learned can be passed on to the reader. Obviously, a story about an experience in prejudice, cheating, safety, or first love has something to teach. At other times the lesson may be less obvious.

When the point of the narrative is evident or clear, the writer does not need to state it. If the narrative is more subtle and the point may not easily be grasped, the conclusion should probably explain or interpret it. In either case, a narrative that has nothing to teach will bore the reader and waste his time. Common, overworked topics, such as "My Most Embarrassing Moment" or "My Blind Date," often seem pointless, though these, too, can have a purpose. The writer should know what the story has to tell the reader, and then make sure the reader gets the point, explicitly or implicitly.

Tale of a Terrible Tuesday Night

I awaken at 3:30 A.M., fully rested, having gone to bed early Monday evening. For two hours I happily read Cather's *The Song of the Lark* in preparation for discussing it with one of my students, a former colleague now retired, in her Independent Study English course.

Breakfasting early at Mason's, I arrive at ACC before 8:00 A.M. and get in a productive hour at the piano. Until my student arrives at 10:30, I talk with colleagues and handle routine paper work. At 10:30, Thelma arrives, prompt as usual, and we spend well over an hour discussing and dissecting the novel, comparing it to the other two Cather novels we've studied. We talk of James' style, comparing and contrasting it with Cather's. I get quite carried away defining style; Thelma is deeply interested.

Since she has a 1:00 P.M. appointment, we have a brief lunch at Mason's. She orders a hamburger; I pig out on surprisingly good beef stew. I see clearly how she keeps trim and how/why I fail.

I head to Tommy's Market to buy fish for dinner and feel fortunate in finding sole, my favorite. Flounder is equally beautiful, but sole has a more delicate, subtle flavor. It's frozen, but fish freezes particularly well; besides, getting fresh fish in midwinter is no easy matter.

Returning home, I open the fish to let it thaw, note with satisfaction the beautiful green of the asparagus purchased Sunday at the Safeway, and begin to put the house in order. The silver, crystal, and linen come down from their storage boxes. I decide on the lace tablecloth over white and the large, bowl-like wine glasses. Black plates will show off the white fish in its white wine sauce and the verdant asparagus. The fresh, white cauliflower, cooked in milk to keep it white, will be served in separate, small dishes. It will be a beautiful meal both in taste and appearance.

I hurry to the "Y" arriving around 1:20 for a workout, a short but intense one as I have a 3:00 class. My body responds well; I'm up ten pounds on the bench; my workout time is down. I leave refreshed, renewed, even rested!

From 3 to 4:15 I do a knockout job of teaching. When I'm good, I'm damn good, and the class, although remedial, is intelligent, mature, and responsive. They like me and know I like them.

At 5:00 I get home, forgetting to pick up my *Washington Post*—the second day in a row I've forgotten and/or been too busy. Even my light days are full. I'm glad Mike and I decided on Tuesday rather than Mondays. I pleaded a heavy schedule on Monday, and *Brideshead Revisited* made Monday bad for him.

He'll arrive at 6:00; I have an hour to pull everything together. I *must* vacuum. Forty-five minutes later, everything is under control. The wine is chilling; the food is on the stove awaiting heat; and I'm sitting sipping a cocktail.

Six o'clock comes. Mike doesn't. At 6:30 I call his home. No answer. At 7:00 I call again. Same result.

I'm so frustrated I feel like weeping. Part of me wants to throw the food away and go out for dinner. But Reason wins; I turn on the stove. Twenty minutes later, I'm dining alone.

The food is delicious. I've never done a better job on the fish, but having no one to share it with diminishes my pleasure.

I put on a Barbara Cook album and find myself listening closely to the words of one song. Suddenly, I can relate to it more fully than ever before:

Dear Friend
by Bock and Harnich

The flowers, the linen, the crystal I see
Were carefully chosen for people like me.
The silver agleam and the candles aglo,
Your favorite song on request.
Each colorful touch in the finest of taste
And notice how subtly the tables are spaced.
The music is muted, the lighting is low,
No wonder I feel so depressed!

N. Kelley

Questions for discussion

1. Why is Tuesday night "terrible" to the author? Do you agree with the author's point of view?

2. Have you ever made elaborate preparations and been disappointed? How did you deal with the situation?

3. Comment on the author's style and use of physical description. Are you able to visualize the food and the supper table?

4. Do the lyrics at the end of the "tale" capture the narrator's mood? How?

A *vignette* is a short, descriptive literary sketch, usually designed to capture a brief incident or scene. The following trilogy captures the charm and subtlety of the vignette's essence.

Honor

Even as a child of eight, I had definite opinions and preferences, many of which would follow me the rest of my life.

I knew then that I preferred butter to margarine, not because it was the "higher priced spread," as margarine advertisements put it then, but because there was a distinct difference in taste, and I liked the taste of butter.

My father disagreed.

"The only difference's the price, Son. There's no way you can taste any difference," he said reproachfully.

"There is so a difference. And I can prove it. Buy a quarter of a pound of each. Put some butter on one cracker and some margarine on another. I'll tell which is which," I argued with all the confidence of youth.

He agreed to our little experiment.

After one taste of each, I correctly identified the butter.

He tasted both, confirming my opinion.

"You're right, Son. I was wrong."

My father was a man of honor.

Little Dog Gone: Little Boy Lost

Like most boys, when I was five or six I wanted a dog. Now I had learned early that one of the ways of getting what I wanted was to cite the fact that my brother George had had whatever when he was my age and that therefore I too should have one. George had had a dog, and so did I. For a short time.

What occasion was it—Christmas or my birthday? I don't remember, but I do remember receiving Brownie, a blond Cocker Spaniel. No ecstasy can equal that of a boy getting his first dog! But no pain can equal that of a boy losing his first dog!

How long Brownie and I had each other I don't remember. What I do remember is that one day after coming home from school I couldn't find him. I called and called and searched and searched. When I asked my mother, she denied knowing anything about him. She had a funny look on her face, a look I later realized as guilty.

She'd been less than enthusiastic about my getting a dog in the first place, having "gone through all that" with George, not wanting to clean up after it, etc. And at the time my parents' marriage was beginning to come apart. And perhaps she saw that down the road a dog would be one more problem for a woman separated from her husband. I don't know.

Never was I given an explanation of why Brownie had vanished or where he had been taken. The matter was ignored, although it was a matter of the greatest importance to me.

My little dog was gone, but more than that, so was I, for I had lost forever the trust and love I had once known for my mother. With Brownie's leaving something else left, and what remained was a wedge that was to deepen beyond healing between my mother and me. She died a few years ago. I don't remember how many or the date, although I think it was in October. I didn't go to the funeral.

Little dog gone, little boy lost—forever.

Summer Vacation Incident

We had been having a wonderful time. I was, perhaps, eleven years old. My parents had separated the previous year, and Dad, then in his early sixties, had taken me to Old Orchard Beach in Maine for a week's summer vacation.

We'd gone swimming and played games in the penny arcade. He'd enjoyed watching me roller skate, and we'd attended nearby Kenneybunkport Playhouse, my first real, live, professional play, an exciting, glamorous, new experience! And the many different restaurants had made meal times exciting and unique. Perhaps the salt air had stimulated our appetites as much as our many activities.

But suddenly, seemingly inexplicably, I was sullen, uncommunicative.

What was wrong? Dad wanted to know.

Sobbing, I finally told him. "I feel bad having such a good time while Mom has to work. She won't get a vacation." I went on and on, pouring out my frustrations and unhappiness, concluding, "It all seems so unfair, that's all. And she's not happy."

Patiently, and kindly and with great sensitivity and tact, Dad explained. "Son, you mustn't make yourself feel bad about enjoying yourself. Would your mother be any happier if she thought that you weren't having a good time?"

"No."

"Well, then the only thing you can do is enjoy yourself as much as you can."

I looked into his eyes.

"I know that your mother is unhappy. But for twenty-five years I did everything I could to make her happy, and I failed. So you mustn't feel bad if you don't succeed either. She's decided that she is happier without me. She must find her own happiness. No one can give it to her."

By then I was calm.

"Now, wash your face and let's go for a walk. Since your mother would feel bad if she thought that you weren't enjoying yourself, the best thing to do is to have a good time and take home many happy memories."

N. Kelley

Questions for discussion

1. What is the "moral" of *Honor?* Has a similar incident occurred in your life?

2. Note the concise style and dialogue of *Honor.* No words are wasted. Why is *Honor* considered a vignette?

3. After reading *Little Dog Gone: Little Boy Lost,* consider a similar incident in your own experience. Was it as devastating an experience as the narrator's?

4. Characterize the mother of the young boy. Is the young boy too sensitive? Did he over-react to the situation? Why? Why not? What would you have done in the young boy's situation?

5. Characterize the young boy in *Summer Vacation Incident.* Do you agree with the father's words of advice?

Suggestions for writing a narrative

1. Write a five hundred word narrative dealing with an incident in your life. Remember that it does not have to be "dramatic" or earth shaking; a simple incident will suffice, something comparable to Mrs. Buckley's "From Up the Crick." Include at least two characters, dialogue, and a physical description of the setting and characters.

2. Write a narrative about the most frightening thing that has happened to you in the past three years: an automobile accident, a fight, an argument with your parents. Did you "gain" anything from this incident? What?

3. Write a fictional account of your wildest fantasy. Be sure to include a description of characters and setting.

■ Chapter 4 ■

Writing the Characterization Essay

Characterization

In expository or dramatic writing, *characterization* combines qualities or features that set a person, a group, or even an inanimate object apart. The writer examines actions, gestures, and dialogue which represent a person's peculiar traits, not only in action but in thought. Often the most interesting aspect of narration, characterization may be achieved effectively in a variety of ways: physical description, personal habits, speech, actions, thoughts, and personal or proper nouns.

Characterization is simply a written version of what a person, group, object, or quality is like through an analysis of a few dominant traits. The character sketch is not only an exercise in analysis, but also the writer's interpretation of his subject. Depending on the subject, characterization may be divided into two basic categories: *type* and *individual*.

Characterization as *type* deals with a group of persons or things which share common features that distinguish them as a class. Although some specific details may be presented to illustrate the characteristics of a class, the type sketch remains a collective abstraction, a general model, instead of a specific individual, for example, the "executive type," a "typical teenager," a traveling salesman, a professional politician. . . .

The *individual* sketch, as opposed to type, deals with specific features in a concrete manner. Particular details in physical description, habits, backgrounds, beliefs, and speech reveal the subject's personality. The writer uses many sources of information in a successful characterization: *narration*, using concrete examples; *brief incidents*, instead of one long narration; *dialogue*, using speech patterns (idioms) to exemplify character;

49

description, using physical details; *opinions of others,* using reactions of neighbors, friends, and family; personal names, using nouns to typify— Mr. Scrooge, Miss Pangloss; *titles,* using specific ranks to connote distinction; *appellations* (nicknames, sobriquets), using a name to describe a character—Lincoln, the "Great Emancipator"; Pete, the "Class Clown"; Rita, "Miss Airhead."

In writing a characterization, choose a subject that you know well, so well that you know things about the subject which will not appear in your final story. Include speech patterns that typify the subject. Become so accustomed to the character's dominant traits that you will be able to add corroborating details to complement your presentation. Determine what you want to convey about your subject and select your illustrations consistently. *Be specific.*

The following list of generalizations was taken from student papers. Are they "good" or poor? Why?

1. Pete is always fun to be around.

2. Mary always had some crazy idea and there never was a dull moment.

3. He straightened out things that confused me. If he could shed any light on a subject he did.

4. If I need someone to talk to, I know she will always be there to listen. If she was busy, she would always drop what she was doing to listen to me.

5. Whenever something was wrong, we always came to her and discussed our problems.

6. She was never like the others, because she was against almost everything they believed.

7. Rita is always the life of the party and never has anything but a smile on her face. (Poor Rita!)

8. My father is always in a bad mood and never tries to understand me.

9. My mother always understood me.

10. Everybody liked Pete because he was such a good friend.

The type sketch

Wolf's Corner, Main Street—USA

The young men stood arrogantly outside of the pool room, talking loudly, leaning against the brick facade of the old building. They had nothing better to do than to watch the people walking up and down Main Street—the shoppers, the businessmen, the employees of the stores and offices. Hundreds of people came under their scrutiny, especially the young, pretty girls. And the young hustlers sized up every one of them. Sometimes their comments were subtle as the girls walked past them. Sometimes a wink or a raised eyebrow signaled their pleasure; sometimes a whistle would escape their pursed, approving lips. When a real beauty sauntered by, they would simultaneously applaud, genuflecting in mock worship and beggary, hands over their hearts, as the blushing female quickened her pace. Fortunately, homely or plain girls drew no comment or gesture whatever. Such girls were simply ignored politely, much to their chagrin.

It was small wonder that the juncture of Main and Franklin Streets, where these connoisseurs stood guard, came to be known as Wolf's Corner. A notorious spot, but harmless enough, although more than one tryst was arranged there. For some enigmatic reason the place seemed to draw the prettiest girls in town.

But the fellows were never downright vulgar with the girls, or insulting, just bold and daring, typical of their carefree youth and ardor. Seldom were the giggling girls offended by the comical comments and gestures. Only the rather homely ones seemed to take umbrage as they walked through Wolf's Corner, quite safe in their leisure promenade.

Questions for discussion

1. What are the obvious characterizations that can be drawn from "Wolf's Corner"?

2. What are the dominant features that identify the young men as a group?

For another example of the type sketch in characterization, refer to Mr. Kelley's essay, "Body Builders."

Eighteen-Year-Old Burnouts

They are attractive, healthy, well-groomed, and stylishly dressed in name-brand clothing which they wear with the ease of those accustomed to the best, the finest. The cars they drive are always impressive; if secondhand, they're well-cared for prestigious models; no bottom-of-the-line bare minimum for these young people! They can dress so well and drive such cars because they live at home, most of them, and because they work, often full-time, to provide these necessities, which used to be considered luxuries.

And they go to college full-time.

"How do they do it all?" you ask, and you speculate on the remarkable energy of youth. But the truth is that they don't do it all; they only appear to. For instance, when torn between the demands of college and work, the latter wins, for it is the source of fuel for the car, clothes for the body, and spending money for the social life.

Some have been so torn since they were sixteen. First, a part-time job, then a full-time summer job, then often a full-time job during their senior year. Finally, the trap closes. By high school graduation, accustomed to having it all, they find it virtually impossible to give it all up to become full-time college students. They don't. They only appear to. So they continue to try to do it all, and they do so at great cost. When the going gets tough, the courses get dropped. How often full-time status shrinks to part time! How often majors are changed to those less demanding, to those whose courses meet at a time convenient for the job!

Many, maybe most, of their jobs provide little reward or satisfaction beyond the paycheck. These are apt to be entry-level, dead-end jobs. Perhaps the best that they provide is an awareness of the ugly reality that, without an education, these young workers will be permanently trapped in such jobs. But they're not really getting an education, for courses are often selected not only on the basis of when they meet but also on how little they require. Demanding courses which cannot be avoided are sometimes passed—barely— A's, B's, and sometimes even C's being luxuries unaffordable to these young people.

They're tired—understandably. Often their eyes hold the message, "Just tell me what I need to know to pass the test, please." They're too tired to be interested in knowledge for its own sake.

What options do they have? The Modern American Dream has turned into a Nightmare and has claimed them. And American society encourages this frenetic activity among its young just as it encourages heart-attack, stroke-producing behavior in middle-aged businessmen. "He's a go-getter, a hard-hitter, works 12-14 hours a day!" These words commend when they should condemn. And parents? They feel satisfied, pleased, brag about their children when they should be ashamed. "Work keeps them out of trouble," they say. But this frenetic behavior foretells future trouble.

They're victims of a disease they caught when very young and had no immunities to fight, a disease which says that appearances are the be-all and end-all of life. Thus, at eighteen, these young people are no longer really young. They're eighteen-year-old burnouts. And they're an American scandal.

N. Kelley

Questions for discussion

1. Do you agree with the author's criticism of young college students? Why? Why not?

2. Who is to blame for this national predicament? Parents? Society?

3. Have you ever withdrawn from a course because it conflicted with your job schedule? Did you, in effect, sell out, as Mr. Kelley suggests?

4. Have you ever taken a course simply to gain knowledge of a subject that appealed to you? What did you gain?

5. Do Americans feel that "appearances are the be-all and end-all of life"? What does this say about our society? Our parents?

Assignment

Write a four-hundred word essay challenging the author's criticisms. Remember to be objective, not emotional, in your rebuttal.

The character sketch

From Up the Crick

Down the road . . . in Woodlawn was the House of Morgan, a saloon and grocery store, owned and operated by Ike Morgan. Everybody on the crick has a story or two about Ike, a ready wit who could impart into a familiar word or situation a racier significance than it had possessed before. Once a young boy bought some peanuts from Ike and began to shell them, dropping the shells on the floor. Ike scolded the boy, "Damn it, kid, can't you see that the old woman just scrubbed the floor?"

The boy said, "Well, I bought them here."

Ike quickly asked, "Well, what the hell would you do if I sold you a laxative?"

Ike's father came from Wales but Ike was born in Frostburg. He opened his saloon in Woodlawn in the early thirties, and it soon became the favorite gathering place for locals and drummers. His wit was nowhere more unmistakable than in the handling of his stories which are terse to the point of severity, yet wholly adequate. Everything necessary is told but with an economy of word and phrase. When once asked if things were slow in the Klondike-Woodlawn area, he replied, "Things are so slow that the crick runs only three days a week."

Ike was quick to poke fun at his wife Mag. Mag disapproved of Ike's drinking and one night she had her brother hid behind a tree where Ike had to pass coming home from one of his toots. The brother saw Ike approaching and began his attempt to frighten Ike. "This is the devil, Ike. This is the devil, Ike. I've come to warn you."

Ike, without hesitancy, said back, "I know. I married your sister."

Another time Mag and Ike had had a fight and Mag left home—just across the road to relatives. Ike dressed up like a woman and went to sweep the steps. Mag hurried over to see who Ike's new woman was.

A customer came into the saloon one night and hollered to Ike, "Hey, Ike, Mag is down on the Klondike Bridge drunk!"

Ike loudly announced, "A case of beer to the one who goes down and knocks her off."

In an attempt to slow down Ike's occasional binges, Mag reminded Ike that a "rolling stone gathers no moss." Ike quickly answered, "Yeh, and a settin' hen has no feathers on her ass."

One day Ike took his sons for a ride to the Youghiogheny, and they asked their father the origin of the water's name. Without any hesitancy he explained to the boys how the Yough was named: an Indian and a white man were riding in a canoe. The white man stabbed the Indian and the Indian said, "Yough." The white man stabbed the Indian again, and the Indian said, "Yough, again." And that's how it got its name.

. . . the gypsies, who for several summers camped out in the area, Ike met them head on. When they would come into his place of business, they would come in groups in order to distract Ike so they could steal. They would pay him for some items, but Ike calmly ordered them to put down their Abrahams and said, "I want for that stuff you've got down in your bosoms."

He once asked one of the area's leading and informed citizens if this area were a direct air route between Washington, D.C., and

Pittsburgh. The man said that he really didn't know, but there were a great many airplanes that crossed daily. He asked Ike why he was concerned. Ike replied, "Well, I'm worried about those Rooshins, but hell, when they see what the stripminers have done, they'll figure that somebody beat them to it."

In response to the question about whether there were any nuts in the area, Ike remarked, "When you cross that bridge down the road, they're all nuts."

Ike was simply a delicious specimen of humorous characterization. Somebody once asked Ike if he ever went to the church directly across from his saloon. His irreverent reply was, "No, and if half of them over there came over here and paid me, they wouldn't be going either." He made fun of life and yet he thoroughly enjoyed it. He made fun of Mag and yet he loved her. Nobody else dare say a word about her. He was a good father to his two adopted sons. His was a good-natured kind of fooling. Ike's stories have been repeated over and over on the crick. He joked without effort and he was one to whom life seemed good. For many he was a welcomed companion for an idle hour and made exaggeration seem more lifelike than accuracy. Many of the things that he said were the natural things to say, too natural for anybody but him to say. A customer once asked Ike for a straw. Ike looked him straight in the eye and said, "There's a broom full of them over in the corner."

Ike saw things with a wonderful clearness, and his effect lingers in the mind not as sayings but as pictures and situations. We crick people liked to laugh and we richly rewarded those who could make us do so.

Mary Colleen Buckley

Questions for discussion

1. How does the author use physical details to characterize Ike Morgan? What is attractive about him?

2. Do you find Ike's humor and wit to be representative of the people living in the "crick" area? Of their way of life? What is good/bad about such an atmosphere?

3. Discuss Ike's relationship with his wife, customers, and friends.

4. In what respect does Ike become a local legend? Is he "larger than life"?

5. Write an essay characterizing an individual whom you know with similar qualities.

The essence of characterization

1. Stress the essential qualities of a person.
   Physical description may not be included at all unless it is essential to the reader's understanding of the inner person.

2. Decide what limitations to place on the subject.
   It is impossible to cover every quality of a person in a short essay, and attempts to cover too much will result in a scattered, disorganized overview. Concentrate on one quality, or a few important ones, which reflect the most outstanding and unusual facets of the individual.

3. Be specific.
   In description, in narration, in other types of essays, specific writing is always preferable to the general. Avoid meaningless general statements, such as "She is a nice girl"; "He is always fun to be around"; or "I never agree with my mother about anything." Also, do not use such clichés as "He is always there for me"; "She will always listen to my problems"; or "He would give you the shirt off his back."

4. Illustrate through specific examples.
   Each time you want to convey something about a character, whether it is a favorable or an unfavorable quality, don't just state it, but show it through illustrative examples.

Four types of characterization essays

1. *Someone you know*—This is the most common type and probably the easiest, characterizing a friend, an enemy, a family member, an employer, a colleague, a classmate, or unusual pet. The examples you use should show the reader why the particular subject was interesting enough for you to choose.

2. *Someone you don't know*—You can write essays on famous persons, celebrities that you admire (politicians, film stars, athletes), historical persons, or even fictional characters. Obviously, should you choose to write about such a person, you should be an expert and your essay should be factual. Yet you should also have a uniquely personal insight into the subject, and some reason why you want to write about that person. Without your own point of view to express, you will write a dry, impersonal essay which will sound either like an encyclopedia report or a gossip column—a

poor result. Interpret the subject's significance—do not merely report on birth, dates, marriages, awards, and so on.

3. *Yourself*—Those who like to write personal essays may write a self-analysis focusing on some aspects of their own characters; such essays may be serious, but may also lend themselves to humor. Typical topics might be "Why I am Selfish," "Overcoming My Shyness," "How I changed," or "How I'd like to Change."

4. *Group*—Group characterizations, also often humorous, discuss a group which the writer belongs to or has observed. Such topics may include occupations (waitress, nurse), or social or academic groups (cheerleaders, football players), or hobbyists (fishermen, bird watchers). The writer must generalize (without stereotyping) to get across the shared qualities of the group, but the writer can still be specific by referring to individual members and activities.

Doris

Doris Gracey, 87, lives alone in a huge old house she inherited from her family. For most of her life she has been by herself in the same place, an unattractive, single woman "without much style" (as my mother says). Now, she can hardly see, and sometimes falls asleep on the telephone. Yet somehow this spry little old lady is happier than most people I know.

Walking into Doris's big house is like walking into a museum or a novelty store. Every room is crammed with souvenirs and mementoes of her travels and many friends, and she has a story to go with each object. She has oriental tapestries and statues, picturesque music boxes, colorful toys, and patterned afghans. Some of these have been in the same place for fifty years, but every Christmas, when I make my holiday visit, a few new items have been added. Doris can tell me the complete story of everything she owns: "It was 1914," she will say, "and I was going to a dance with some friends, and I carried this fan and handkerchief. . . ."

Most of all, the lady has dolls. There must be hundreds of dolls of every size, male and female. Many she makes herself; others are gifts; some are even human-sized store mannequins. She has spent much of her life making wardrobes for them. It seems she can make doll clothes or shoes or purses out of almost any old household object including foam, egg cartons, or milk containers.

Doris has made many dolls into famous literary or story characters, like Alice in Wonderland, Cinderella, and Snow White. Others are old movie stars—a Greta Garbo doll, a Jean Harlow. Some, including the mannequins, she has endowed with names, personalities, and life histories of their own. Her favorite, the five-foot, ten-inch Lulu, has a number of ensembles to suit her busy lifestyle. Every Christmas, Doris shows off at least one new doll, and a new outfit for the ever-popular Lulu.

Doris has found the secret to a happy and exciting old age. Not only does she keep herself busy with hobbies, but she keeps her home interesting enough that many people want to visit her.

Questions for discussion

1. Characterize Doris Gracey. Do you find her interesting? Why? Why not?

2. Do you consider Doris to be a stereotype of a senior citizen living alone? Is she typical of an old spinster?

3. What do the dolls symbolize? Why is Doris preoccupied with them?

Aunt Jean

Aunt Jean was one of five sisters, each of whom was known for a particular quality. One was the "pretty" one; another was the "smart" one; Aunt Jean was the "dependable" one. Her parents always said, "Jean keeps her promises." She probably would have preferred to be considered the "smart" or "pretty" one, but Aunt Jean spent her life keeping promises, being dependable, and influencing me to have these qualities. I've always wanted to be like her.

Being a childless widow, Aunt Jean "adopted" me and her other relatives. With a good income, she lavished presents and treats on us. She took me out for expensive dinners countless times, and was also a "party lady" who corrupted me with my first *legal* drink, and numerous later ones. Until well into her eighties, she lived up to her role as the "dependable relative," available to take people shopping or running errands. She also frequently sent checks to me and others, or appeared at the family home with baskets of food.

In the spring of 1964, at age seventy, she developed cancer. The doctors gave her six weeks to live. She refused to accept death and made her most important promise. She told me that we would be out "hitting the bars" by summer. I didn't believe this, but she was right. In fact, she went back to her accounting job, worked until she was eighty, and died at eighty-seven, having outwitted the doctors by seventeen years.

Two years before she died, she had made a colorful afghan for my mother's sofa, and promised me one. Aunt Jean was finally running out of energy, but she worked slowly on the afghan that she had promised to me. Finally, it arrived, big as a circus tent, bright and colorful, the most cheerful item in my house.

A month later, my favorite relative died, having kept her last important promise in life.

Questions for discussion

1. What are some adjectives that can be used to characterize Aunt Jean?

2. Do you see a symbol in the afghan promised to the writer? What is it?

3. Should we abide by the promises we make? Why?

4. This essay could have been entitled, "The Promise." Do you think Aunt Jean's character influenced the writer? In what ways?

5. Are such ethical qualities a thing of the past with the older generation? Do you know anyone with similar qualities?

Streisand: "Nothing's Impossible"

"The trouble with her is, she settled for *more*." This is how one of Barbra Streisand's friends described her. Let other people be content with less. Streisand, a known perfectionist, always wants more, which means testing new abilities and trying the unknown. "She's OK if you like talent," said another admirer. Streisand has stretched her talent more than any known female entertainer.

Considered ugly and an oddball throughout high school (as were many geniuses), Barbra Streisand became a Broadway and recording star within two years of graduation. In 1963, at the age of twenty, she put her first album in the top ten.

Streisand was one of the few non-rock musical artists to survive the Beatles and British rock invasion which wiped most other music off the charts. (Herb Alpert also survived, but only briefly.) Streisand was younger than the Beatles, but she kept having top-five albums on her own terms, singing older music, the show tunes of their parents' generation.

By 1970, she had won nearly every award available—Grammys, Emmys, and an Oscar in her first movie. And still she wanted to branch out, take more chances, reach more people. She began singing rock tunes and—surprise—they were "hits." She even had a couple of disco hits. "Enough is enough" claimed one. But it wasn't. The surprising star made a *classical* album. Meanwhile, she won another Academy Award, this time for composing. Has another performer covered so many bases?

In 1983, she capped her previous achievements by becoming the first woman to produce, direct, (co)-write, and star in a major movie. The result, *Yentl,* was a subtle, gentle, serious, and profound study of sexism, and one of the most beautiful movies ever made.

"Nothing's impossible," said Streisand as Yentl. The woman's phenomenal career proves it.

D.B.

Questions for discussion

1. Do you agree with the statement, "Nothing's impossible"? Explain.

2. To what do you attribute Streisand's resounding success?

3. Do you strive for perfection? In what ways? Is it possible to achieve that level in our personal or professional lives? Why? Why not?

Mozart—Child Prodigy

I have always liked Mozart's music, and, after seeing the movie *Amadeus,* I decided to study his life. Mozart may be the most famous example in history of a genius child prodigy. Before his teens, he was famous throughout Europe as a composer and as a performer. Unfortunately, as with many child stars today, his early fame made it difficult to grow up and contributed to his early death at thirty-five.

Mozart could read and write music before he could read or write letters and words. When he was five, Mozart told his father that he had composed a piano concerto. His father looked at the scribbled music and said, "Yes you have, but it is too advanced and difficult for anyone to play."

Afterwards, Mozart played his own difficult concerto, saying, "If it were easy, it wouldn't be good."

At that time his father gave up on his own musical career and began to exhibit his son in Germany, Austria, Italy, and France. Though his talent was admired, the child was treated like a circus exhibit or a freak of nature.

The child Mozart did not have much of a social life, seldom got to play, and for some years did not even have a home, as the father moved him from one performing place to another. Perhaps this is why the man Mozart remained something of a child, always anxious to play and dance and laugh, not able to face responsibility.

Mozart did not earn much money in his life, and, what he did earn, he spent quickly. He never achieved financial responsibility, nor did he exhibit "adult" mature behavior, but he kept composing every kind of music that existed. What amazes listeners is that so much of his music is calm, serious, serene, and peaceful . . . when his life was not.

He and his wife had six children, four of whom died pathetically as infants. (Mozart's parents had seven children, with five dying early.) Both Mozart and his wife were frail people who were plagued by ill health.

If I have had a hard day, if work or distractions have gotten to me, if my nerves are bad—a half hour of Mozart's music is the most soothing remedy I know.

D.B.

Questions for discussion

1. What impact has music had in your life? What type of music do you admire? Why?

2. What is a "child prodigy"? Do you know of any in your experience?

3. Why do so many child "stars" have a difficult time as adults?

4. If you had a child genius, would you sacrifice his early years pursuing fame and fortune as Mozart's father did? What would you do if your child were a Mozart or a Michael Jackson?

Someone I Admire

Ed was born in 1945 with brain damage, cerebral palsy, and other physical defects. He did not develop as other babies do, being unable to walk, talk, read, write, dress, or feed himself until long after normal. Throughout his childhood, doctors at many hospitals told his parents that Ed was retarded, a vegetable, that he should be institutionalized because he had no chance to go to school or lead a normal life.

Many parents would give up on a child when told such devastating news. But Ed's family believed that he *could* learn. They insisted on sending him to school and on helping him. They consulted with his teachers and explained his problems honestly, so that Ed could understand why he was "different" and how to cope with his shortcomings.

Nothing came easily for Ed—not school, not play, not social life. But he became determined to have the life the doctors said he couldn't have. His parents helped, but in the end it was Ed who graduated from high school; it was Ed who got a job in a restaurant; it was Ed who moved into our apartment, made many friends, and proved all the wise doctors wrong.

Ed has learned and has taught me, his brother, that people can do anything if they want to badly enough. Now, at thirty-seven, he is a junior in college, majoring in psychology with a "B" average, intending to become a counselor to help others. Ed is probably the brightest, certainly the bravest, person I know. This college student, who is also president of a marathon running club and on the county board of health, wasn't supposed to have a life at all. If our parents had taken the doctors' advice, Ed would be a "vegetable" in a hospital now, helpless. Instead, his life has been a series of victories.

It makes me wonder how many other parents have listened to doctors, how many lives have been wasted away because some "expert" said the child was beyond hope, that the child would never amount to anything. And it makes me angry and impatient when a "normal" student complains about work and says, "I can't do this." Ed, who I think turned out to be a genius, has proven that anyone can be one.

Questions for discussion

1. Do you agree with the writer's assessment that Ed is brave? How?

2. Why does the writer admire Ed? Do you?

3. Does the writer give the reader specifics concerning Ed's "victories"?

4. Do you know of a similar situation or person who overcame great personal odds to be successful? Who?

The Measure of All Things

From the number of Irish people emigrating to America in the early twentieth century, it would seem that everyone had an Irish grandmother. Actually, I had two. My mother's mother, Mary MacDonald, from Iona by way of Armagh, had died long before I began to swim in the amniotic fluid. My father's mother, Catherine Feeney, from Ballymoate, County Sligo, was separated from her granddaughter by a thousand leagues of open, wild Atlantic and a world war. Nevertheless, the presence of those two formidable women did not diminish. As heroines of nursery tales, they easily displaced Little Red, Goldie, and all that ilk. "Tell about the time

Uncle David was going to be spanked." I grew up in their ambience. The Greeks may have held that man was the measure of all things, but I came to measure experience in terms of those two near-mythical grandmothers.

Grandmother Catherine's picture did not impress me. My father's mother managed to look simultaneously fragile and dumpy in her long, black working-class best, her white hair pulled straight back from her forehead and gathered carelessly in a bun. Her rimless glasses were far from fashionable then.

This plain, small woman had survived the loss at sea of her first husband, master of a merchant vessel, followed by the loss of their children in some of Ireland's interminable "troubles," a sorrow she kept secret to the end of her life.

Emigrating to Scotland during subsequent "troubles," she met and married my grandfather. In fact, she was pregnant with my father and walking home on a fine, soft day from work in Wishard—a mere twelve miles, mostly hilly—when a sudden storm blew in from the east, wind and rain off the North Sea, the Grampians, and the Lammermoors. My grandmother developed pneumonia, then rheumatic fever, both of which my father was born with. If she lived, the doctors said, she would be a lifelong invalid. And there were times when she could not lift her arms to brush her hair, which was long enough to sit on. So, every day when my grandfather came home from the mines, he sat brushing that mane of light reddish-brown hair with the silver and mother of pearl brushes that had been his wedding gift.

But between bouts of bronchitis and other "bad spells," Catherine Feeney bore and nursed four more children, raised several who were not her own, extended hospitality to people who had left Ireland—for various reasons. She cleaned like one of the Furies, cooked for Gargantua, never missed a day's work or a day's mass, cared for those poorer and weaker than she. And she nurtured her children in the fear of the Lord—Saturday confession, the family rosary, no smoking, no playing cards on Sunday or any day when the "devil's cards" led to squabbling among the children.

But it was her character and my grandfather's that inspired implicit trust in their children so that, to this day, when a question arises, it is often answered by what they did or would have done. "Ah, sure, the old ones knew best."

Grandmother Mary MacDonald was equally tiny and nearly blind, although none of her children knew about her poor eyesight until she was dead. Apparently a teacher in Ireland had struck her across the eyes with ruler, more than once. She was tiny, but she had the posture of a princess. She had been brought up with the children of Prince Arthur, Duke of Connaught, whose bailiff her father was, and educated for a short time in a French convent where she had learned sewing—fortunately, for she loved beautiful clothes. For herself and her four daughters, she could copy any dress she saw, even from a *Tatler* photograph. She never had a house without a piano and people gathered around it, singing or listening. Her cooking—another result of her brief French education—has been the subject of fond reminiscence and imitation for two generations. Widely read, politically aware, she wanted votes for women; she tried to prevent her oldest son from joining the Gordon Highlanders to fight in World War I. In the labor unrest in Scotland, her sympathies went with the workers. She was witty and beautiful, clever at managing money and people. At her death, my grandfather and the children discovered she had accounts they knew nothing about. As for managing people, well, there was the case of my grandfather.

Apparently, my grandfather had the habit of spending an hour in a friendly pub before returning home for the evening. My grandmother remonstrated with him gently. He was not persuaded to change his ways. She decided, therefore, to TEACH HIM A LESSON. Burning the gaslight in their bedroom low and making sure the fire did not blaze up too brightly, she set the scene for his homecoming, overturning a table, a chair or two, but leaving his favorite chair beside the fire where he usually sat and smoked his pipe, often falling asleep. Next came a judicious tearing of her night clothes, followed by an application of soot, india ink, and raspberry syrup to her face, arms, and gown. Finally, she took a bottle of whiskey and spilled enough on the rug, bed, and curtains to make the room reek. Leaving the bottle and a glass strategically near Grandfather's chair, she went to bed to wait.

Enter Grandfather, more than a little the worse for wear. He stumbled over to his chair, slid down into it, and promptly fell asleep. Grandmother waited until she was sure that he had fallen into a sound sleep. She began to moan and cry, softly at first, then louder and louder. The noise roused Grandfather. Still in a daze, he made his way to the bed. "Oh, my darling. Oh, Mary, what have I done to you?"

Grandmother never explicitly told him that he had come home drunk and beaten her, but he would have gone to his grave believing that if my mother had not told him the truth in 1927, four years after my grandmother's death. He shook his head and laughed.

Dr. Noreen Hayes

Questions for discussion

1. What do you find heroic about Grandmother Feeney? What does her physical courage reflect about her background? Do you think that such women exist today? In America?

2. What was Grandmother MacDonald's motive in "fooling" her husband? What does this tell us about her? About her husband?

3. In addition to characterization, the essay is also a study in comparison and contrast. Which of the two Grandmothers do you find more appealing? Why?

4. What does the author mean by the title? How does it apply to her characters?

5. Write a five hundred word essay characterizing two relatives of yours.

The Ones That Got Away

Looking back over the students of the sixties, I remember two with particular vividness. Call them Isaac and Ishmael. Both might have been born children of the promise; in neither instance, however, was the promise kept.

Isaac habitually sat bolt upright in the first chair in the first row of his eight o'clock English 101 section, his intense dark eyes never still. His thin, sallow face registered instant agreement or disagreement with whatever was being said. He could hardly wait to participate, yet when he did speak, he began by groping for words in his three-inch thatch of black hair—he was the first non-black I knew who had an Afro. Suddenly his long, never too clean fingers found something under his precarious yarmulka. Then the words rushed out—harsh, high pitched, authoritative. He hated to repeat himself, as he often had to, but he would not change his delivery. He wrote the same way, in large, childish script with obvious muscular difficulty and extreme pressure on the pen.

Orwell, Thoreau, James Baldwin—whatever we read, Isaac enjoyed, arguing for or against the writer or his classmates, but always against capital punishment and the Vietnam war, always in favor of civil rights and Robert Kennedy, his idol, or the relic of another idol. He had no trouble finding an idea. But he needed to organize his thoughts, to gauge his audience, to catch details—words omitted or misspelled, missing commas.

And what of Ishmael? He came late, when he came, to his three o'clock class, slipped into the back, in a corner near the door, hunched his broad shoulders over his student desk until all I or anyone else could see of him was the wavy brown hair on the crown and back of his head. But I knew what he was doing. He was staring at his hands, the fingernails bitten to the quick. At least, that's what he did in conference in my office. I don't know how I persuaded him to come in, but if he had not come, I would never have heard his deep, slow, deliberate voice, for he never spoke nor moved in class. Six feet of him, sprawled in my office chair, the clean-cut All-American boy in jeans, t-shirt, and sneaks—he seemed totally relaxed, carefree. Indeed, he was carefree: he didn't care about anything or anyone, so he told me. Nothing we read interested him. "I don't have any reason to write. Give me one good reason. When it comes right down to it, I got no reason to do anything, no reason to go on, well, you know, like, just to go on."

And he didn't write, not at first. I had him up to nine sentences by the time he left. And his sessions with somebody in the Counseling Center had helped him to talk more easily on a one-to-one basis. He knew all about guns and pit bulls. If blacks left him alone, he'd leave them alone. Capital punishment was all right with him. If he were ever convicted of murder, he'd take the chair any day over a life sentence. He thought about joining the marines, going to Vietnam. He loved America; he knew that, and he hated the Communists. Besides, they would draft him anyway, and he might as well get it over with. He had also thought of joining the American Nazi Party. And he didn't know about Robert Kennedy.

They both dropped out.

Every day Isaac fidgeted more. His bones appeared too big for his 5' 4" frame. His knickers and other Ivy League duds were conspicuously torn, patched, stained. He grew a funny little moustache like a paste-on Charlie Chaplin, then a beard. The day I signed his withdrawal slip, I noticed he had shaved it off. He had cut himself badly and his hands were shaking. Although he promised to keep in touch, I didn't believe I would hear from him.

I didn't hear from him, but I did hear of him. Cheryl, another student and Isaac's friend, met him by chance in a Chicago parking lot. He was "doing fine," working with his uncle, one of Mayor Daley's cronies. He invited her to his apartment; in fact, he made her promise that she would come. Reluctantly, she kept her word. Food, dishes, clothes lay in heaps. There were no furnishings except a life-size portrait of Timothy Leary and a number of incense burners. She was crying the day she told me that Isaac was in an institution—she didn't know where. His family had put him away.

Ishmael left me a note: Dear Miss Hayes they are going to kick me out of this great place for fiting in the dorm, so I am leving first.

I will be going in service try to let you know the branch.

We lost them both.

Last week in Washington, I tried to find Ishmael's name on the Viet Nam Memorial. Isaac would have told me indignantly I was saying kaddish for them. Amen. Amen.

Dr. Noreen Hayes

Questions for discussion

1. How does the author use physical details to characterize Isaac and Ishmael? What is the significance of their names?

2. Do you sympathize with Isaac? With Ishmael? Why? Why not?

3. Using Dr. Hayes' pattern of comparison and contrast, write an essay characterizing two individuals whom you know. Include physical description and dialogue to convey important elements of your characterization

The Face at the Window

Every time I come home, the living room curtain moves and a face appears at the window. The face vanishes, reappears, vanishes, and returns as I come up the walk and turn the key in the door.

The ecstatic face belongs to Harley, my super-enthusiastic hundred pound German Shepherd, who possesses one of the world's biggest, eternal smiles—the open-mouthed grin. I recall that smile, which just may be the happiest sight in my daily life.

Harley waits at the window for me to come home and flicks the curtain aside when he hears the bus stop to let me off. I think he checks the window all day whenever a vehicle stops or a car door slams that may be bringing me home. When I really do get there, he begins his welcoming ritual: first the face at the window; then he runs to the door and back to the window, door, and window again until I'm inside the house.

Harley, born in July 1991 in my house, seems always to be in a good mood. He barks at other dogs and most people, which frightens some because of his hugeness, but he really likes dogs and people (and my cats, who don't feel quite the same affinity for *him*). His bark seems to be saying, "Please notice me. Stop and play."

I have never seen him mean or cross, angry or hostile—although he did have a cautionary word for one of my friends who injudiciously tried to take a bone out of his mouth. Harley gave a "Don't even think it" look and my friend prudently withdrew. Harley is generally happy, except for the weekly occasion when I must reprimand him for eating yet another sofa section, or for removing and scattering the stuffings from a pillow. Most of my pillows have been reduced to pathetic shreds.

My big, perpetual puppy, he of the round-the-clock open-mouthed grin, was named "Harley" after a delightful song by Kathy Mattea, an outgoing singer who just happens to be my all-time favorite. It seemed very right that my favorite pet and my favorite singer should come together this way, two extroverts, and I hope someday to meet the singer and tell her about it.

Meanwhile, I cherish all the quality time I get to spend with my undisciplined, untamed, hyper-energetic, loving dog. My only hope is that I get to see his grinning face at my window far into the twenty-first century.

D.B.

Questions for discussion

1. What other adjectives could you use to characterize Harley? Why?

2. What does the tone of the essay convey to the reader?

3. How would you characterize the author of the essay?

Self characterization

Phobia

I'm not sure which came first or when, but my chief phobia and my pet peeve are the same: I am afraid of time, my worst enemy which changes everything, eventually taking away everyone I love, everyone I like. Annoyed by anyone who makes me wait or waste time, I have a compulsion to be occupied constructively at all hours, not to waste a precious moment. Therefore, I maintain a hectic schedule that never slows down. There is so much to be done and enjoyed, so little time.

Often accused of not being spontaneous because I plan what I do as far in advance as possible, I have a fear of empty, unplanned, unoccupied time. Every day I have this constant, nagging feeling of too many plans, but I'm lost without them.

I have often wished to stop time, to freeze it right there, when my life was going the way I wanted. Many days I would like time to slow down so I could fully enjoy an experience. Unfortunately, I can't remember a "slow" year or "slow" time in my life; it always hurries heartlessly on, changing or taking away whatever I like. Do you understand why I get angry with people who waste time?

After my mother died, my aunt gave me a box of letters Mother wrote to her over a fifty year period. On a warm August day, I sat under a tree and read her letters. This high school girl's writing style was already its completely formed adult self. She wrote of presents received for graduation—probably the nicest gifts she got during the Depression. There was a letter written in 1939, when she was a newlywed setting up her first apartment with my father. She had just bought a picture of a writer at work called "Inspiration." That same picture still hung over the typewriter when she died, fifty years later. I thought fifty years was too little time, passing too fast, for her to enjoy the picture, which I now own.

There was a letter written when she was pregnant with me, wondering who and what I would be. There were other letters written about her literary sales, my high school and college years, and the time I started teaching.

And as I sat under the tree in August 1989, holding all those pieces of my life and before my life, they seemed like pieces of time. On that hot day, I got a chill. I shivered, and I haven't stopped yet. I am terrified at the swift passage of time which took away that Depression schoolgirl, that eager newlywed. She didn't have nearly long enough time. Neither do I.

D.B.

Questions for discussion

Does the author express thoughts or feelings that seem universal? What are they? Do you feel the same way about the passing of time?

Assignment

Select one of the four types of characterization analyzed and write a three-hundred word essay on that subject.

Chapter 5

Writing the Process Paper

No matter what our station in life, inevitably we will be called upon to give directions, to advise someone on a particular type of procedure, or simply to tell someone how to do something. From following directions in a recipe to giving instructions on how to change oil in a car, we accomplish the procedure only if we adhere to a step-by-step sequence, from the very first step to the last. This "how to" approach is perhaps the easiest type of paper to write for two reasons: The purpose (theme) is the writer's intention to explain the steps of the process in natural chronological order; therefore, the organization of the paper is simply a matter of putting the steps in their proper order. It is important to do the right thing at the right juncture in clear sequence. Still, certain guidelines must be followed.

Use the second person.

In writing a process paper, you should use the second person (you) because, generally, you are addressing the reader. Although the use of the second person imperative is more effective in a process, it is not recommended for other types of exposition.

State the process.

Identify the subject by stating the process to be performed and by relating the importance of the process. Remember the reader by answering such questions as, "What is the importance of this procedure?" and "Who performs this task?" For instance, "How to Apply Makeup Properly" is of value only to those who wear makeup, and probably only to a certain percentage of that interest group. Nevertheless, the "importance" of the subject may be of general interest, rather than a frivolous topic, such as "How to Pick Your Nose at the Supper Table without Offending the Guests."

Explain the steps clearly.

If the process is relatively simple, the organization of the paper follows the development of the steps in the process. Each sequence should be analyzed, developed adequately, and explained clearly. If the subject deals with a complicated technical procedure (How to Construct a Nuclear Reactor), then the process will probably be subdivided into several processes with an organization of their own, each fully developed and in the proper order, but related to the original theme.

Define your terms.

If any special terms relative to the process occur, do not take for granted that the reader knows the definition of such terms (jargon). Define each term as it occurs, or, if such a system proves too clumsy, offer the reader a glossary at the end of the composition. Remember your purpose is to communicate clearly and not to befuddle the reader.

Be complete.

Do not omit any step by assuming that the reader will fill in the blanks. Clarity and completeness are essential.

Generally, the last step in the process provides the writer with the necessary conclusion for his essay. But this stylistic device more often reflects a relieved finale rather than a graceful conclusión. Two of the better ways to end the paper are by summarizing the major steps or by commenting on the importance of the process. *Do not* end your essay with the last step of the process.

Be interesting.

As in all writing, but especially concerning the process paper, try to make your presentation interesting to the reader. Vary your sentence patterns; do not digress; present your information in concrete terms in clear language; do not use stylistic flourishes or pretentious language. As an aid to clarity, warn your reader against certain errors sometimes or often made in the process, thus providing contrast and interest to your composition.

Tips on How to Study

Knowing the correct procedure in preparing for a test or simply in retaining knowledge is vital in high school and college. Following these steps will better prepare you for that dreaded test or classroom quiz. Although the amount of time needed for study will vary with the individual student and his course load, plan to spend an average of one and a half hours for each hour spent in class. Planning your study schedule is your first step.

Second, gather all of the materials which you will need before you begin to study. This includes books, notes, pen and paper, and a dictionary. A complete inventory of essential material at hand is important in saving time. If you must get up and search for a pen or an eraser after you have begun to study, you not only waste time, but you interrupt your concentration.

Third, before you begin studying, make sure you are rested and alert. Do not attempt to study if you are half asleep, nervous, or emotionally upset. Your mind must focus on the material. Related to this factor is your physical readiness. If you anticipate a long session, provide yourself with a refreshing liquid (coffee, tea) for periodic stimulation. As for food, avoid snacks (potato chips, ice cream); they're too troublesome. While you can't truly concentrate if you're hungry, gorging on junk food isn't conducive to the learning process.

Fourth, find a place where nothing can distract you from the task. Shun a room where people are talking, whispering, laughing, or walking about. Obviously, the noise of television or radio must be avoided completely. A serene atmosphere is mandatory for full concentration if your mind is to absorb the material. No, the "peace" of libraries is too often fractured by noisome students. Lock yourself in a room where you are free from any sort of invasion. Try to study in the same place every day—you will concentrate better and spend less time settling down.

A fifth step in the proper study habits involves obtaining and arranging the proper furniture. A clean desk is important, large enough to spread your books and writing material without having to dig through piles of material for easy reference. A wooden chair with a hard back is preferable over a comfortable, plush chair. *Never* study on a couch or sofa! Before you know it, you'll be waking up with your face on your textbook rather than above it. The *proper lighting* is vitally important. Generally, one of the best methods in reading and writing is to have the light placed over your right shoulder, a soft light, not one that glares off the book's pages.

In summary, keeping a study schedule, collecting the necessary materials, preparing yourself mentally and physically, studying in a suitable place, and obtaining and arranging the proper furniture will better prepare you to succeed in your academic career.

How to Change Oil in a Car

Keeping the oil clean in a car's engine helps to preserve its expected life and helps the car get better gas mileage. Changing the oil in the engine is an important but easy task.

To begin this process, gather all the needed tools and supplies. The most common tools needed are an oil filter wrench, a wrench (which may vary in size) to remove the oil pan bolt, a funnel, a pan to drain the dirty oil in, a can opener, and two ramps. Four or more quarts of oil, depending on the model of car, and an oil filter are also needed.

After gathering these necessities, move your car to a vacant area where you will not be disturbed and place the two ramps in front of the front wheels. Drive your car up on the ramps just enough to elevate the car sufficiently for you to be able to work underneath the engine. Draw the emergency brake and block the rear tire. Now is the time to crawl under the engine and remove the oil pan drain nut, which is located on the left side of the oil pan. Make sure there is a pan under the engine to collect the oil which drains from the engine.

Next, remove the dirty oil filter which is located next to the oil pan. After the oil has drained out of the engine, move the old oil and filter out of your way. Put the oil pan bolt back in the pan and tighten it.

Open a quart of oil and pour it into the new oil filter before inserting the filter. Rub some oil on the top of the oil filter gasket to ensure a good seal when it is tightened. Being careful not to spill any oil, take the filter and screw it back on, tightening it by hand only. Using the funnel, add the remaining three or four quarts of oil to the engine.

After that, start the car's engine and check for leaks near the oil pan bolt and the oil filter. Now remove all the tools from under the car and back it off the ramps. Remember to release the emergency brake and to remove the tire block. Check the oil level after the car is on level ground and add oil if necessary. Dispose of the old oil, the oil filter, and the empty cans. Put away the ramps and the other tools that were used.

Keeping your car's engine oil clean is important. Changing the oil and the oil filter can be done easily and inexpensively. This is a major step in keeping your car performing at an optimum level.

How to Apply a Tourniquet

The average citizen is seldom confronted with a situation in which he must administer lifesaving measures. Although most first aid procedures are simple and easy to employ, if performed incorrectly they can cause the victim to suffer serious additional harm. The tourniquet is an example of a first aid measure that may be employed by an informed citizen to save a life.

A tourniquet is used as a last means to control hemorrhaging, or the abnormal bleeding which threatens someone's life. The tourniquet is used only if the application of a pressure dressing fails to control bleeding. Because most adults can tolerate the loss of one pint of blood, bleeding is considered to be uncontrolled if the blood loss is in excess of one pint.

The type of injury which might anticipate a need for a tourniquet is an amputated, mangled, or crushed extremity. With this type of injury, large arteries are severed and the victim can bleed to death in a matter of seconds. Arterial bleeding may be distinguished from venous bleeding by the presence of bright red blood spurting from the injury; venous blood is dark red and flows from the injury. A tourniquet must be used to control arterial bleeding.

Unless you keep a first aid kit at hand, it is unlikely that you will have a tourniquet available in an emergency situation. Many items—a tie, a belt, a stocking, or a torn piece of fabric—may be used. Never use a piece of wire or rope because they are too damaging to the tissues. If a torn piece of fabric is used, tear it long enough so that is will extend around the limb with enough fabric left over to tie two knots. In addition to the piece of fabric, a firm rod, a pen, a pencil, a spoon, or a stick, is also needed. The rod is used to tighten the tourniquet.

When applying the tourniquet, place the fabric one inch above the injury. Placing the tourniquet below the injury will not control the bleeding, and placing it too high will cut off the blood supply in too great an area. Wrap the material loosely around the extremity. If the material is long, it may be wrapped several times without danger to the victim. You should be able to insert two fingers between the fabric and the victim's skin.

Next, tie a loose knot in the material and slip the rod through the center of the knot. Tighten the knot and tie a second knot over the first knot. The rod must be held firmly in place so the tourniquet can be tightened.

To tighten the tourniquet, grasp the rod in one hand and turn it clockwise. When the pressure of the tourniquet exceeds the pressure in the artery, the bleeding will stop. Do not tighten the tourniquet any more than necessary to stop the bleeding. Maintain a constant amount of pressure by holding the rod in position. Note the exact time when the tourniquet was tightened; such information is important in the physician's evaluation of the victim's condition.

Because the circulation of blood is stopped in the area below the tourniquet, gangrene (the death of tissues due to a loss of blood) can set in, endangering an extremity that might otherwise have been saved. To prevent gangrene, loosen the tourniquet for five seconds every twenty minutes. To loosen the tourniquet, simply rotate the rod counter-clockwise until the bleeding returns.

Count to five and tighten the tourniquet by turning the rod clockwise. As soon as the bleeding ceases, stop turning the rod and hold it in position until the victim is in the hands of medical personnel.

The tourniquet is a lifesaving device that may be employed in extreme circumstances. If applied incorrectly, the tourniquet may cause the victim to lose a limb that might have been saved. It must be remembered that a tourniquet is used only when direct pressure over the injury cannot control bleeding, is always used with arterial bleeding, is applied one inch above the injury, and is loosened every twenty minutes for five seconds.

Questions for discussion

1. Do you agree with the author's approach in "How to Study"? Could you have added more ideas on the subject?

2. Is the essay on "How to change Oil in a Car" clear to you? After reading the instructions, could you change the oil in your car?

3. In "How to Apply a Tourniquet," did the author make allowances for what to avoid in safeguarding the victim? Are the steps clear in the process? After reading the essay, do you feel qualified to attempt such a procedure on a possible victim?

How to Develop Black and White Film

The process required to develop a roll of black and white film is not complicated and needs little effort. It is primarily a matter of having the proper equipment and chemicals and following a few basic steps, the details of which depend upon the specific type of film being developed. The following process will be different from most others on the same subject, for there is no set pattern and few restrictions.

Three chemical mixtures are necessary to develop a roll of black and white film into a negative. All three are mixed with quantities of water specified on the brand's package. The first is the *developer,* which does precisely that: it develops the film. The second is the *stop,* which stops the chemical process. The last mixture is the *fixer;* it finishes the process by preparing the film to be washed in water. This entire process is done in a tank sealed from light. The film itself is wound into a reel to avoid touching any part of itself at any point.

Although easy enough to do, loading the film on the reel is the most hazardous step, for this is the point where it is easiest for something to go wrong. In preparation for this step, be certain that no light can come into the room where the loading process occurs. Pour 290 milliliters of developer into the tank and place the tank, the tank's lid, and a pair of scissors at a place where they can be easily reached. If the film has a leader (a piece of film protruding from the canister), this can be loaded into the reel before turning out the lights. If the film does not have a leader, use a can opener to pry open one side of the canister, and then load as before, doing both steps in total darkness. Whichever method is used, once all of the film is on the reel save that which is attached directly to the canister, and use the scissors to splice the film, getting as close to the canister as possible. Then place the reel into the tank; seal the tank with the lid, and turn the lights on.

For the next seven minutes (more or less, depending on the type of film used), agitate the tank at twenty-second intervals by lightly twisting and shaking it, and tapping it softly on the table at one-minute intervals.

The tank itself should be constructed so that the top may be taken off and yet the film is also protected from the light. This is so because, at the end of seven minutes, the top is removed, the developer poured out, and the stop poured in. Leave this in for thirty seconds, agitating as before, and remove.

Next, pour in the fixer. Leave this in for ten minutes, again agitating as before. When the time has elapsed, remove the fixer and the tank top and place the film under running water for thirty minutes. This will remove any chemicals remaining on the film. After thirty minutes, hang the film out to dry in an area where it will be free from wind or sun contact, with a clip on each end in order for the film to hang straight. After about fifteen minutes, the film will be dry and the printing process may begin.

If you follow the previous steps, a roll of black and white film may be developed with little time and effort. With a knowledge of the basic steps and an adherence to the necessary restrictions, you will develop clear pictures.

How to Apply Makeup

Most females know that applying makeup can be a detailed, tedious process, and that preparing for this process may take as much concentration as the process itself. The right surroundings and tools are important, with the tools close at hand to avoid breaking your concentration. If done properly, applying makeup can become an easy routine.

Before applying makeup, make sure your face has been washed thoroughly. After moistening your face with warm water, place approximately one teaspoon of facial cleanser in the palm of your hand. Work the cleanser into a lather and apply the lather to your face with both hands in a circular fashion. After washing the lather off your hands, splash your face with cool water until all of the soap residue has been removed. Then pat your face dry with a clean towel.

A good lighted mirror should be used when you apply makeup. Sit in a firm chair in front of the mirror and adjust the light according to the amount needed. The magnified mirror should be used for obscure places at the desired angle.

First apply the foundation and the blusher. After using the makeup sponge to apply the foundation, apply the powder to your face. Do the forehead, the nose, the cheeks, and finally the chin. When doing the chin, make sure that the makeup is blended over the neckline to prevent definite lines showing. Pick up the blusher brush and blow on it so that any remaining blusher is removed. Rub the brush across the blusher two times. Apply the blusher where your cheekbones are most prominent. Sweep the brush from this point back towards the top of your ear and all the way to your hairline. After doing this on both sides, blend the blusher into your skin by lightly rubbing it with your fingertips. The blusher should not be bright, but it should look natural to you.

The next step is to apply eye shadow and mascara to your eyes. After selecting the eye shadow, take out the brush and wipe it across the shadow one time. Close the eye which you are going to work with and brush the shadow across the entire eyelid. After doing this, open your eye and close the other one. Repeat the same process. After doing this, gently blend the shadow into your eyelids with your fingertips, making sure that it looks natural to you.

The final step involving the eyes is to apply mascara. After selecting the shade you wish, tilt your head back and look down into the mirror. Brush the mascara around or across the eyelashes of both eyes, making sure that no lumps of mascara stay on your lashes. If a lump of mascara is still on your lashes, just brush it off with the wand. Then tilt your head forward and do the same thing to your lower eyelids.

The final step is to apply the lipstick. After selecting the shade of lipstick you prefer, rub the lipstick across your lips, staying on the natural line of the lip. After applying the lipstick, take a tissue and wipe off any extra from around the edges or in the corners of your mouth.

If the previous steps are followed carefully, applying makeup should become a relaxing habit. The more times you go through the routine, the easier it becomes. Always make sure that the proper tools are at hand. After applying makeup several times, you will begin to develop your own style and will become an "expert" on your own makeup. The best way to learn all that you can about makeup is to experiment with it.

Diane Zamagias

How to Tolerate Students

"Tolerate" usually means to "put up with." It is not a positive word. One who only tolerates something does not like it. In my opinion, a teacher who merely tolerates students probably should not be teaching them, and does not get much enjoyment from his job. To be a good teacher, and to enjoy it, one must, more than tolerate, *like* the students. I have worked with a number of teachers who did not like students, and I have always tried to avoid talking to them, because their attitude is negative and depressing.

To like students it is obviously necessary to like people in general, especially young people. A person who finds it difficult to like people should find another profession instead of education. Still, there are some teachers who seem quite friendly to their families, neighbors, and each other. Yet on the subject of students, they become hostile. What is their problem?

Having observed numerous teachers through the years, beginning or experienced, I've noticed that many of them commit two related errors. First, they quickly forget what it was like to be a student; and, second, they put themselves on a pedestal.

All teachers were students once, and most go into teaching only a few months after they finish school—but how quickly they forget! Students can have many problems of their own trying to "tolerate" teachers who are unclear, contradictory, unprepared, senile, or inexperienced. Teachers can treat students like immature babies, or they can go to the other extreme and talk "over the class's head," expecting too much, thinking the work will come as easily as it now does to them. If the teacher puts himself in the student's place, remembering what it was like for himself, he can avoid most of these communication problems, resulting in better teacher-student relationships.

Similarly, putting oneself on a pedestal is probably the most common teacher error. Some strange magical transformation often takes place in young beginning teachers: they start to believe that their education makes them a better as well as smarter person; they develop large egos and can never be wrong or corrected. (This conceited attitude is frequently encouraged by older, experienced teachers, who convince the younger ones it's the right way to feel.) Therefore, teaching becomes an "ego-trip," with the teacher showing off his knowledge. Naturally, it is difficult for the teacher to like or even tolerate his students, whom he sees as inferior beings—having forgotten that he started that way, too.

I have had many quarrels with fellow teachers—and made my share of enemies among them—because I've seen students talked about and treated with such insulting disrespect. Now I try to ignore it and concentrate on doing my own job. By my definition, that means liking the students. When a time comes in my life that I don't like students, or feel I'm better than they are, that's when I'll quit.

Still, no one's perfect. Try as I might, it is impossible to like every student out of 100 a semester. There will always be from five to ten percent who alienate by distractions, disinterest, or disrespectful behavior. However, by remembering the points in this essay, I'm happy to say I've been teaching twenty years (twelve at ACC) and greatly enjoy the job and the students.

Dudley Brown

Questions for discussion

1. Do you agree with the author's point of view concerning some teachers' treatment of students?

2. Must a teacher "like" students to be a "good" teacher? Why?

3. Do you know of any teachers who actually dislike students? Write a five hundred word essay analyzing the teacher(s) and the situation(s). Be specific. Avoid the subjective approach in your paper.

How to Submit a Manuscript

Before mailing a manuscript to a publisher, you should follow certain standard procedures which the publishing houses adhere to across the country. Following conventional rules will not only save you time and money but provide a more favorable response from that publisher you're trying to influence.

Most publishers require a query letter regarding short stories or novels. *Never send an unsolicited manuscript to a publisher!* With the query letter, include a brief outline or synopsis of your work, together with two or three chapters from your manuscript. Your letter of inquiry should include the book's title, length, and subject matter. A short paragraph about yourself (experience, previous publications) should be included. Type your inquiry letter—neatly, without any errors. Be sure to include a stamped, self-addressed envelope (SASE).

If the editor or publisher responds favorably and wishes to examine your manuscript for possible publication, mail your manuscript in a box—either a typing paper box or one similar in size. Naturally, the manuscript must be typed, preferably on one side of each page. Most publishers will accept photocopies if they are neat and "clean." The pages of your manuscript should be numbered and placed into the box loose, without clips or staples.

Always take the time to address your manuscript to a specific editor or to the appropriate department. Never write, "To Whom It May Concern."

When submitting a manuscript, always enclose the correct amount of return postage. If you wish the manuscript to be insured, indicate the type of return mail preferred and give special instructions in an accompanying letter.

Generally, book manuscripts may be sent by first class mail or by a special fourth-class manuscript rate (not as fast but less expensive). Since these rates are subject to change, consult your local post office to be sure of the current rates. Envelopes and packages should be marked accordingly; remember to mark return envelopes and packages also. To insure your manuscript, inquire at the post office.

Remember that you are responsible for "keeping track" of your manuscript. If you do not receive a reply from the publisher for six or eight weeks (generally) after submission, write a courteous letter concerning the matter. Once again, enclose a stamped, self-addressed envelope to insure a prompt reply.

One last reminder before you mail that precious manuscript out into the cold world of publishing: always keep a copy under lock and key.

Suggested topics for writing a process paper

Select a topic from the following list and write a five hundred word essay.

How to change a tire on a hill

How to bake a cake
(select a specific kind)

How to get to the college from my house

How to apply makeup

How to feed an infant

How to hem a skirt

How to shine shoes

How to change oil in a car

How to tune up a car's engine

How to apply a tourniquet

How to apply CPR

How to clean a gun

How to make a sandwich

How to bathe a dog

How to cut down a tree

How to wash clothes

How to develop film

How to clean battery terminals

How to study

There are several types of non-technical essays.

1. *Creative* process can deal with creative writing, art, music, and how the creative process may be done, for instance, "How I Write a Poem," or "Painting to Music."

2. *Self improvement* tells the reader how to be a better or a happier person in some way—"Building Time," "Learning to Accept Criticism," "Controlling your Temper."

3. *Overcoming an obstacle or a problem* may include such topics as "How to Cope with Depression," "How to Survive Loneliness," "Dealing with your Parents' Divorce."

4. *Avoiding something undesirable* may relate to topics such as "How to Avoid Quarrels," "Staying out of Debt," "Avoiding Peer Pressure."

5. *The wrong way* type of process paper may be humorous or instructive. It tells how to do a process incorrectly, for example, "How Not to Write an Essay," "How Not to Get Dates."

6. *Intellectual* process deals with academic matters, such as "How to Pass Biology," "How to Study," "The Art of Tutoring."

7. *Humorous* content process may overlap with most of the other types, since most of them can be humorous. Examples of this type might include "How to be Unpopular," "How to Ruin a Date,"

"Manipulating your Parents," "How to Con a Teacher," "How to Get Fired."

8. *Personal relationships* may include topics such as "Coping with In-Laws," "How to Keep a Mate," "Getting Along with Six Brothers."

9. *Appreciation* deals with sharing something you like, for example, "How to Enjoy Opera/Classical Music," "How to Enjoy Reading," "Appreciating Exercise."

Note that many of these categories can combine or overlap. Topics given under one category may fit equally well in another.

For class discussion

How many other topics can you suggest for each type? (Also note that process topics need not begin with the words "How to"!)

Exercising Your Mind

The last few years have seen a fitness craze, with all kinds of people who never exercised before now running, biking, stretching, lifting, or doing aerobics. One of the most important types of exercise, though, has been neglected. Most runners, riders, and lifters are still afraid to exercise their minds.

"Afraid" is the key word. People fear the unknown, and what's in a mind is still unknown to us. Most people are afraid to test their skills or ability because they are afraid that, mentally, they can't do much. People have little intellectual confidence. They will not test their limits, like the explorers of old who were afraid to venture too far for fear of falling off the edge of the earth. Columbus, for one, found out differently, and so do geniuses, who explore their own brains and learn that, in fact, their minds have no limits—this could happen to many of us if we only had faith in our potential. Most geniuses remain undiscovered, even by themselves. You might be one.

The brain, like the body's various muscles, responds well to being disciplined, stretched, challenged. Too many people approach a difficult course or test, book or term paper with the attitude, "I can't do it." But runners did not run marathons on their first try, either. They do a little more each day and work up to goals. The same technique works with the brain. Periodically, try something a little harder than you did before—read more pages, write a longer paper than assigned, do extra work that looks difficult. Your mind will expand to include what you do. It won't break, and it won't snap back. Then what you try next will be easier. The mind wants to stretch, to grow. If you don't try, some of it remains unexplored and eventually dies of neglect. But, over a period of time, you can make yourself grow intellectually. On the other hand, just as you get weaker and less developed if you stop exercising your body, so your mind will close off and get "rusty" if you use and challenge it less—which many people do, through lack of self confidence.

Many athletes know the capabilities of nearly every muscle and how to develop it. A bicyclist or a race car driver will learn every part of his machine and how to keep it at peak efficiency and performance. A guitar player or other musician wants to know every note of his instrument and to keep it tuned. Yet these same people keep their minds untuned and do not have a clear notion of what they can do. Often, they are afraid of failure. Yet we fail only when we set limitations on ourselves. Saying "This is too hard for me" is a self-imposed limitation and self-fulfilling prophecy.

There is a definite parallel between physical strength, health, and mind. If you develop the physical energy to exercise, your mental energy and capabilities are correspondingly increased. A good student who doesn't exercise will do better if he does—and vice versa. Most of us need to seek a better balance and equality between the mental and the physical in our lives.

D.B.

Appreciating Music of the Sixties

When I first saw this topic, I thought of a "smartalecky" answer which would close the discussion at once: one can appreciate music of the sixties best by simply listening to some of today's music and hearing how much worse it is. The fact is that most musicians, fans, and critics consider the sixties to be the "Golden Age" for all forms of Rock music, white and black, and it has never recaptured the lost glory of those days. But I am not sure one can appreciate the music fully if one was not there at the time.

When I look at old record charts from 1964-67 (the "great years"), it seems that most of the records listed have survived as classics. What made the sixties so exciting, as opposed to today, was that as many artists were creating new styles, and new records on the radio were truly different, showing a touch in lyrics here or arrangements there that had never been tried before. By contrast, there is seldom a new sound in today's music. Most artists specialize at some tried-and-true version of an already existing style.

Many stars of the sixties are deservedly legendary. The Beatles, the Rolling Stones, Bob Dylan, the Beach Boys, and the Who are only the outstanding of many examples. Every time these people released a new song or album, which is usually the case today, it never sounded like their previous one, and it contained some experiment in some new direction, which neither they nor anyone else in rock had tried before. The survivors among those people are still coasting today on the goodwill they earned in the sixties, and most of today's "new" groups are still using the styles those giants created. But, if you hear their music for the first time today, it cannot sound as startling and thrilling as it did then; it no longer sounds new, having been copied so often since. Lesser artists, such as the Byrds, the Yardbirds, Simon & Garfunkel, and the Doors, were also producing strikingly original work which broke new ground, but which would not sound so new to a first-time listener.

The sixties were also the great years for black musicians, and their story is parallel to that of White Rock. The sixties' records of such geniuses as Smokey Robinson, Marvin Gaye, the Temptations, Aretha Franklin, Diana Ross and the Supremes, James Brown, Sly Stone and others created and defined the styles used by most black musicians since. The music of such contemporary stars as Prince or Michael Jackson is almost completely based upon the sixties' creations of the above mentioned artists.

Sixties' music was better than today's music because it was more creative, original, and thus more heartfelt and sincere. It didn't need MTV or videos to put it over since it usually came from the heart. I like and buy much of today's music even though it often seems shallow, heartless, or flashy. I wish, musically, we could live again the excitement and intensity of the creative sixties, when music was good enough to stand on its own without visual aids. But, if you missed it then, I'm not sure you can catch up with it now. Appreciating sixties' music fully, for the first time, requires hearing and understanding what was new and different about it— a difficult, though not impossible task—if you have a teacher for it, someone who can communicate the excitement of the time.

Questions for discussion

1. Do you agree with Mr. Brown's evaluation that sixties' music was "more creative, original, and thus more heartfelt and sincere" than today's music? Can you give examples to prove your point?

2. Why doesn't the writer mention Elvis Presley and his effect on sixties' music? Was Elvis merely an imitator of black music?

3. Do you agree that Rock music has a damaging effect on young people's morals? Why? Why not?

How *Not* to Write an Essay

Experts say it is harder to do most tasks wrong than right. If an English teacher, or a good writer, sits down to write, deliberately, the worst possible essay, he finds it difficult to "plant" all the errors and mistakes he's in the habit of avoiding. I'm sure it would take me more time to produce a "wrong" essay than a right one.

If I wanted to write a poor essay, I'd start the day before—preparing myself mentally. I'd stay out late, drink plenty of cheap liquor, sleep two or three hours, and arrive ready to start with a hangover, a headache, and a thoroughly rotten attitude. Not only would it be hard to concentrate, but I'd have such negative feelings that whatever I wrote would come out cranky and nasty.

From the vast selection of topics, I'd take the one I knew and cared little about. That way I'd be sure to make only the most trite, obvious, general statements, with nothing personal or first hand. Obviously, I wouldn't plan the paper at all, just write what came into my troubled head in no particular order.

Since I pride myself on an extensive vocabulary, the next point would be difficult. But I'd have to remember to fill my paper with the dullest, most boring, and overused words in the language—words like "nice" and "thing" and, of course, every sentence would have to contain "is" and "was," verbs guaranteed to put the reader to sleep.

Finally, and the worst of all, I'd have to remember to include generous numbers of fragments, run-ons, a few agreement errors—which my career depends on avoiding. I must put these in, resisting every temptation to clean them up or correct them.

If I can do all of these sins at once, I should be able to produce a "classically" awful paper. I see that I've failed *this* time. But then it appears that these instructions were unnecessary—because I just started to read the new essays I received today, and I find that some people already know how to follow every one of these rules.

D.B.

Questions for discussion

1. Using "How *Not* to Write an Essay" as a guide, what is your reaction to the various points made?

2. What is a "run-on" sentence? What is a "fragment"? Do you avoid such errors in your writing?

3. What are some strategies a writer can use to organize his essay? Do you utilize such strategies? Why not?

Suggestions for writing the non-technical process paper

1. Write a three hundred word essay on selecting a boyfriend/girl-friend.

2. Write a three hundred word essay on preparing for college.

3. Select one of the topics listed under types of non-technical essays and write a three hundred word essay.

Chapter 6

Comparison
and Contrast

A *comparison* implies the weighing of similar or parallel features between two or more objects, people, ideas. Literally, a comparison draws on how things are alike or equal. *Contrast,* on the other hand, is a form of comparison which points out the differences between two or more things.

Perhaps the most functional and popular of expository forms in college writing, the comparison-contrast analysis may be organized in one of four ways: the point-by-point alternating pattern within the sentence, alternating paragraphs, similarities and differences within the same paragraph, and simple division of the essay into two parts.

Point-by-point alternating
pattern within sentences

The two brothers were alike in some ways, but their differences were many. Richard was short and feisty, whereas his brother Jim was tall and reserved. Richard loved to flirt and tease the girls, unlike Jim, who was painfully shy around the opposite sex. Outspoken and frank in his opinions, Richard was a loud and cocky extrovert while Jim never ventured his opinion on any subject and kept his thoughts to himself. Richard left home at nineteen and married when he was twenty; Jim stayed with his parents until he was twenty-three and never married. Successful in sales of real estate, Richard became a wealthy man, but Jim devoted himself to the teaching of literature and never amounted to anything approaching financial success.

Alternating paragraphs

Richard was short and feisty, a young man who loved to flirt and tease the girls, Outspoken and frank in his opinions, Richard was a loud and cocky extrovert. He left home at nineteen and married when he was twenty. Successful in real estate sales, Richard became a wealthy man.

His brother Jim was tall and reserved, painfully shy around the opposite sex. Jim never ventured his opinion on any subject and kept his thoughts to himself. He stayed with his parents until he was twenty-three and never married. Devoting himself to the teaching of literature, Jim never amounted to anything approaching financial success.

Division within paragraphs

The two brothers were alike in some ways, but their differences were many. Richard was short and feisty, a young many who loved to flirt and tease the girls. Outspoken and frank in his opinions, Richard was a loud and cocky extrovert. He left home at nineteen and married when he was twenty. Successful in real estate sales, Richard became a wealthy man. His brother Jim, however, was tall and reserved, painfully shy around the opposite sex. Jim never ventured his opinion on any subject and kept his thoughts to himself. He stayed with his parents until he was twenty-three and never married. Devoting himself to the teaching of literature, Jim never amounted to anything approaching financial success.

The fourth method of writing comparison-contrast is by dividing the essay into two halves; one half gives an analysis of the first subject, and the last half gives an analysis of the second subject.

The effectiveness of the comparison-contrast essay depends on how well the paragraphs are organized. The topic sentence must clearly state the point of comparison or contrast. Then the development must allow the reader to see how each point has been handled with adequate secondary support.

Two Pets: Tiger and Linda

My pampered cats, Tiger and Linda, celebrated their birthdays/anniversaries in the household last week. Tiger, age nine, and Linda, five, both joined me in early June. They are not alike in any major way, and their differences in preferences and habits, behavior with guests, and behavior with me always fascinate and educate me and my friends.

They share almost no preferences in play, possessions, or food. Little, gray, fluffy Linda is almost perfectly behaved and disciplined. She likes to play quietly and neatly, and gets most upset if she spills or knocks anything over. Big, orange-striped Tiger, who resembles Morris, is a rowdy kitty who loves to make mischief, rearrange the house, and show his scorn for "rules." Each has certain toys, and games with those toys, which the other won't go near. Neither cat eats as much as most I've known; while both are finicky and picky, each has a certain few favorite foods which I must keep in stock; I can't try to serve the same food to both. Casual Tiger loves to "kiss" people and eat snacks from their hands, while neat Linda apparently considers human skin unsanitary. She shows affection by "bumping" heads or noses.

Linda, the shyest cat I've known, hides when people come to the house, but she listens to their voices and, if they sound familiar, she will come out and greet her human friends, curling up on their laps—only if the number of people is three or less. Strangers usually have to visit several times before she trusts them enough to go near. Outgoing Tiger is a showoff who loves crowds of people, the more the better. He likes to get in the center of a group and do some impressive tricks and even dances. Yet he won't get close or affectionate with any person except me, so most of my friends come to prefer Linda, who shows feelings for the people she learns to trust.

While cats are reputed to be independent and less devoted than dogs, both my cats seem to have dog-like attachment to me. They both demand affection, petting, or play from me. They seem jealous of television, music, books, schoolwork, or any activity that causes me to ignore them. The difference is that Tiger picks out set times, every couple of hours, when I must drop everything for him, and he'll hassle me until I do. Linda does not operate on such schedules. She wants attention every waking moment, would be happy to spend her whole life being brushed and petted, and begs for notice whenever I'm home. Such is her devotion that, when I'm away for a few days, she goes on hunger strikes, refusing to eat until I come home. I often wonder what would happen if I left for months—would she force herself to eat, or starve? I've never tested this. As they get older I keep noticing subtle differences. With two pets so amazingly unlike, it's gratifying that they get along as well, are fond of each other, and seldom quarrel. Certainly, both have added much beauty, warmth, grace, and humor to my life—more, I sometimes think, than I could ever give them.

Dudley Brown

Questions for discussion

1. What method of comparison/contrast does the author use in his essay? Is it effective? Why?

2. Does the author overstate his case concerning the "human" qualities of Tiger and Linda?

3. Is the style of the composition "easy" to read? Why?

4. Are cats "independent and less devoted than dogs"? Support or attack such a point of view in an essay.

5. How are Tiger and Linda similar? How different?

Paul's First Job

Working in the pool room caused subtle but perceptible changes in the young man called Paul. His demeanor and attitude became more confident, more stable, as the months passed. Once timid, he gradually became overtly aggressive, especially concerning the opposite sex. The maturity, and immaturity, of the crowd that infested the pool room gradually worked its will upon him, affecting him and his future outlook on life forever. Gradually, a mysterious metamorphosis overtook him, molded him, forged in him a new spirit, a new consciousness—a unique ethos—more worldly, but fundamentally and cruelly selfish; more earthy, but basically sensual; more practical, but innately shrewd. The pool room would prove to be an institution of higher learning with its open door policy, welcoming the untutored sophomore to share in its course offerings.

Paul would learn many things before he graduated. He would learn of courage and cowardice, of truth and deceit, of love and base lust, of generosity and greed, of kindness and cruelty, of hope and despair, and, ultimately, of life and death. It was an education that no college or university could bring to fruition. No. Only the pool room offered the true course of knowledge—the direct route to wisdom, devoid of textbooks and the fatuous paraphernalia of a formal education. The pool room offered him the empirical method of Newton to obtain knowledge of life and death. No degrees were offered, no Phi Beta Kappa keys glistening; those he would earn later and regard with indifference and even scorn. No esteemed, renowned professors in gaudy robes would applaud his progress here. But his worldly educators would teach him well, completely, with a knowing smile or hearty backslap as his reward. His true alma mater lay before him in the ghetto of pool hustlers, gamblers, and con men, not the lofty towers of academe.

The romantic gradually became a pragmatist, a skillful opportunist, a manipulator, a user of men and women. He had shed his illusions, his dreams, for the sake of expediency. He was no longer a fair-skinned youth reading and thrilling to lines of obscure poetry. Paul had become a man.

Questions for discussion

1. What is the basis for comparison in "Paul's First Job"? Is the comparison implied? How? To what?

2. Discuss the author's style. Does it read smoothly? Is it difficult to read and to comprehend quickly?

3. What does "alma mater" mean? How can a pool room be an alma mater?

4. Judging from the tone of the essay, is there hope for Paul?

5. How is the pool room compared and contrasted to a college?

Mickey's Funeral

Slowly they made their way to the casket. Paul was the last to kneel at the side of the bier, mumbled a short prayer as the others had, although self-consciously, and crossed himself. He dreaded having to look down at the corpse but he wanted to say goodbye. Perhaps somewhere, somehow, ol' Mickey might hear him. Mickey had been so fond of eavesdropping when he worked in the pool room. Paul gazed at the serenely lifeless body—the balding head forever at rest on the silken pillow; the stiff limbs lying at peace; the white rosary clasped forever in his tight right hand, those once clever fingers insensitive to feeling now; the prominent nose and thick lips eternally frozen in a plastic smile; the sunken eyes, large now in death, closed to sight.

Paul remembered how Mickey loved to laugh and kid around, winking at him whenever he would decide to taunt Deadeye, hopping on and off that favorite wooden chair of his. In death Mickey was more emaciated than when Paul had seen him in the hospital. All the more appalling was the plastic, orange hue of his once pale face, making him look almost demonic as he lay in the white silken drapery of the coffin under a giant crucifix of a tortured Christ on the wall.

Time was Mickey covered the bald spot on his head with a cheap brown hair piece. The boys in the pool room used to roar when Mickey got excited during a ball game on television and the hair piece slid to one side of his head. And those hands—stiff now—were once so nimble at palming an ace or a pair of loaded dice against an untutored yokel who just happened to stray into the pool room. And Mickey was always chuckling when he won at craps or pool; when he smiled, his lips seemed thin and his nose not at all large and chiseled. His blue eyes glistened when he read the results on the ticker tape machine. Mickey always seemed to be so cheerful, except when he found his wife with. . . .

Paul leaned over impulsively to kiss Mickey's forehead. His lips may as well have kissed the marble of a tombstone, so hard and cold the impervious flesh. "Goodbye, Mickey," Paul whispered. "I'm sorry." Then Paul stepped back into the arms of his friends who were cursing softly, bitter at the cruel metamorphosis of Mickey Ryan.

Turning to leave, Paul managed one last look at the corpse. "Embolism, huh?" he whispered, answering his own question bitterly, "Bull!"

Questions and discussions

1. What is the basis for comparison in "Mickey's Funeral"? Is the comparison implied? How?

2. Do you see any elements of humor in this selection?

3. How is the dead Mickey Ryan compared to the living Mickey?

Today's Fast Pace Compared to Yesteryear

The world certainly moves faster today than in my childhood, let alone my parents'—not only transportationally, but professionally and educationally. People are expected to work faster, do more, while new knowledge is multiplying at a rate confusing for both teachers and students. Of the changes this fast pace has caused in our life styles, the one I regret the most is the *decline of creativity* in recent generations. People used to make more and do more for themselves than they have time for today.

People often feel that they do not have time to read or write. One reason freshmen college students fear English courses is because they lack our ancestors' practice in reading and writing. Television has taken much of the blame (maybe too much) for the decline in literacy skills. Whatever the reason, the fact is that fifty and certainly one hundred years ago, people who did not graduate from high school possessed reading/writing abilities which today's college students have to struggle to get. Our grandparents had time to read books, write letters (today, people prefer expensive phone calls), and keep journals and diaries. In my family, we have a fascinating series of diaries by several of my relatives which span a period from 1860-1950. These people had time to write every day, so they probably had little fear of it.

Today's hurried life has made people less self-sufficient because they make so little for themselves. Besides providing much of their own food, many of our ancestors made their homes, clothes, furniture. The latter, in particular, has proven to be more substantial and lasting than today's expensive store-bought furniture. But one of the most interesting changes has been in children's toys. Those used to be homemade too. During the Depression, unable to buy toys, my mother and her brothers made hundreds of homemade toys out of modeling clay, painted and baked and hardened. They made a whole town with houses, furniture, and over 300 occupants, which won prizes at fairs. These were saved and became my own favorite toys a generation later. I am sure that they provided more, longer-lasting satisfaction than the thousands of "E.T." toys bought this Christmas, let alone the annoying video games, which I think represent some new low in intellectual creativity.

If I had to choose one example to symbolize the decline in creativity, I'd choose greeting cards. I don't know when these began to be sold in stores, but I know what used to happen. People made them, individually, for the person and the occasion—birthday, Christmas, wedding, funeral, whatever. People drew them and wrote their own messages. We have a collection of beautiful, personalized "cards" (usually several pages in a notebook) made by and for members of the family, with pictures and poems.

Today, we take a minute of our busy schedules to go into a store and select an impersonal card made up by somebody that doesn't know who will get it. We buy "prepared," packaged emotions or congratulation, thanks, sympathy, to express the feelings we don't have time to think out. At least, most people do this. I send very few greeting cards because I still like to make my own, in little booklets, with personalized messages. It's my own small protest against the un-creativity greeting cards represent.

I am not a person who yearns for the "good old days." In most ways, I would not trade places with another generation. But I do wish all of us had more time to improve our lives by creating more of what's in them.

Dudley Brown

Questions for discussion

1. What is the author's basic premise? Do you agree with his argument?

2. Find the topic sentence of each paragraph. Does the author present enough examples to prove each topic sentence?

3. Write an essay dealing with how things were (or appeared) when you were a child to what the situation is today.

4. Discuss the author's criticism regarding this generation's lack of creativity—in the arts, in writing and reading, in basic skills.

5. Write an essay disputing the author's point of view; or, if you agree with his thesis, write a similar essay using your personal experiences.

Sexual Attitudes—the Fifties Compared to Today

During the fifties, open conversation about sex was unheard of among my peers. Perhaps the attitude in the boys' locker room was different, but the girls never discussed their sexual feelings. And our teachers never made comments or even joked (even subtly) about sex. In fact, if they did, they put their jobs in jeopardy. Sex education in the public school system was not allowed, and even our biology books lacked vivid pictures of the human anatomy. Details involving the reproductive system were discussed in broad terminology.

Dating separated the "good" girls from the "bad." Proper girls never kissed on the first date. Girls who did were assumed to have other interesting moral attributes. Petting was not done with a "good" girl until the wedding date had been definitely set. Yet there were always those few girls who were considered "fast," and they were the ones who gave the boys those first amorous encounters.

Pregnancy in high school was practically unheard of, and a girl who did get pregnant had to leave school. If one were married, it was unacceptable to attend school. Believe it or not, the carnal knowledge such girls possessed was thought to corrupt the other students.

Parents had a closed-mouth attitude regarding discussions of sex with their children. Children were still being told about a stork bringing babies to families, or of the doctor bringing the squealing infant in his black bag! Though I was fortunate to have a mother who answered my questions, most of my friends never even mentioned the word "sex" to their parents. A trip to the doctor just before marriage was often the first really educated information a girl received about sex.

In the fifties, many men wouldn't have considered marrying a woman who wasn't a virgin. Although they (the men) may have been knowledgeable, only a woman who was "pure" was good enough to be a wife. This thinking seemed to continue in the way a father felt about his daughter's virginity. "Shotgun" weddings were sometimes a reality.

Today, sexual attitudes have made a drastic change in people's thinking. Sex is the main conversation among teenagers. I doubt if many of them even know how to blush. What was once locker room talk is now discussed openly between boys and girls. Sex education is taught at the elementary level and textbooks have explicit pictures of the human body. The four-lettered words once used only rarely are now thrown about so easily that they have lost all of their meaning. Vulgarity has become popular—not only in the living room but in the class room.

Petting and dating now go hand-in-hand, and girls always kiss on the first date. If a girl and a boy date for any period of time, indulging in sex is not unusual. The only girls who are considered "fast" or "trash" are those having sex with many boys—and even those labels are becoming rare today.

Pregnancies in the high schools are increasing, even soaring. With all of the information available about birth control (which we didn't have), it is astounding that there are so many unwanted pregnancies. Abortion? We never considered the idea. But getting an abortion today is almost as easy as getting a tooth pulled, except for the cost.

A man would have a difficult time in this day and age finding a virgin to be his bride. However, men no longer consider that to be important.

Perhaps the contemporary sexual revolution isn't all bad. But I still feel that some things should remain sacred. Sex for the fun of it, with no real feelings of love, has lost something important. Ignorance certainly is not bliss, but somewhere, some time soon, I hope that we can reevaluate our thinking. I often wonder why our bodies were made to be the most easily tempted at a time when the sexual taboos are the greatest.

A Tale of Two Kitties

Three years ago, I was given a stray kitten called Pooh. He was one of the popular orange-striped tabbies often named "Morris cats" after the Nine Lives celebrity they resemble.

Later, I acquired a humongous German Shepherd dog named Harley. Pooh disliked my dog so much that he began spending days and nights away from home.

Sometimes I thought I saw Pooh on a shady porch in another block up the hill. But, when I went to pet him, this cat did not recognize me and retreated with hostility.

Several months passed before I discovered that this cat was one and the same cat as mine; however, the elderly lady, Mrs. D., called him Sunny because he was bright like the sun. Comparing notes, we learned the Pooh/Sunny was leading a double life—two of his nine lives at once. Whenever he tired of my dog, he left for Mrs. D.'s house. Then, when he was well fed there, he came back to my house and ate again. All of this commuting up and down the hill kept him fit and trim.

Now that our two kittens turned out to be the same one, Mrs. D. and I agreed to continue sharing "them" and to split medical expenses if necessary. But Pooh still would not speak to me when he was up at her house in his other identity. Being Sunny, he preferred to keep his lives separate. I thought that he was quite a clever kitty—or two.

This double life, which fascinated and amused me, continued for about a year. Whenever she didn't see the cat for several days, Mrs. D. called me to be sure he was all right. I began to suspect that maybe he had other lives going on at other houses. During the fierce blizzard of 1993, Mrs. D. called to inform me that he was safe and staying there for the duration.

About a month ago, Pooh/Sunny suddenly began living and eating at my house "full time" and made up with the dog. Now Pooh acts very much like a cat with only one home and one life. I assume something has happened (possibly ill health) that has made it impossible for him to stay at Mrs. D.'s house. That's too bad, because this arrangement was one of the "coolest" things I've seen a kitty do.

D.B.

Questions for discussion

1. What elements of comparison/contrast do you find in this essay?

2. After reading the essay, do you wonder why dogs and cats are often referred to as "dumb animals"?

3. What elements of humor do you find in "A Tale of Two Kitties"?

Two Heroes

Michael Stipe and Garth Brooks probably don't appreciate each other's music and would be surprised to appear in an essay together. But here they belong as two of the most charismatic, committed musicians of their era—two who have reached the top intelligently, have taken chances, and stood for something.

In and out of music, both men have been unafraid to speak/sing up for potentially unpopular causes. Both men have actively supported gay rights, especially risky for Brooks as a country star in a conservative field. His song *We Shall Be Free* was banned from many country stations for this reason, while his pro-gay remarks in a Barbara Walters' interview cost him some fans.

Stipe's comments on this and other issues have been less risky, as he is a rock star, a position which still seems to permit more liberal freedoms than country music. Nonetheless, his interviews and some REM group lyrics have had a more humanistic, constructive tone than much of the negative, violent rock music of the early 90's.

Musically, both men have refused to remain in a rut, releasing unpredictable records in a variety of changing styles. Recently, REM went from the quiet, melodic san sounding *Automatic for the People* to the loud, rocking *Monster* and both were enormous hits. Stipe and Brooks have proven that they can retain their enormous following without touring and, in the fickle contemporary music world, have retained/enlarged their audience for over ten years of changes.

Brooks, sometimes accused of not being country enough, keeps bringing in more styles, mixing in Bob Seger type rockers, Billy Joel balladry, barroom blues, and a bit of cajun beat on his wonderfully varied *In Pieces* album. In his shows, Brooks keeps "pressing the envelope," defying traditions, yet always honoring his own heroes—lavish in his public praise of country or rock stars he likes.

Their honesty, their daring, their insistence on change, their ability to bring new adventures to their audiences, their lack of venality—these qualities make REM. Although Michael Stipe and Garth Brooks are unlikely essay mates, they are thoroughly deserving heroes of the decade.

D.B.

Questions for discussion

1. Why does the author refer to Stipes and Brooks as heroes? Do you agree? Why? Why not?

2. Do you have any "heroes" that you could compare and contrast in an essay?

3. What is your definition of "hero"?

Overall Points on Comparison/Contrast

1. Balance is important. Both topics should be treated approximately equally in terms of space. One should not totally dominate the other.

2. The introduction and conclusion should usually mention both topics, rather than beginning with only one or ending with only one.

3. Most essays seem incomplete if they do not do some comparing and some contrasting, not all of one or the other. Theoretically, no two topics are 100% identical or different.

A Comparison/Contrast of commonly misused words

Adverse and averse

In the statement, "He was not adverse to war if the cause was just," the word *adverse* (acting against) is a malaprop, mistaken for *averse* (having an aversion to). The mistake is easy to make for two reasons: the words sound very much alike, and both words have a loose association with the idea of "being opposed to." A correct use of *adverse* would be "George had an adverse reaction to her kisses."

Comprise and compose

A thing cannot be "comprised of" something else. The word *comprise* is synonymous with the word *include*. The whole comprises the parts; the parts compose the whole. (Incorrect: Water is comprised of hydrogen and oxygen.)

Note: *Malaprop* is a French word which means *out of place*. Mrs. Malaprop was a character in R.B. Sheridan's play *The Rivals*. The word is usually a humorous misapplication, for instance: He had no *symphony* for me.

Sensual and sensuous

Sensual denotes the gratification of the senses or indulging in gratifying base appetites. The word is used to convey a deficiency in moral, spiritual, and intellectual interests: The late days of the Roman Empire reflected the decadence of its sensual excess. *Sensuous,* however, although pertaining to qualities that appeal to the senses, more often applies to aesthetic enjoyment of art, music, nature, and the like: He enjoyed the sensuous beauty of the autumn day.

Suggestions for writing a comparison-contrast paper

1. Write a comparison-contrast essay dealing with high school and college.

2. In five hundred words or more, compare and contrast one of the following: two relatives, two teachers, two pets, two boyfriends/two girlfriends.

3. Write a five hundred word essay comparing what you are now to what you hope to be in the future. Consider career goals, salary, marital status, children, and so on.

Chapter 7

Arranging Systematically— Classification

Classification is a systematic arrangement of related groups or categories according to established standards. A basic technique in organization, classification deals with the logical division of a group of plural objects to provide a useful order. Formal classification observes three rigid requirements among its divisions: completeness, coordination, and non-overlapping.

Completeness means that everything must be included; nothing in the study may be left out. In classifying types of outlines, for instance, all three types must be discussed: topic, sentence, and paragraph. In classifying verbals, the teacher analyzes the three types: gerund, participle, and infinitive. To conduct a thorough study means that no item may be excluded.

Coordination refers to equality in rank or significance. The categories must be on the same level, not only in terms of rank, but in grammatical form. In the composition of "typography," a classification would be hand composition, machine composition, and typewriter composition, *not* hand, machine, and typing. *Typing* is not coordinate because it is a noun, whereas *hand* and *machine* are adjectives. You must decide upon which method to use concerning your classification, making sure that all of the types are *parallel* or balanced. For instance, one method by which poisons may be classified is according to their chemical and physical types: acids, alkaloids, industrial solvents, inorganic chemicals, organic chemicals, poisonous gases, and poisonous foods. But another classification of poisons would be according to their physiological actions. In a classification of "toy" dogs, you would include Chihuahua, English Toy Spaniel, Griffon, and so on. But to include the Old English Sheep dog would destroy the ranking of "toy" dogs by disrupting parallel structure since the Old English Sheep dog is considered a "working" dog.

The list of items in a classification must be *non-overlapping;* an item must be placed in one category and not in two or more categories. If an item can be placed in more than one category, you must search for another way to distinguish your items. Remember that the categories must be presented in the best order in accomplishing your purpose logically and clearly. For instance, if you were to classify the clothing you wear according to seasons, your categories would probably overlap; you would have more success in classifying your clothing according to materials (fabrics) or color rather than function. In classifying the bourgeoisie (middle class) during the Middle Ages, a list of artisans, merchants, and intelligentsia would be guilty of over-lapping, since a merchant or artisan could easily be placed in the intelligentsia category.

Methods of presentation

The order of presenting your groups in a classification paper may be handled in different ways, depending on your purpose. In a process paper, a *step-by-step* or chronological order would probably be the best method to use. Another method would be citing the items in their *order of importance.* In classifying types of puppets, for example, you could divide according to complexity, starting from the simplest to the more involved or complicated: the finger puppet, the hand puppet, the stop-motion puppet, the rod puppet, and shadow puppet, and, finally, to the marionette. If you were to classify the rooms in your house, one basis could be according to *function.* Another basis of classification could be *spatial,* according to a physical or geographical approach. In classifying the common types of pumps, you could organize the groups *alphabetically,* instead of function or complexity: centrifugal, density, direct pressure displacement, jet, reciprocating rotary, and vacuum.

Whatever method you use in writing a classification analysis, remember that the categories must be complete, coordinate, and nonoverlapping.

Classification: Intelligence

As a teacher, I don't believe in stupid people. Like the writers Emerson and Thoreau, who have influenced so much of my thinking, I believe everyone is basically, potentially intelligent, although some people have not found it yet. Of the four main kinds of intelligence—practical, academic, social, and creative—everyone possesses at least one, probably more.

Practical intelligence, the kind I obviously lack, is also known as "common sense." People with this intelligence can fix broken appliances, change a tire, keep a neat house, shop wisely, and cope with their bills. These people are usually organized and, as they say, "together"—so I've heard—I don't believe there's ever been one of this kind in my family.

Academic intelligence is often contrasted with, or pitted against, the practical kind, in an "either-or" thinking which suggests that one can't have both, though I can't see any reason why not. People of academic intelligence are, of course, the ones who know how to study, memorize, get good grades. But if a person possesses only this kind—and some good students do—he will probably have trouble getting along in everyday life. This may be why some people become bookworms, perennial scholars, and closet themselves safely in libraries.

Social intelligence is not discussed or admired much, but I find it important. These are people who know how to get along with others, handle tricky or awkward situations, know what to say and when to shut up. They are probably popular, being good hosts and guests, tactful and well-mannered. More important, they should make reliable and long lasting friends.

The world has advanced (*if* it has, another topic!) due to the fourth kind, the most respected, creative intelligence, which is responsible for inventions and great art, literature, music. People with creative intelligence are those commonly termed "geniuses"—and often eccentric, since they may lack the other types. Many creative people are impractical, unsociable, and/or poor students, but they have the best chance of being remembered.

Although intelligence is usually considered positive and constructive, it can be negative, destructive, when some of the above kinds combine to produce a clever criminal, a crooked politician, or a power-mad dictator.

Has anyone ever combined every type of intelligence? I cannot think of an example. Everyone must have some combination of the above, but a blend of practical, academic, social, creative intelligence—constructively used—strikes me as an ideal dream of perfection.

Dudley Brown

Questions for discussion

1. Do you agree with the author's premise, "As a teacher, I don't believe in stupid people"?

2. Are there other ways to classify intelligence?

3. Are the categories which the author presents coordinate, non-over-lapping, and complete?

4. Do you agree that many "creative people are impractical, unsociable. . . ."? Does the implied syllogism necessarily follow?

5. Write a five hundred word essay classifying types of students.

The Pool Room Crowd

About eleven thirty the crowd started arriving. It was a flood of diverse elements: the coal miners, thick, coarse men, but with an indigenous cheerfulness; steelworkers, with their bent lunch pails under their arms; construction workers, weathered faces distorted, bulging with chews in their mouths; salesmen, with their neat, pin-striped suits and glossy shoes; a few doctors, neat, impeccable, disdainful, eager for a fast lunch-hour game of pool or cards; and the old timers—Greeks, Italians, Poles—tired with life, exhausted with age, grubby looking fellows who seemed to find a home in the pool room. And then there were the hustlers, so pitifully obvious. It was not their manner of dress which made them stand out from the others, nor their young age. It was in their eyes, that quality which set them apart from the convivial working man and the snobbish white collar class. For their eyes had a stark, desperate quality in them, like the fox, predatory, stealthy, cunning, yet wary. Subtle and patient, they were the pros, the manipulators, sensing an easy mark in the card and pool games.

Questions for discussion

1. How many categories does the author list in his classification of the "Pool Room Crowd"?

2. Are the categories over-lapping?

3. Analyze the author's style in terms of sentence structure, types of sentences, modifiers, participial phrases, non-restrictive elements, diction.

4. What do the words "impeccable" and "indigenous" mean?

5. Does the author stereotype the categories in his classification?

6. Write a five hundred word essay classifying crowds which gather at picnics, student centers, ball games, bars, and/or churches.

Body Builders

Wearing tight jeans and an even tighter T-shirt, he stands like a sturdy paperweight holding down the corner of Main and Center. Short but incredibly solid, he does not need tight clothing to advertise his hobby, his avocation, his consuming passion: body building. His huge chest and enormous arms bulge from the shirt. But they're so immense, they shrink the rest of his body, making him look like a badly stuffed teddy bear. His proportions are all wrong; his body lacks balance. Surely if he moves, he'll fall over! He can't be missed, and though he appears oblivious to the looks he gets, he enjoys the attention. He has placed himself in the center of town.

He can walk! He can talk: "Whatcher bench?" (translation: "How much weight are you pressing on the bench press?") But like his perceptions and interests, his conversation is extremely limited. This high school dropout is a small town's answer to six times Mr. Olympia winner Arnold Schwarzenegger, and a poor answer he is. For he has become a stereotype, whereas Arnold Schwarzenegger has revealed himself as an interesting, witty, perceptive man, a well-developed person as well as an exquisitely proportioned and defined body.

Body builders hold a fascination for many people. Are they only dumb hunks? Are they more than great masses of muscle? Some are the former; some, the latter. But there are really three types of body builders, and these types are distinguished by their approach to the art. Each type, whether a Sociable Sam, an Occasional Oscar, or a Regular Robert, may be seen in any health club, gym, or YMCA.

Enter a weight room and you'll notice Sociable Sam first. But you'll rarely see him alone, for he "works out" primarily for camaraderie though he pretends he's doing it to "get in shape" or to "keep in shape." Of the three types of body builders, he spends the greatest amount of time though he does the least amount of actual working out. In groups of three or more, he shares his jokes and adventures and appreciates those of the others. Although he may work out by exercising or lifting weights, he's happiest in team sports, especially basketball. He convinces himself that in the game he's doing as much for his body as he would with exercise or weights. He does work out one muscle to its fullest: his tongue. Yet he's a pleasant guy, a "hail-fellow-well-met" sort. But one can't help wondering how much he gets done on his job!

Certain seasons of the year bring Occasional Oscar. Look for him in May (to get in shape for the summer), in September (to get in shape for the winter), or in January (he's made New Year's resolutions). His resolutions last for two weeks at best. He overdoes from the very beginning, pushing and straining and sweating himself into exhaustion. Sore and stiff, he'll usually "lay off" for a while, and the "while" stretches into months. He has good intentions, no discipline, and no wisdom. Having childish expectations, he becomes discouraged when they're not met, and so he gives up until the season changes. He returns occasionally, works unwisely again just as he diets unwisely, and continues to delude himself. You see, in his way, he's a Platonic idealist: He likes the idea of body building more than the sweaty reality of it. Does he approach his job with such irregular spurts of attention?

All seasons, all weathers—nothing stops Regular Robert. He's not always noticed immediately; the Sociable Sams are being so raucous and the Occasional Oscars are grunting and groaning so dramatically. But Regular Robert is there. Always, He works out three times a week on a regular basis. He is faithful; he is disciplined. If he works out with a partner, it is for safety reasons, not for sociability. His workouts are patterned; having a regular rhythm, they seem almost a choreographed dance. He is usually quiet, non-conversational. He appears anti-social, but he is not. He is purposeful, and he uses time wisely. On rare occasions, he'll participate with the Social Sams or offer a word of encouragement to the Occasional Oscars. Having discipline, he usually has a fine body. Having a fine body, he has the male luxury of being gentle and soft-spoken. Unlike the Sociable Sams, he need not brag or play one-upsmanship games. One watches him work out with admiration and respect. Surely here is a man who, if he approaches his professional life with the same dedication he approaches his body building, must be highly successful!

Few are the stereotyped hunks; still fewer are the Arnold Schwarzeneggers. But many are the Sams, Oscars, and Roberts who people the gyms and weight rooms of the world, each contributing his own unique quality to body building.

Norman A. Kelly

Questions for discussion

1. Do you agree with the author's classification of body builders? Why? Why not?

2. Comment on the writer's style—his use of similes and images, sentence construction, and diction. Do you find any humor in this essay? Where?

3. The author compares each body builder's approach to the physical

discipline as a reflection of that individual's probable success in his professional life. Do you agree with this estimate? Why? Why not?

4. Write a classification essay of five hundred words dealing with a similar type of activity: football players, basketball players, and so on.

5. Do you see the dangers involved in stereotyping people according to the type of sport in which such people are involved? What are some of the complications in such a process?

Weddings

Throughout life, certain events begin a new stage of an individual's development. As common as birth, childhood, adulthood, and death, the sacred wedding also represents an important point that begins a change in life. Although a wedding symbolizes basically the same meaning for every couple, each ceremony is not performed in the same manner. Generally, there are three types of wedding ceremonies: church, "garden," and the elopement.

Performed by a minister, the church ceremony takes place in a church (obviously) or another place of worship. This type of marriage is planned months in advance and usually takes place after an engagement period between the bride-and-groom-to-be. It can be an expensive ceremony which includes formal apparel. The bride usually wears a long, white gown with a matching veil and carries a bouquet of flowers or a Bible. The groom wears a white tuxedo and a boutonniere that coordinates with the bride's bouquet. The wedding party customarily includes a maid of honor, a best man, a flower girl, a ring bearer, and several bridesmaids and ushers, all of whom accompany the bride and groom during the religious ceremony. The traditional dialogue recited, ". . . in sickness and in health, till death do us part," is an element that has been passed down through centuries and through generations. A large number of family members and friends gather to witness this sanctified-by-the-church type of wedding ceremony.

The "garden" type of wedding is performed outside—in a park, on the beach, in a garden, in the woods, or a similar type of environment under the open skies. It can be performed by a minister or other licensed official. As with the church ceremony, however, the engagement period may encompass a period from a year to just a few weeks. Sometimes it may be a spontaneous event. It is semi-formal and less expensive than a church wedding. The bride usually wears a knee-length dress and flowers in her hair. She may also carry a small bouquet of flowers. The groom wears a three-piece suit or just a "nice" pair of slacks and a shirt. The wedding party generally consists of a maid of honor and a best man along with the bride and groom. The ritual that is recited is sometimes composed by the wedding couple in lieu of more traditional forms. Also, a smaller number of family members and friends attend the "garden" wedding than the more formal church wedding.

Another type of ceremony deals with the wedding couple who decide to elope. Such a decision is made quickly, usually, and the wedding may be performed on the same day as the decision was made. It may be performed by a justice of the peace or another licensed official and is witnessed by one other person. Since it is an informal and brief procedure, the attire of the bride and groom varies and is usually what they are wearing that very day. As an inexpensive function, it is usually witnessed by no members of the family or friends.

Although these various types of weddings indicate the legal binding of a couple, each ceremony is rendered differently to provide a suitable choice for the bride and the groom. And if the procedures are different, the end result is the same.

Questions for discussion

1. Do you agree with the author's classification concerning three types of weddings? Do the categories overlap? Are they mutually exclusive?

2. Could there be another type of wedding ceremony which the author does not acknowledge?

3. Can you think of ways to enlarge the details of each type of wedding ceremony to provide a better division of the categories?

Types of Employers

After many years of employment in several different health care facilities, I can look back at the numerous employers I have had and classify them into one of four distinct stereotypes: the "autocrat," the "father", the "figurehead," and the "democrat." The types can be distinguished by the manner in which they direct their employees.

The autocrat is the domineering employer who considers himself to be an expert and sole authority. He lacks confidence in any of his employees and considers his role to be the indisputable force driving his subordinates rather than leader of the team. Because the autocrat believes that his employees are morons, he stifles employee input regarding business matters. All decisions are made by the authority figures who reside on Mount Olympus.

Communication between the autocrat and his workers is in one direction: downward. Directives are issued in place of suggestions; formality frowns upon any type of informal behavior. Because the employees know that their opinions are considered unimportant, they avoid the autocrat and refrain from making any constructive suggestions.

Next, the figurehead is the type of accommodating employer who lacks a strong self image, anxious to be liked and accepted by all of his employees. Undemanding, the figurehead nevertheless sees himself as the master of his servants. Major decisions concerning business affairs are made by the figurehead. Minor issues, however, are decided upon by the group and approved condescendingly by the master.

Communication between the figurehead and the employees is in a two-way direction—upward and downward—but employees seldom voice their true feelings and concerns, generally, because they feel intimidated.

The parent is the "protector of the flock." He is the paternalistic employer who sees himself as a father figure. Protective of his employees, he unfortunately treats them like children. Employees are rewarded for "good" behavior, and privileges (coffee, breaks, extending lunch breaks for a few minutes) are withheld for "bad" or poor behavior.

Because the protector knows what is best for his employees, all major decisions are made in the absence of employee consultation. Although the parent encourages open channels of communication among his "family," communication tends to be uni-directional—from the top down—but reassuring and informal.

The fourth type of employer is the democrat, the consulting power who sees himself as "team builder." The democrat believes that he functions to support and to advise the group; he has a great deal of trust and confidence in his employees. This enlightened individual invites employee participation in all aspects of business and believes in a team approach to decision making.

Communications is free flowing in all directions—friendly, informal, and constructive. Without fear of criticism, employees voice their opinions honestly and frankly.

The paternalistic, accommodating, and domineering leadership styles have a pronounced negative effect on employee morale. Although each individual may react differently under these styles, I believe that creativity is suppressed and productivity is reduced. The consulting leadership style, however, has a positive effect on all employees because the workers feel needed, that they are contributing to the total success of the business, and that they have a voice in the formulation of policies which directly affect them.

Questions for discussion

1. Do you agree with the author's classification regarding the four types of employers? Do the categories overlap? Are they mutually exclusive?

2. Could there be another type of employer which the author does not acknowledge?

3. Can you think of ways to enlarge the details of each type of employer to provide a better division of the categories?

Suggestions for writing a classification paper

Choose one of the following items and write a five hundred word essay of classification.

types of teachers (college)	types of furniture in your house
types of friends	types of waitresses
types of jewelry you own	types of restaurants
types of church-goers	types of love
types of courses you are taking	types of customers
types of clothing you own	types of teachers (high school)
types of CDs you own	types of food you like/dislike

■ Chapter 8 ■

Writing the Definition Paper

Whenever you write an essay, you must understand the words you use and remember the reader for whom your words are intended. Writers often misuse words, abuse words, and lack full knowledge of the terms which they use. In writing essays, reports, or business letters, you must understand the terms which you use, not rely on a hazy conception of their meaning, but you must have a working ability to make words effective in the process of communication. Anything less is simple laziness and ignorance, which may later cause you embarrassment.

Formal and informal definitions

There are two categories of definitions—the formal and the informal. Although the informal category is more frequently used, the formal definition is longer, more detailed and, in writing and research, the more functional of the two. An informal definition may be a single word substitute, a phrase, or a sentence, depending upon the purpose of the writer. Informal definitions, naturally, are brief and incomplete.

Examples of informal definitions

The word to be defined: *secret* (the term)

> Single word definition: Private, covert, hidden (synonyms)
> Phrase definition: Eluding observation or detection
> Sentence definition: A secret is something kept hidden from others or shared confidentially with a few.

The word to be defined: *carcinoma* (the term)

    Single word definition: Cancer, malignancy (synonyms)
    Phrase definition: A cancerous tumor
    Sentence definition: Carcinoma is a Greek word which
                          means "a malignant tumor of epithelial
                          origin."

The word to be defined: *natuary* (the term)

    Single word definition: Ward
    Phrase definition: A hospital ward (classification)
    Sentence definition: A natuary is a ward in a hospital for
                          women during childbirth. (distinguishing
                          characteristic)

The word to be defined: *measles* (the term)

    Single word definition: Disease
    Phrase definition: An acute contagious viral disease (classification)
    Sentence definition: Measles is an acute, contagious viral dis-
                          ease marked by an eruption of distinct
                          red, circular spots (distinguishing charac-
                          teristics)

A *formal definition*, on the other hand, *thoroughly* explains the subject to make it clear and distinguishable from other subjects, even those related to it. In an extended explanation of a term or subject, a three-step definition process is necessary.

1.   The term (word, concept) is regarded as the *species.*

2.   The class (group, category) is regarded as the *genus.*

3.   The *distinguishing characteristics* set the term apart from those words or concepts similar to it.

Therefore, in a formal definition paper, you must identify the subject (term) as a part of a group (classification); you must then explain the features of the subject which distinguish it from the other parts in the same group.

To define a subject thoroughly, you may use several different yet complementary methods.

Synonyms may be used to define a term quickly and effectively, depending on your purpose. Although there are no "perfect" substitutes for the original word and its meaning, the synonym is one method popularly used: "Potent" may mean "powerful" or "capable." "Registrar" may mean a "recorder" or "keeper of records."

Specific details or *distinguishing characteristics* of the subject are necessary to achieve clarity: A viola is a stringed musical instrument of the violin family; it is slightly larger than a violin and tuned a fifth lower, thereby having a deeper tone. . . .

Analysis is a separation of the whole into basic parts to determine the nature of the whole; fundamentally, analysis is a methodical breakdown of constituent elements. For instance, in a definition of *carburetor,* which is a device used in gasoline engines to produce an efficient explosive vapor of fuel and air, the writer would separate and describe its basic parts: the throttle lever, the fast-idle cam, the idle-mixture, the idle screw, fuel inlet, choke rod, and the idle speed screw. In biology, a *cell* is defined as the smallest structural organism capable of independent functioning. Analysis would break down the cell into its component parts: nucleolus, nucleus, centrosome, ribosomes, endoplasmic reticulum, and so on.

Another important method of definition deals with *process* or operation—explaining how something works or functions—for purposes of clarification. For instance, "sputtering" is accomplished by spitting (emitting) small particles (saliva, perhaps) in sporadic bursts. "Breathing" involves the process of drawing air into and expelling it from the lungs.

Comparison shows similarities between one subject and another: A wizard is a male witch, comparable to a magician.

Contrast, on the other hand, is a method whereby different aspects between subjects are emphasized:

> A simile is a figure of speech in which two essentially unlike things are compared, typically by using *like* or *as:* He was like a lion in the fight. A metaphor is a figure of speech in which a term assumes an implicit analogy without the use of *like* or *as:* He was a lion in the fight.

Often referred to as extended metaphor, *analogy* is a form of comparison between things otherwise dissimilar. The logical inference in an analogy is based on assuming that, if two subjects are alike in some respects, then they must be similar in other respects. Such syllogistic reasoning must be cautioned against, naturally, but the analogy may be used effectively in the process of definition, especially when supplemented by complementary methods.

> To the ancient Greeks and Romans, making love was considered to be analogous to making war: the physical confrontation between two fighters in a personal encounter (the man versus the woman); the anxiety and passion of the conflict on the field (a meadow or a bed); the juxtaposition of the combatants (the passion of two antag-

onists); the struggle to gain physical dominance (generally, the male as aggressor, the frenzied sexual writhing); the ultimate conquest (the climactic resolution or victory); finally, the fatigue experienced by both participants.

Another practical form of definition is the use of *negative detail*—clarifying a term by telling what it is not. For instance, "love" is not "lust"; a "sphere" is not a "square"; a "smile" is not a "leer."

Classification is a systematic division into groups or categories according to established criteria. The dog (term) is a highly variable carnivorous, domesticated mammal (genus) probably descended from the wolf. The Ionic (term) order of Greek architecture (class or genus) is uniquely characterized by the spiral volutes of its capital. Any plural subject may be classified: tools, furniture, fish, dogs, and so on. One must simply determine the class to which the subject belongs. If the subject is singular and not to be described according to class, the process of definition would then be a form of analysis called *partition*. For instance, the human eye as an organ of sight may be partitioned (divided) according to its parts: the optic nerve, fovea, sclera, choroid, retina, and so on.

Another useful method of definition is an *illustration* or example of the term being defined: The Humanities include such courses as history, art, architecture, literature, philosophy. . . . Also, a proper noun names a specific person, place, or thing: Mr. Rogers, Cumberland, the Walt Whitman Bridge.

Also of extreme value as a method of definition is the use of maps, charts, pictures, diagrams or sketches (appropriately labeled, of course). If a *visual aid* can be used to enhance the reader's understanding, use it.

For a fuller comprehension of the meaning of a term, the writer does well to understand the linguistic origin of the term. *Etymology* is the study of history of word forms. By tracing a word's development in the language, you are able to define its meaning to suit your purpose. The *Oxford English Dictionary*, among other important sources, provides useful linguistic information. For more contemporary or modern words, use a specialized dictionary, text, or source to investigate the origins of such words as "radar," "racketeer," or "beatnik."

The origin of a word also leads naturally into the word's *uses, causes,* and *effects.* For example, Eros (Cupid, in Latin) was the Greek god of passionate love. From "Eros" comes the word "erotic." From Aphrodite, the goddess of love and beauty, comes "aphrodisiac." Venus, the Roman counterpart of Aphrodite, gives her blessing to "venereal," or the "disease of love." In terms of etymologic origin and history, political and religious, vast concepts and philosophic doctrines have been coined: Geocentric, heliocentric, and egocentric. The uses, causes, and effects of such terms have played an enormous part in the history of man and are still in evidence today.

Choosing a method of definition depends on the nature of the term to be defined. If the term is abstract, for instance, the writer may set about his task of definition in a relaxed manner, without the objective severity common to encyclopedias, dictionaries, and textbooks. However, the writer must be logical, setting aside subjectivity or prejudice in favor of the objective if he is to succeed. The following essay, "A Definition of Conceit," by Dudley Brown, exemplifies informal definition of an abstract concept.

"Conceit" is a quality widely misunderstood. Though many people are accused of being conceited, few actually are, and those few hard to detect. Most people labeled "conceited" are something else instead.

Conceit means to have an *exaggerated* notion of one's talents, abilities, importance, status, etc. This exaggeration is important. If a person is obviously talented, able, important, or brilliant, and knows (admits) it, this is not conceit, just a healthy awareness of the truth. Perhaps modest concealment is more attractive to others, but to accuse genuinely gifted people, who flaunt it, of "conceit" is misusing the word.

Two kinds of people get falsely accused of conceit. First, there are people who are loud, boastful, who brag about their looks or social/sexual conquests, when others know they're losers. However, these people are usually not conceited; they believe the opposite of what they're saying. Inside, they're insecure, unsure, so they cover it up with a confident appearance, which is false.

Second, many shy people are falsely accused of being conceited ("stuck-up") because they seldom speak to people and seem self-contained. Often these people are suffering; other times you simply have to get to know them. But to accuse them of conceit is an unjust misunderstanding.

If no one I've mentioned is actually conceited, then who is, and how are we to recognize the trait? I've concluded that true conceit is extremely rare and almost undetectable. In fact, most people are the opposite; they're too modest, unconfident, and constantly underrate themselves. (As a teacher I see this every week.) And to detect a conceited person, we'd have to read his mind, see what he *really* thinks of himself. Who can do that?

I'm not sure I've ever known a conceited person, since everyone who seems so fell into one of the above categories. But the conceited individual is probably a quiet, confident soul, too sure of his imagined worth to call attention to it, who goes about his business with deadly, certain efficiency—not realizing he's often wrong. He's too self-satisfied to be bothered by snubs, hints, or criticism, so nothing disturbs his dream picture of himself.

Questions for discussion

1. Do you agree with the author's definition of "conceit"? Why? Why not?

2. Could other definitions of "conceit" be included in the essay?

3. Do you agree with the premise that "Everyone is conceited about something"? Are you?

4. Write an essay analyzing a person whom you regard as conceited, not a person whom you dislike, but one who is guilty of arrogance or pride.

5. Is the word "conceit" synonymous to "pride"? Write an essay analyzing the difference.

Loyalty—a Definition

My parents and uncles grew up near the Ohio River, where they loved to swim, fish, and to go boating. A favorite expression of theirs, one of the highest compliments that they could pay a person, was to say that he was "someone you could ride the river with." My relatives meant that, if the current got rough or the boat overturned, the person being described would not abandon them but would stay and help. It was their definition of *loyalty,* and it describes someone I've always wanted to be.

A loyal friend shows respect for the different tastes and lifestyles of others. It is not necessary for two people to agree, to get along, if they accept areas of disagreement. A loyal friend will not attack another's religion, politics, musical taste, housekeeping, lifestyle, clothes, or other friends. It is fine to have mature discussions about these matters, but not to adopt an ethnocentric "Mine-is-Better" attitude, which usually leads to one person's trying to change another. Refusal to accept or respect a friend's differences, to me, is a form of disloyalty.

A common form of disloyalty is what I call the "He said-she said" game. How often does a friend deliver this unwelcome news bulletin: "Did you know what Jane said about you?" or "Pete says you're the biggest slob he ever saw." Jane and Pete probably did not want these messages repeated. Not only are *they* disloyal for making these criticisms to someone else, but so is the person who repeats such remarks. A loyal friend will (1) not criticize me to others without telling me first, and (2) will tell me the compliments he hears about me and forget the insults.

Should criticisms be made in a friend's absence, the loyal friend will defend the victim of such remarks. I have observed entirely too much negativity and not enough praise when people discuss others, but a loyal friend should be ready to speak up for the absent one. It is not pleasant to me being in a group which attacks someone I like. It's even less pleasant if I lack the courage to say, "This person is my friend, and I don't like to hear my friends attacked." A loyal friend gets the subject changed—fast.

A person who can accept my differences and disagreements, who will not participate in malicious "He said" games, whom I can count on to defend me in my absence—this is someone I feel I can "ride the river with," and someone who deserves, and gets, the same loyalty from me.

Dudley Brown

Questions for discussion

1. What is your definition of loyalty? Of friendship?

2. Do you agree with the author's definition of loyalty? Why?

3. What other qualities distinguish friendship?

4. What would you do if your friend asked you for twenty dollars? If you didn't have the twenty dollars and your friend needed the money desperately, what would you do? Would you borrow the money to give to your friend? Why not?

Definition of "Program"

The word "program" was introduced as "programme" by the French in the 19th century. Later, the word was changed from its Greek-Latin derivative, "programma" to program, which is most commonly used today. (*Oxford English Dictionary*, 1933)

"Program" may mean a plan or scheme (Roget, 1979, p. 129). It is not vague or unorganized, but a sequential step-by-step set of instructions with which the computer solves a problem (Eppert, 1979).

Programs vary greatly in their degrees of complexity. They may be used to solve relatively simple problems, such as creating a name and an address listing, or they may be used to solve more complex problems, such as producing a payroll register (Eppert, 1979).

Programs may be written in what are referred to as programming "languages." Such languages include RPG (Report Program Generator Language), COBOL (Common Business Oriented

Language), FORTRAN (Formula Translation Language), and ALGOL (Algorithmic Oriented Language).

There are five distinct steps which should be followed when the operator writes a program. The first step is defining the problem. The operator must have a thorough understanding of the problem to be solved. The second step is determining the best method of solving the problem. This task normally involves checking the programming logic which must be used in order to get the correct results in a program and, quite often, is the most difficult step in solving a problem on the computer (Shelly and Cashman, 1981). The techniques used to determine the logical processing which is to take place within a program include flowcharting (pictorial representations), decision tables, and narrative instructions. The third step is writing the program. The operator shows which operations are to be performed and the sequence in which these operations will be executed.

Once the program is written, the fourth step is completed. This involves testing and debugging (finding the error) the program. The program must be checked for errors, both in the use of statements and the logic which will be performed. To do this, the operator must design data which can be used to test all aspects of the program. After test data has been prepared, the program may be tested by the computer. The number of test "runs" which will be required to debug a program completely is normally dependent upon the size and complexity of the program.

When all aspects of a program have been tested for errors and the program has been determined to be correct, the fifth and final step should be completed. This last step is documenting the program, which is the process of recording the facts concerning the program and describing the routines and programming techniques used. This documentation must be done so that any other programmer will be able to make changes in the program in a minimum amount of time—if the need arises.

A computer program and an outline for an essay are similar in that they both require careful planning. However, the similarity ends there. The outline for an essay shows only the main points of the paper without an identification of details, while the computer program shows in detail the step-by-step instructions needed for solving a problem.

The computer is a powerful, fast machine, but it has no magical powers. It is only a tool which is unable to devise a plan or decide to act. The computer can do only what it is told to do, in exactly the way it is told to function. In 1971, Marilyn Bohl stated that the computer "is only as effective as the program that controls it."

References Cited

Bohl, Marilyn (1971). *Flowcharting Techniques*. New York: Science Research Associates, Inc.

Eppert, Ray E. (1979). *Business and Computers*. The volume library. Nashville, Tennessee: Southwestern Co.

Program. (1933). *The Oxford English Dictionary*.

Roget, Samuel R. (1979). *Roget's Thesaurus of Synonyms and Antonyms*. New York: E. Kroiz Publishers.

Shelly, Gary, & Cashman, Thoma. (1981). *Introduction to Computer Programming*. Fullerton, California: Anaheim Publishing.

Questions for discussion

1. What method of definition is used in the first paragraph?

2. How many methods of definition does the writer use in defining the word "program"?

3. Comment on the writer's style. Is it clear? Why is such a style important in this type of expository essay?

4. What does "etymology" mean? Is its inclusion necessary in the definition of the word? Why?

"Herpes Simplex"

"Herpes" is derived from the Greek *herpein,* meaning "creeping," "to creep," or "to spread." (*Random House Dictionary*, 1975) The word "creep" accurately states the nature of herpes.

Etymology

Herpes simplex is literally a more simple herpes caused by a virus and characterized by groups of blisters containing clear fluid found on the skin or mucous membranes. (*Webster's Third New International Dictionary*, 1961) These eruptions do, in fact, creep or spread over the surface of the skin. The official name of the condition is Herpes simplex virus disease or HSV, but it is often referred to as simply "Herpes."

Identification

Historically, the initial symptoms associated with Herpes, such as burning, tingling, or itching sensations, have been noted since ancient times. Wickett (1982) states that the disease was named in 1736 by a French

Distinguishing Characteristics

physician, Jean Astruc, whose research was lost for 200 years and has only recently been rediscovered.

In the early 1960's, the Herpes simplex virus was isolated. Two strains were identified—Type 1 and Type 2.

Wickett (1982) found that HSV Type 1 includes the oral herpes and herpes labialis which produce infections with a tendency to occur in the facial area, particularly around the mouth and nose. In fact, HSV Type 1 is the fever blister or cold sore commonly experienced by millions of people throughout the world annually. Several hours after the initial symptoms of tingling, burning, or itching sensations about the edges of the lips or nose occur, small red papules develop, followed by the eruption of fever blisters filled with fluid, several of which may merge to form a large blister. Within a week after the onset of these symptoms, thin yellow crusts form as healing begins. In about a week, the crust disappears, and only a little inflammation remains, fading slowly over a period of a few days.

Wickett goes on to analyze HSV Type 2, identifying the second strain of the Herpes simplex virus to include the genital region. The effect of HSV Type 2 is the same as that which occurs with HSV Type 1. However, unlike HSV Type 1, with HSV Type 2, a local swelling of lymph nodes in the area close to the site of the infection (the groin) takes place, which, according to Wickett, lasts during the entire period of the active infection and may remain for some time afterward. Also, body temperature elevation of 99.8 to 100.5 degrees is not uncommon. The fever ordinarily lasts during the first five or six days of the attack and then returns to normal. A third additional symptom experienced with HSV Type 2 is the constant problem of headaches, which last during most of the episode. The discomfort is persistent but not severe, often experienced in

Classification

Synonym

Specific Details

Process

Comparison

Contrast

the front portion of the head. (Wickett, 1982).

Herpes simplex is caused by a DNA virus which may control the life force of any cell it infects. Every cell in our bodies has its own DNA (genetic code) which is the driving force that determines the ultimate purpose of that particular cell (Wickett, 1982). Because of the Herpes simplex virus's ability to take over the life force of the cell, the original purpose of that cell is lost, and the virus becomes the dictator of the actions of the cell, thereby causing destruction of the cell. At this point, the virion (virus particles) spew out into the bloodstream to embed themselves in other cells and repeat the entire cycle of destruction, thus spreading the disease.

Cause

Effect

On an important point of contrast, Herpes simplex virus disease is not Herpes zoster. Herpes zoster is an acute infection caused by the varicellazoster virus (VZV), not the DNA virus. Also called "shingles," Herpes zoster affects mainly adults or persons past middle life, is the infection of nerve centers, and forms blister-like eruptions in the area of the nerve distribution (*Mosby's Medical and Nursing Dictionary*, 1983).

Negative Detail

Herpes is a nasty disease which acts differently in various individuals. But it can be beaten. Research is progressing toward the development of new medications for the treatment of this dreadful disease, and it is only a matter of time before science will have the answer to the Herpes virus.

Conclusion

References Cited

Herpes. (1983). *Mosby's medical and nursing dictionary*. New York: Science Research Associates, Inc.
Herpes. (1975). *Random house dictionary*.
Herpes. (1989). *Webster's seventh new international dictionary*.
Wickett, William, M.D. (1982). *Herpes: cause and control*. New York: Pinnacle Books, Inc.

Suggestions for writing a definition paper

Using ten of the formal methods of definition listed in this chapter, define one of the following terms.

arthritis	preposition	picnic
tragedy	tooth	poetry
geography	thermometer	gangster
automobile	pneumonia	finite
telekinetic	microcosm	philanthropist
secretary	politics	sapphire
venereal	clearcutting	terminal
aphrodisiac	ecclesiastic	harmony
tort	comedy	radar
morphine	aristocracy	philosophy
narcotic	democracy	psychology
panic	typewriter	gasket
asterisk	computer	physics
semicolon	hospice	narcissus
hospital	cancer	gremlin
lexicon	culture	disk
denture	geriatrics	concert
liturgy	misogynist	rhythm
sensual	electricity	digital
academy	parentheses	essay
pedagogue	police	engineer

Note: Check with your instructor before beginning research. Perhaps your instructor would want to add to the list or give you permission to research a term that you prefer.

Chapter 9

Searching for Causes and Effects

Do you agree with this statement: "For everything that happens, there is a reason for its happening"? Does a cause always precede an effect? Or, is there a reason for everything that happens? If your answer to such questions is yes, then we may formulate a doctrine: For every effect, there is a cause or causes. Perhaps the cause is not apparent or readily discernible, but it is always there. Our task is to search for it.

Consider the following narrative illustrating cause and effect.

As Mr. Burro was walking along the pathway beside the Humanities Building, he fell—face forward, his limbs awry, his books, papers, and pencils, in accordance with the universal laws of gravity, falling beside and atop his prostrate form. Dazed, Mr. Burro surveyed his forlorn condition, assessed the damage done to his fatuous dignity, and began to rise slowly.

A comely coed who had witnessed the incident, Ms. Brenda Comely, hurried to the fallen instructor and began to gather his scattered possessions. "Oh Mr. Burro! Are you all right? I noticed that you fell."

Gradually righting himself, Mr. Burro replied, "Yes, Ms. Comely, I am all right. And yes, I did fall."

Continuing to gather the strewn papers, she looked into his pale face. "What happened, sir?"

"Oh, nothing. I just fell." He dusted the dirt from his trousers and smiled weakly.

Several students began to gather around them.

Upon hearing this, Ms. Comely shook her head as if Mr. Burro were teasing her. "But there must be a reason for your falling on the pathway beside the Humanities Building!" Her tone was mildly accusatory.

Mr. Burro reached for the books which Ms. Comely was holding. Slightly annoyed, he replied, "No. I just fell. No reason. Thank you." He turned to walk away, but Ms. Comely held his arm.

Being a student of inductive-deductive reasoning via advanced studies in philosophy, Ms. Comely was adamant. "But everyone knows that there can't be an effect without a cause! What caused you to fall?"

"W-well," Mr. Burro stammered as more students arrived to investigate the reason(s) for this latest of academic follies.

"Did you trip over a piece of concrete?" one curious student asked.

"Ah, no . . . I don't. . . ."

"Did your knees buckle under the weight of your textbooks?" another student of logic asked.

"Well, I. . . ."

Another student impetuously drew closer to examine Mr. Burro's breath. "Have you had anything to drink? Perhaps a beer or a stiff shot of ouzo?" the suspicious hedonist asked.

"Certainly not! I never drink on the job!"

Ms. Comely persisted. "But there has to be a reason why you fell! We must search for the cause!"

"OK! How's this for a cause? I simply lost my balance," the harried man argued.

"Did you suddenly get dizzy?" another interlocutor wondered aloud.

"No, I. . . ."

"I know!" Ms. Comely shouted victoriously as she leaned over the bruised man's shoes. "Here is the answer, the probable cause!" She held up a torn piece of black shoestring for the throng to scrutinize.

"Ahh," the curious group signed in relieved unison.

Mr. Burro blinked nervously as Ms. Comely loudly declared the results of her research. "The reason that Mr. Burro fell, obviously from the evidence at hand, is because he tripped over his shoestrings, actually tearing the loose end from one. It's as simple as that," Ms. Comely beamed.

"It is so simple!" the students cheered as two of them hoisted her upon their shoulders and marched to the Student Center, Ms. Comely triumphantly twirling the offending bit of lace between her fingers.

Mr. Burro, still dazed slightly (effect) from the previous fall (cause) smiled grimly, spied his image in the giant urinal called the reflecting pool, and sighed, "It's as simple as that!"

Obviously, the preceding narrative is a parody of a cause and effect analysis, but a relevant one: for any event, no matter how insignificant, a cause exists. An inescapable fact is that we are concerned with causes and effects throughout our daily lives. For instance, why did this particular student fail English? Why was *E.T.* such a popular movie? What caused the automobile accident on the Industrial Boulevard? What are the causes of inflation? Why does Pete sneeze as soon as he wakes up in the morning? If you wish to analyze the problem concerning the national shortage of nurses in America, for instance, you could begin by writing a topic sentence stating the problem:

Studies have shown that there is a correlation between the shortage of nurses and the poor quality of hospital care.

This topic sentence could be developed in one of two ways. By establishing the topic sentence to be the cause (the shortage of nurses), you could present all of the effects reflected in the poor quality of hospital care (effect and cause analysis). Either of these approaches to the subject (topic) is correct.

In writing a cause and effect analysis, you must acquire the discipline of logical reasoning. The actual effects resulting from the causes are revealed only after careful examination of the facts. There are many pitfalls to be guarded against when you begin to write a cause and effect paper.

Beware of the post hoc, ergo propter hoc line of reasoning.

Post hoc (after this), *ergo propter hoc* (therefore because of this) provides us, generally, with little more than superstitious nonsense. If a black cat scampers before us as we toddle down the street, we tend to blame the innocent feline for any sort of mishap which subsequently befalls us. (Note our preoccupation with "black" as the harbinger of evil: blackmail, blacklist, blackball, black comedy.) Through the ages, old wives' tales warn us about walking under ladders, breaking mirrors, crossing oneself to avoid the evil eye, and so on. Usually, however, there is an historical germ of truth in such myths which the passage of time has distorted. For instance, lighting three cigarettes on a single match as taboo dates to the First World War and trench warfare.

Do not let bias or emotion effect your judgement.

Since everyone (it seems) is a victim of some sort of prejudice or pre-conceived preference, being objective is often difficult. Nevertheless, let the facts speak for themselves. For example, for years after the Great Depression, many Americans still felt that Herbert Hoover caused our national economic problems, totally ignoring many other factors contributing to that international depression. Also, the plethora of Polish jokes in this country is unfortunate because of cruel stereotyping which creates national prejudices not only against Poles, but logically against all racial and national minorities. The fact that a hoodlum of Greek descent stole your milk money when you were a child should not establish, in your mind, that all Greeks are thieves.

Avoid an inference that does not follow the premises.

Do not be hasty by "jumping" to conclusions. A *non sequitur* is a fallacious statement that does not logically follow from anything previously stated. To say that your dog died because you did not go to church on Sunday is not a logical inference.

Do not assume something which has not been proven as true.

Begging the question is a form of syllogistic reasoning which has little to do with reason. As the "tight wad" father argued, "Why should I waste my money sending my daughter to college? She's only going to get married and have kids anyhow!" And then he added, after a moment of sober reflection, "Girls don't need a college education like boys do!"

Instead of settling for one cause, search for multiple causes.

The student who says, "I failed English because I was always late with my assignment," may have stated a possible cause which contributed to his failure, but he is obligated to investigate other reasons. To say that slavery alone caused the Civil War is to ignore other major factors: states' rights, economic sectionalism, the election of Lincoln, and so on.

Be sure to confront the real issues.

Do not ignore the question by shifting the real causes and effects to false, misleading ones. To elect a candidate to public office because he is a war veteran or because he is a "good family man" is foolhardy. The real question must not be obscured: does he have the qualifications suitable for public office? If a senator dies in office, should his wife be elected to that office for the unexpired term—simply because she was his wife?

Coincidence may be a factor.

We often assume that two unrelated occurrences which happen at the same time have a causal relationship, ignoring, more often than not, mere coincidence as a probable factor. If a police car seems to be following your vehicle for several miles, turning left when you turn left, turning right when you turn right, you probably begin to perspire, suspecting that you have somehow violated the law—until the police car turns off or passes you. The simple truth is that you were both traveling in the same direction for an unrelated reason.

Distinguish between the probable and the possible.

Be sure that the suspected cause is capable of producing the effect.

Thanksgiving Day! I was looking forward to a succulent turkey dinner with all of the trimmings. Pete the Poodle shared my apartment with me; he was my bosom buddy—well trained, obedient, and a gentle companion.

It was about two o'clock when the huge, twenty-pound turkey was finished cooking. I removed it from the oven and placed it on the kitchen table. Lying patiently on the floor, Pete the Poodle, who weighed only about six pounds, watched me silently, his furry white head between his paws, his tongue licking his lips in hungry anticipation of a hot, delicious Thanksgiving dinner.

Suddenly the telephone rang. Greta, a friend who lived a block down the street, needed me to help her move some heavy furniture in her apartment. I agreed to hurry over to help her. As I was leaving my place, I told Pete, "Now I'll be back in about twenty minutes, Pete. Take care of the place, and when I come back we'll eat supper, OK?"

Pete yelped enthusiastically as I was leaving through the kitchen door. Once again I reminded my faithful watchdog, "Take care of things until I get back, Pete."

"Rrff!"

With that affirmative response from Pete, I felt secure and hurried down the street to Greta's pad.

I returned half an hour later, my mouth tingling with anticipation over the thought of a delectable meal. A twenty-pound turkey would provide a meal for me and Pete for at least two days. As I slipped my key into the kitchen door's latch, I noticed that it was open. Had I forgotten to lock up the place? Not to worry, I reminded myself that Pete, my valiant guard dog, was there to defend my meager possessions.

As I entered the kitchen, I shrieked involuntarily. My turkey, or what had been my turkey, was a hollow shell of bones and bits of gristle! The stuffing had been devoured; the mashed potatoes lay like mounds of grey putty on the floor; blobs of cranberry sauce checkered the white table cloth. My holiday dinner had been consumed by some strange, rapacious beast! Stunned, I fell to my knees beside the table. There, lying contentedly upon his side, his stomach bulging with the contents of a forbidden repast, was Pete the Poodle. His eyes were half closed in contented slumber, his paws and nose slick with what I presumed to be traces of my devastated Butterball. Stirring slightly, Pete looked dimly into my frenzied eyes.

"You traitor! You Judas! You greedy pig! Why did you gobble down the whole damned turkey?" I shouted as I reached to throttle the little cannibal's throat.

Sensing immediate danger, Pete bolted from his resting place, scurrying up the stairway to hide in one of his secret cavernous retreats, safe from my avenging anger. I did not pursue the devious monster.

Returning to the ruins of the table, I looked at the bleached bones of what remained of my supper. With tears of frustration streaming down my cheeks, I gulped down some scraps of stringy dark meat that dangled from a stripped turkey leg. Moral? Never trust a poodle to guard your turkey dinner.

I didn't talk to Pete for days.

What is the obvious conclusion which the narrator has drawn? Do you find his reasoning, spurred by emotion and anger, to be sound? Did Pete the Poodle lack motive? Was he sufficient cause for the narrator's determination of the effect? What are some other possibilities?

Use caution in assuming that stipulated causes will produce definite effects— sometimes the reverse may result.

The Volstead Act (Prohibition) was passed by fervent moralists in a calculated effort to stop the drinking of alcohol in the United States. Not only did drinking increase in the country but other serious problems were created by its passage and subsequent enforcement: bootlegging, the rise of gangsters such as Al Capone, the increase in street violence, the corruption of elected officials, and so on. When the Japanese bombed our fleet at Pearl Harbor, they presumed their act would crush us in the Pacific and totally demoralize Americans at home. Yet the effect the Japanese had expected did not materialize and actually boomeranged. Not only did the Japanese warlords unwittingly succeed in unifying a divided country immediately, but America rushed into emergency war-time production to replace the obsolete fleet destroyed at Pearl Harbor; their strategic faux pas brought us into the war openly on the side of the British and Allies.

Avoid rationalizing.

It is often tempting to use false or superficial reasons to explain one's behavior, ignoring deliberately the true motives. The employee who was fired because "the boss didn't like me" may be citing a possibility, but a doubtful one if the employee had been doing his work properly. Many people smoke cigarettes, they say, because it "calms" their nerves, a form of rationalization used to camouflage their lack of will power in breaking a foolish habit.

Do not confuse cause for effect or effect for cause.

Determine objectively the logical order of cause and effect. Discuss the following concepts: "God will be whatever man wants Him to be," or "Man will be whatever God wants him to be." In other words, who was created in whose image? To cite a common problem most of us have heard before, "Which came first, the chicken or the egg?" Consider the geocentric-heliocentric-egocentric concepts of our solar system. Analyze the confusion of cause for effect or effect for cause in the following narration. Try to understand the "hayseed's" logical dilemma as he stands in a 1930's bread line.

I was standing in the bread line freezing my bejeebers off when I heard this guy with a lot of authority say that the only thing I had to fear was fear itself. Now that made sense to me. Or at least I thought it did when I heard it. Not being an educated person—move up, buddy—I began to explore the meaning of these words which I admit sounded pretty good to a poor country boy like myself without two nickels to rub against each other.

In other words, being afraid is the only thing to be afraid of. Right? You gotta stop bein' afraid of bein' afraid. Bein' afraid is bad because it causes you to be more afraid and that's the only thing to be afraid of. The guy is sayin' that you shouldn't be afraid of bein' afraid. And if you are afraid, then that is the time to be afraid 'cause then you got a serious problem—bein' afraid. OK, I can see that. So don't be afraid of bein' afraid. Or, as we would say out in the sticks, don't be afeared of bein' afeared. Fear is fearful. Don't worry about fear. But—if you are afraid, then you got somethin' to worry about. Therefore, don't worry. If you're not afraid of bein' afraid, then you shouldn't worry anyhow. So don't let the fear within you strengthen the fear you're tryin' to get rid of. I guess you got a fight on two fronts: the fear you're tryin' not to worry about, and the fear of fearin' you can't lick the fear you're supposed to be lickin'.

Thank you, ma'am. Pardon me while I sit down and eat this hard bread here on the curb. Just like the guy in front of me. In the bread line. I had to push him and tell him not to be afraid to move up. You know. And you have to admire the guys who went busted on Wall Street jumpin' off some of the buildin's here in New York. You can't be afraid to take a plunge. Smash fear into pieces. Positive action I guess is what they call it.

But some people don't understand this guy's philosophy. Like this skinny woman with two kids in the bread line a while ago. I walked up to her and told her that the only thing she had to fear was fear itself and she kicked me in the ass. Some people really need an education. You know.

But—a thought just occurred to me sittin' here on the curb eatin' my bread. What do you do with a coward?

Questions for discussion

1. What is the point of the hayseed's semantic scrambling?

2. Does the author deliberately set out to confuse the reader or to illustrate a principle?

3. Why does the destitute woman with the two children attack the narrator?

English Anxiety

English anxiety is probably one of the few kinds I've never had, but I suppose all anxieties result from similar causes: a feeling of inadequacy or inability to cope with the subject. I can recall my severe anxieties on such subjects as biology, geology, math, French, driving, bill paying, tax figuring, and—especially, worst of all—physical education. All of these were/are areas for which I had no liking, understanding, or ability—or so I thought. In truth, English anxiety—or any of the above—is a "self-fulfilling prophecy": a person becomes convinced in advanced that he can't do it, so of course, he doesn't.

Is English anxiety different from any other kind? I doubt that the psychological or emotional symptoms are different, but each kind may have contrasting causes. For instance, my old physical education anxiety had two causes: growing up in a home where sports were never discussed or stressed in any way, so that I was ignorant of sports and felt them unimportant; second, as I was the smallest person in the class, hence easily picked on and battered. English anxiety, on the other hand, would have nothing to do with a person's physical traits, but could result from growing up in a home where English, words, communication were given no emphasis or priority at all, whereas they were almost the only conversational subject in my family, who were all writers, teachers, or journalists.

English anxiety may be a fairly recent phenomenon. I don't remember any of my classmates having it twenty years ago, a time when language abilities and test scores of eighteen-year-olds were much higher than they are today. Most experts say that the present college generation is a "non-verbal" one, raised on television, movies, rock music and other media in which correct usage is not important. But one formerly popular pastime has been in a long decline: reading.

Twenty, forty, and a hundred years ago, young people read more than they did today—not just comics or newspapers, but books. The number of students who don't read books for enjoyment is the most shocking (to me) change in the last twenty years. Books familiarize us with words and with style. So I would guess that the lack of books in young people's lives has caused so many of them to suffer English anxiety when faced with a blank piece of paper to fill. Sad but true, T.V., music, and movies aren't much help in filling up that piece of paper, are they?

The rise of English anxiety has had one unfortunate effect on my life. It has made me embarrassed to say I'm an English teacher when introduced to people. They almost always have a negative reaction—automatically. They either say, "English was my worst subject in school," or "Guess I'd better watch my English!" When I entered this profession, I thought it had some status I could be proud of, but this is not how new acquaintances treat it. It's as if they have such a negative image of English; it extends to the people who teach it, and I have to *prove* that, in spite of my hateful job, I might still be an interesting human being worth knowing. I blame English anxiety for the situation, and I resent it.

Since I never had English anxiety—and I never cured any of the ones I *did* have—I don't know how to cure it. But I have three suggestions to a person who suffers from it: 1. Start reading good books and appreciate the language as you read. 2. Keep a regular diary or journal of your feelings, without worrying about corrections. 3. Don't go into an English class or essay—or any other course—with the preconceived notion that you'll do poorly; that's exactly the way to ensure you will.

Dudley Brown

Questions for discussion

1. Do you agree with the author's premise concerning the cause of anxieties? Why? Why not?

2. Is there a particular course which causes you to suffer anxiety? What can you do to correct the situation?

3. Write a five hundred word essay analyzing the cause(s) of your present anxiety and the effect(s) upon you.

Suppertime

To write this paper I had to think backwards—what I do now and why!

I suppose that my decision would center around suppertime. Now, to explain from the very beginning: I was born premature and weighed two pounds; as a result, I was a pretty skinny kid. So, my parents were naturally over-concerned about my getting enough to eat. In retrospect, I can say suppertime was not enjoyable for me. It might have started well, but in the end I was stuck in the kitchen alone until I cleaned my plate. I was really glad the dog was there sometimes so I could give him my food. I guess it was not quite as bad as I described, but several incidents occurred that I will never forget.

So you see, at the time I dreaded suppertime and its ensuing routine.

My decision amounted to a determination to eat supper when, where, and only if I felt like it. Thus, when I left home at eighteen, I did not (and still do not) make a routine of supper. Even today, I will eat supper on the spur of the moment and will not make big preparations concerning it. I detest it when I do go home, having to schedule my day or plans so that I am home for suppertime. Therefore, more often than not, I will just tell my mother not to make anything for *me*. I will eat when I am hungry and when it is convenient for me, not others! I think it is absurd to have to schedule or rush just to be at a certain place at a certain time for a meal.

I suppose the best detailed example I could give is my current style of living. I come in from work and open the freezer door and then decide what type of TV dinner, hamburger, pizza, or hot dogs I want. Sometimes I will leave work and just go to McDonalds; other times I will eat at the Sugar Bowl before class or Mannys after class or cook something around 11 P.M., or perhaps not at all. So—I adjust supper to me, not me to it. I realize that I cause problems for other people (for example, my parents or girl friend) when I go home and they ask when or what I want to eat the next day or that night, and I will usually say, if pressured, "Just forget about it."

In regarding to what could have been done at the time to counteract this decision, my only response could be for my parents to have accepted it when I said that I did not want any more or anything to eat.

I suppose that I have not done anything to change my decision, but then I see no reason to change it. Of course, when I think about it now, my present situation of going to school full time and working full time does not allow me much free time of my own. In other words, since I have to be at certain places for twelve hours of the day, suppertime is the only "time" I really have some control over adjusting the situation *to suit me!*

Frank J. Hager

Questions for discussion

1. Should people eat when they are hungry or at certain socially acceptable periods of the day? Defend your answer.

2. Is the writer correct in his assessment of the past regarding a cause and effect analysis? Were his parents responsible?

3. Do you agree with the implied deduction that children should not have to "clean" their plates of food? Why?

4. Judging from the tone of the essay, do you think that the writer is socially maladjusted? Why? Why not?

5. Write a five hundred word essay analyzing a similar situation from your childhood and its effect(s) on you presently.

Gossip—Cause and Effect

Most people love to gossip. Though it is commonly associated with females, men do it just as much while calling it something else (business talk?). Occasionally, I encounter someone who claims he/she doesn't like to gossip or even listen to it. Immediately I mistrust this person and feel I don't want to know him better. The few people who don't gossip are basically self-centered and uninterested in others, for people gossip due to their curiosity about other people.

I was brought up to believe—as I still do—that gossip is a healthy sign of interest in the world beyond the self. Through observing others and talking about them, I've learned more about human nature, which in turn helps us to understand ourselves and those close to us. If we care at all about other people, it's natural to be curious about their private lives, habits, and relationships. Gossip does not have to be malicious or unpleasant, as some think, It can be kind, or compassionate, or merely humorous. Usually, it's educational, or at least if there is any truth in it; another false notion is that most gossip is false.

My home was always filled with gossip, mostly the humorous kind. My mother and all her friends were fascinated by every little quirk and oddity of the people in town. I grew up listening to and enjoying hours of laughing telephone conversations about people's quarrels, secrets, petty crimes, and occasional kinks. All this was much more interesting than listening to a parent go on and on about her own boring problems, which seldom happened.

Most people think they do not like to be gossiped about, which is wrong, too. If no one talks about me, I must be a boring, dull person that no one notices. Who wants to be like that? The people that get talked about are those who make a strong enough impression to stand out. Chances are, others secretly want to be like them.

People who claim to dislike gossip may be well intentioned, but they strike me as pompous and "holier-than-thou," if not hypocritical. Gossip has acquired an unfairly bad reputation. It makes the world far more interesting—and outgoing—than a gossip-free world where each person minded his own trivial business. I hope people will never get so self-absorbed that they lose interest in others, in gossip.

D.B.

Questions for discussion

1. Do you agree with the author's view on gossip? Why? Why not?

2. Would you be offended if you were the object of gossip? Explain.

3. Is most gossip false? Explain.

The cause and effect essay

There are at least three types of cause/effect essays: those on cause only, effects only, or cause *and* effect. It is possible to concentrate solely on causes or effects. You may, for instance, write an entire essay on why you made a decision (cause), or on the results or outcomes of that decision (effects). Sometimes the causes may be far more interesting than the effects and vice versa. Also, you may write on the causes of a decision or event which is too new or recent to have had lasting effects.

Much writing about cause is *speculative*. That is, the writer does not have factual knowledge of causes, but is simply giving his opinion of them. For instance, given a topic on "Why People are Ethnocentric" or "Causes of Depression," many writers will have different explanations of the causes. The writer should then be aware that what he writes is his opinion, not factual. As with other kinds of writing, select a topic you know well enough so that your opinions will be informed.

Effects of Quitting Smoking

It was a sudden, unplanned impulse in June 1983 when I threw away my cigarettes and announced that I was quitting "cold turkey" after twenty-five years of non-stop, heavy smoking. I told all of my friends because I knew they'd make me too ashamed to start again. The effects were immediate and violent.

Constant smoking must be an energy drainer because I found myself full of excess, restless energy. I needed to be in motion constantly—running or pacing around. I could not sit in one place because I could not stay still. Concentration was difficult. I was teaching summer school and could hardly sit still long enough to grade papers. After reading one paper, I was up and around the room again. The next few weeks were the only period of my adult life when I did not read a book, because I could not sit down to do it. I felt like I was a prisoner of my restless body, but if I could just get through this state, it would all be worthwhile.

However, I also could not sleep. I developed nightly insomnia. I always used to have cigarettes by the bed, and, when I woke up, I'd smoke one—and now they were not there. These were the worst of times, lying awake at three A.M. wondering when I was going to be able to relax and sleep again. One night I got up and moved furniture around until I got tired.

Three weeks after I quit smoking I had to travel to a high school reunion, my first long bus trip without cigarettes or sleep. Of course, by now my intake of gum and candy was about five times what it was before. During the reunion weekend I managed a small triumph. I read my first book in a month. I actually stayed in one place long enough to do it.

But still I could not sleep and I had far too much energy. I finally had to go to a doctor for some tranquilizers and nerve medicine—which I took for six months. It took this long for my body to get over the violent change I had forced on it. But after the effects of quitting smoking wore off, I knew it was, as I had suspected, worth it.

D.B.

Why I Learned to Read.

Like most people of my age, I learned to read when I was in elementary school. Unlike many people today, however, I learned a love of reading so strong that I made it a lasting part of my life—one of most pleasant pastimes. Why?

That I learned to read is hardly surprising. After all, I grew up in a time when radio was the secondary form of entertainment; reading was the primary. By the time television became common, reading for me had become the primary means of both information and pleasure.

We had a radio but television was still rare. The people across the street finally got one, and I remember Kate Smith singing "When the Moon Comes Over the Mountain." It seemed to come over every afternoon!

My mother was not a reader although, of course, she could read and did read—primarily the newspaper. My father was the reader who taught me to love reading. And yet I don't recall his wading through weighty tomes like *War and Peace*. He "dropped out" of school in the eighth grade and didn't finish high school until he was in his sixties by going to night school. But he read—*The Reader's Digest*, especially, and he loved "Increasing Your Word Power," a column still popular with *Reader's Digest* readers.

It was he who showed me that reading is indeed fun, for every evening after he returned from work and before supper we would sit in one of the big, overstuffed living room chairs and he would read to me—the comics in the daily paper. I grew up reading "Dagwood" and other comic strips of the time. We would "read" together and laugh together. To this day, my day doesn't begin right if I can't read the comic strips. And I often think of him.

A second major reason for my learning to read was the influence of my church. Trinity Methodist Church, like all Methodist churches, had a responsive reading as part of every church service. The minister would read a section and then the congregation would read the section in bold type. The pattern alternated. Since the responsive readings were arrangements of the King James translation of the Bible, the rhythm and music of the language appealed to me—I wanted to be able to participate, too!

So I learned to read. I was not precocious. I was just an ordinary child who was fortunate to have a father who loved to read and a church which clearly valued reading. To win the approval of both and to participate in the worship of the service, I learned to read.

It is said that the two greatest influences in a child's life are family and church. In my case, the saying proves true.

N. Kelley

Questions for discussion

1. William Wordsworth said, "The child is father to the man." Discuss Professor Kelley's essay in the context of Wordsworth's statement.

2. Do you agree that children watch too much television and, therefore, reading and writing levels in America have declined? Defend your answer.

3. What is your reading level? How can you improve?

4. When did you begin reading? What types of material did you read? What do you read now?

Suggestions for writing a cause and effect paper

1. Write a five hundred word essay analyzing the reasons why you decided to attend this particular college rather than another college or university.

2. Analyze the reasons why you are pursuing your present field of study and your future goals.

3. Write an essay analyzing the basis for a particular prejudice of yours. Try to be objective.

4. In five hundred words, search for reasons why you are presently involved with a certain boy or girl. Be specific.

5. Write an essay investigating the cause(s) of an accident in which you were involved and its effects.

■ Chapter 10 ■

Convincing the Reader: Argument and Persuasion

Technically, argument and persuasion are two different strategies you may use to win the reader over to your viewpoint concerning a debatable issue. Through logic or emotion, the persuasive essay attempts to convince the reader to believe something. Through strong conviction, the writer intends to influence the reader by putting forth reasons for or against a belief or course of action. An argument implies intent to persuade another in debate.

Argument appeals mainly to the reader's sense of reason; *persuasion* appeals mainly to the reader's feelings and values to create action or to win support for a particular course of action. If used wisely, argument and persuasion, combined, are effective strategies in creating compromise, in winning agreement, or in eliciting action.

The basic point of an argument or persuasive essay is to demonstrate or establish a point of view through **logic** and **rhetoric.** Logic is impersonal, objective. However, rhetoric involves personal appeals to the reader's feelings, prejudices, and sympathies. Logic goes beyond the appeal of rhetoric, an art which may be unsupported or inflated discourse. A good argument combines both components. Facts, logic—without style, without rhetorical appeal—will be dull, unattractive, and boring—the ultimate sin.

Forms of logical argument:
Deductive and inductive

Deduction is reasoning from one principle to another by means of accepted rules of inference, wherein a conclusion follows from the premises. The best known deductive arguments are called **syllogisms:**

All philosophers are wise.	(Major premise)	All P's are Q's.
Socrates is a philosopher.	(Minor premise)	S is a P.
Therefore, Socrates is wise.	(Conclusion)	Therefore, S is a Q.

If the premises are true, then the conclusion will be true; but an argument may be valid even if its premises and conclusion are false:

All dogs are green.
Plato is a dog.
Therefore, Plato is green.

A good deductive argument must have two features: a valid argument and true premises. Deductive logic guarantees the truth of the conclusion *if* the premises are true:

All men are mortal.
Socrates is a man.
Therefore, Socrates is mortal.

Inductive logic reaches a conclusion about all the members of a class from examination of only a few members of the class, reasoning from the particular to the general, the opposite of the deductive method. Although the conclusion is supported by the premises, the truth is not guaranteed:

Every A we have seen is a B.	Every Greek man we have seen is bearded.
Therefore, A is a B.	Therefore, all Greek men are bearded.

Nevertheless, even though most of our knowledge and science depends upon induction, induction does not guarantee the truth of the conclusion. Thus, the previous example should read: It is probable that all Greek men are bearded. Induction does not guarantee certainty, only probability.

Argument by analogy is a form of logical inference based on the assumption that, if two things are alike in some respects, they must be alike in other respects. Of course, it doesn't necessarily follow that the objects will be similar. Although arguments by analogy may be useful, the problem is one of reliability.

Argument by counter-example is an example that contradicts a generalization.

Reductio ad absurdum is an argument in which one refutes a statement by showing that it leads to self-contradiction or an insupportable conclusion.

Fallacies in argument

Mere assertion

Simply stating your opinion or view is not an argument proving it.

Begging the question

Do not assume as true what you want to prove: Wives must obey their husbands because the Bible says so.

Ad hominem argument

Instead of arguing against an opponent's position, one attacks his/her character on a personal level. Do not attack the person you are arguing against on the basis of lying, appearance, intelligence, or possessions.

Ad populum argument

Instead of offering facts or reasons, one appeals to the prejudices of the audience or reader.

Dubious authority

Do not use the wrong person or someone who is unqualified to give expert testimony.

Emotional appeals

The appeal to pity and other emotions are not legitimate arguments for any particular position, reflecting failure to use a logical basis to support one's position.

Either/or

Do not oversimplify the problem by stating/implying there are only two possibilities.

Generalizations

Do not base conclusions on universally applicable notions, which may be vague, indefinite, or unspecific.

Oversimplification

Do not suggest a simple solution to a complex issue.

Writing the persuasive essay

To persuade the reader, take one side of an issue to convince the reader that your position is reasonable. Select an issue (political, social, cultural) of interest to you and write an essay taking a solid stand, making sure that you use logical principles to defend your point. Avoid issues which have been over-done (e.g. lowering the drinking age to eighteen, capital punishment) or too complex for a short essay (abortion, euthanasia).

One of the following topics may whet your interest.

Exercising regularly	Volunteering
Eating sensibly	Becoming less selfish
Spending more time with your parents	Studying regularly
Budgeting money or time	Giving to Animal Welfare

Think of some specific accepted societal practice or tradition which you consider unjust or barbaric, and explain why it should be banished or ended. Try to convince your reader by appealing to logic and reason, or emotions or prejudices, or a combination of logic and rhetoric.

Try to anticipate possible objections and be ready to answer them. One effective method is, after you have stated your thesis statement and plan of development in the introductory paragraph, to start another paragraph in which you bring up your audience's possible objections to your thesis statement. Proceed to attack such objections in the rest of the essay.

Suppose you are writing an essay in favor of studying regularly. An outline of your essay might look like this:

Introductory paragraph

Tell how you "fell behind" in your classwork.

Thesis statement

Planning your weekly homework schedule, figuring a system to do your homework, and taking notes in class will allow you to get the most out of your limited study time.

Supporting paragraph 1—Possible Objections

Topic Sentence: There are many problems people have when organizing their study time.

Objection 1: I am overwhelmed by the amount of work.

Objection 2: By the time I get to study for my most difficult class, I am too tired.

Objection 3: The material in class is covered too quickly to follow; I'm lost.

Conclusion: Just a little effort in organizing can save a great deal of time.

Supporting paragraph 2—Make your case.

Topic Sentence: Plan what homework you need to accomplish each week by making lists; be specific.

Supporting paragraph 3—Time Management

Topic Sentence: Doing your most difficult work when you are relaxed and fresh will allow you to use time effectively.

Supporting paragraph 4—Take notes in class.

Topic Sentence: Taking detailed notes will allow you to remember to examine the important details from class. Be specific.

Concluding Paragraph—Call for action.

Topic Sentence: Tell yourself to make a commitment to keep up with your homework; once you lag behind, "catching up" is difficult.

Note: The conclusion may summarize and also request that the reader take action in response. You may wish to pose a serious question to the reader or outline what steps need to be taken to solve the problem.

- Assume that the reader is intelligent but neutral regarding your viewpoint. Persuade by using logic, reason, and appeals to emotion.
- Support your position to the hilt. Do not give any indication that you are hesitant or unsure of your position. Be confident in your authority and truth of your thesis.
- Limit your topic as one you can manage within the time allotted.

- Try to develop a thesis from first-hand experience or observations. Of course, credible sources and scientific data strengthen your position.
- Avoid controversial areas such as politics and religion—too many emotional and prejudicial pitfalls.
- Your tone should be moderate. Be reasonable, sincere, and courteous.

Components of the argument essay

1. The assertion or proposition must be stated clearly as your thesis. Of course, the debatable topic may defend or attack a position, recommend a solution to a problem, or challenge traditional beliefs or values:

   - Cigarette smokers should fight for their rights.
   - Professional athletes are over-paid—big time!
   - Marijuana should be legalized.
   - Monogamy is out-dated in America today.

2. Divide your thesis into sub-terms with adequate support.

3. Anticipate the stronger opposing arguments and deal with them briefly with evidence supporting your position.

4. Organization is vital. Build your arguments steadily to a strong conclusion and resolution. Save the best for last.

5. Appeal to the reader by conveying a sincere, reasonable tone based on credible support.

6. Emotional appeals are powerful if directed at the reader's beliefs and values—if such appeals are appropriate to your argument:

   - Animals are being cruelly tortured for what passes as "science."
   - Boxing should be outlawed to save young men from a life-time of permanent injury and premature death.

7. If statistics are used, decide which statistics are best suited to support your position. Be accurate. Do not confuse the reader.

8. Utilizing personal interviews with experts helps your case.

9. Do not hesitate to cite your sources in supporting your position.

Persuasive essay editing—check list

1. Is there a clear "should statement" in the introduction?

2. Did you address any negative perceptions before beginning the essay?

3. Are there at least three good arguments in the essay? What are the arguments mentioned?

4. Is each argument presented in a clear and organized way? If not, which one(s) need(s) explained in more detail?

5. Is there at least one counter-argument presented? What is it? Is the rebuttal an effective one?

6. Do you appeal to emotions through the use of personal narratives or shocking examples? If not, what examples might work?

7. Did you remain professional and ethical throughout the argument? If not, point out areas that may need to be re-worded.

8. Is there a specific "call to action" in the conclusion? What is it?

Ideas for possible argument essays

Think about an argument paper on the following topics.

Police officers	Abortion	Cloning humans
Welfare	Financial Aid	Corporal punishment
Pornography	Pete Rose	President Clinton
Homosexual rights	Monica Lewinsky	Heavy Metal music
Gun control	In-class essays	Michael Jackson
Vietnam	Polygamy	Ethical relativism

Earned Opinions

An "earned" opinion is a "deserved" one. It means the person is informed, knowledgeable, or experienced enough to voice or write the opinion. The opposite would be an "unearned" or "undeserved" opinion. In this case, the person was **not** sufficiently informed, knowledgeable, or experienced enough to make his/her opinion worth saying or writing—so why bother? Most of the poor Letters to the Editor which embarrass me (for the writer) are the result of unearned and undeserved opinions. I strive in my life not to be caught giving the "wrong" kind. Actually, I try not to do it at all. I encourage my students to evaluate themselves and their own opinions in this regard. I grade them on this matter, but the proper use of "earned" opinions is important in life in far more ways than grades. The understanding and practice of sound, well-informed opinion is an important lifetime character trait.

D. Brown

Questions for discussion

1. Think of an interesting, original issue which has two or more sides. Make a list of pros and cons (for and against). The lists must be equal.

2. Explain the difference between an objective statement and a subjective one. Give a few examples.

Letter to the editor

The following letter was sent to the Editor in rebuttal to several other commentaries concerning a young boy's skill in shooting Mourning Doves.

Sportsman or Vandal?

After reading the series of articles and letters concerning the killing of a Mourning Dove by a local young man, I felt a compulsion to share my humble thoughts with you. I do not mean to criticize or attack anyone; my purpose is to respond to what has been written regarding a spectacular local event, one that has aroused not only me, but my neighbors.

Isn't it ironic that a dove, traditionally a symbol of peace and love, one representing the United Nations no less, should be the focal point of violence and anger?

I do not wish to quibble with Mr. Bludd's comment about where the "sports story" should have been located in the *Cumberland Times-News.* It is a great human interest story. Thanks to Mr. Bludd's clarification of the number of doves the young lad bagged, I am struck with awe. After reading the front page article some time ago, with the "American boy" smiling proudly over the carcass of the dove, I simply shrugged, passing it off as a lucky shot on his part. However, after reading the details by Mr. Bludd (I thank him for enlightening me), I was truly impressed. Imagine shooting **ten** of those menacing pests from the sky! Now that is truly front page news, worthy of the cover of *Sports Illustrated,* an achievement that rivals the Twelve Labors of Hercules! I see a gold medal in the Olympics for this young hero. Please continue to hone those awesome sharpshooting skills.

Of course it's front page news, Mr. Bludd, ranking with the achievements of Buffalo Bill, Annie Oakley, Kit Carson, and Davy Crockett, renowned serial killers of dumb creatures such as bison, eagles, rabbits, stray cats and dogs, and Indians—none of whom had any right to live because they were weak. We applaud such achievements in the sport of hunting. I especially liked Ms. Prudy's letter to the editor supporting our young hunter and upsetting nature: "The strong are to survive, now the weak and sick are being fed and there isn't going to be any strong gene's" [sic]. I agree with her. Dead animals are much more interesting than live ones.

I was favorably impressed by her references to Scripture in "backing up" her eloquent attack on Ms. Whiting, who feeds birds at her home. We all know that "might makes right" and the strong will survive and the weak will perish. Amen! I thank Mr. Bludd and Ms. Prudy for directing me to the right opinion on these matters. I am ashamed to admit that, for the past twenty-five years, I have been feeding birds and squirrels who come begging for food, especially in the winter. Obviously, I was remiss in feeding these dumb creatures with faulty genes because Scripture and Ms. Prudy forbid it. Not to worry, my friends, After reading Ms. Prudy's letter, and fearing the wrath of the Lord, I dashed out of the house and trashed the bird feeders. Let the little beggars starve. I shall not feed the robins, the cardinals, the blue jays that chatter incessantly when I am trying to take an afternoon nap. I will not be responsible for upsetting Nature. Besides, "God put food on the Earth for them," Ms. Prudy asserts. Who am I to compete with Divine Providence? In the winter, they can peck through the ice for some dry grass. I intend to save a small fortune. Perhaps I will even be able to buy a Winchester or Remington rifle (American-made, of course) to "blow" those colorful parasites away. Perhaps, if I buy a license, I may "bag" a few and get my picture on the front page of the newspaper (in color, if you please), lording it over ten stupid, weak, gene-deficient birds with my trusty rifle gleaming in the sunlight.

I was fascinated with Mr. Bludd's account that the young lad had been hunting since he was ten years old with his father (Mr. Bludd). The story really warmed my heart. Looking back on my mis-spent youth, I must admit that it was fraught with "sissy" pursuits like hunting for a good book to read, a poem to enjoy, a little league game, some football (we had no television), nothing dramatic like "popping" a bird in full flight from the sunny skies, watching it jerk and flutter to the ground. Instead of a gun, I had a home-made slingshot and a small rock. I aimed at a sparrow once, but missed (technology was poor then), and I gave up the thrilling sport of hunting because of my poor eyesight. Small wonder that I envy the young American boy with his uncanny skills.

Furthermore, my parents erred in making me do my homework at the tender age of ten. They should have taken me hunting to rid the skies and fields of the vermin infesting God's universe. And we all know what a dove in flight can do to a newly waxed car. Unfortunately, my parents deceived me by forcing me to study, to learn, to appreciate all creatures, big and small. I can not forgive them for their insensitivity to what we now recognize as our natural right: **the family that kills together stays together.** I commend Mr. Bludd for his insight. He states, quite rightly, that, if fathers took their sons hunting, there "would be less crime and violence in the world." (He does not mention daughters; this is a man's world, and hunting is a macho sport.) I really liked his logic that hunting leads to less violence in the world. That makes sense. And Ms. Prudy is also correct when she encourages the young men of this area to "keep on hunting and enjoy your sport."

Indeed, don't worry about killing off the species—there's always something out there to shoot at. Just keep playing with that rifle, kid. Soon, if you butcher enough dumb animals, weak, inferior, and stupid, you can call yourself a real man. (It's too late for me.) And if you get thirsty out there in the wild tracking down those dreadful nuisances which blight our skies and fields, have a cold beer and wait. Bambi is coming around the next tree. Forget about art and poetry and music and the reverence for life; those are sissy things you will learn to overcome in your quest as the "Great White Hunter."

Furthermore, Mr. Bludd is correct when he scolds Mr. Smith for sending the editor a letter criticizing the sporting event of the century. I applaud Ms. Prudy when she righteously derides Ms. Whiting for "daring" to belittle our famous young hunter. Even in a democracy where freedom of speech is encouraged, honored, and protected, such "bleeding hearts" should not be allowed to express their honest opinions in an open forum. We can not permit compassion, tenderness, and love for a dumb, innocent subspecies to be printed in the newspaper. Such dangerous thoughts might make some of us think before pulling the hair-trigger on that noble Uzi. Mr. Smith and Ms. Whiting have no right to express their outrage and feelings over what they mistake to be a form of cruelty.

I must reprimand the editor, respectfully, for publishing their letters defending the weak, the frail, and the innocent. Shame on you, Mr. Smith and Ms. Whiting for your compassion! Mercy, tenderness, and kindness are anachronisms in a world lit by the cruel bolts of lightning. Wake up! Take up hunting and smell the gunpowder. It is a noble sport. Destroy your bird feeders! Pick up a Winchester with a telescopic sight, and blast those feathered rascals from the sky. God, according to our wise biblical scholars, will thank you for it.

We worry about people like you. Even Shakespeare expresses his concern in *Macbeth:*

"Yet do I fear thy nature;
It is too full o' the milk of human kindness."

And don't you dare continue the immoral practice of feeding those hungry birds!

"If a man destroys a work of art by man, we call him a vandal.
If a man destroys a work of art by God, we call him a sportsman."
(Krutch)

Questions for discussion

1. What is the tone of the article? Is it effective? Why?

2. Does the author convey satire or bitterness? Explain your answer.

3. Do you agree with the writer's viewpoints? Why? Why not?

4. Is the young boy a sportsman or a vandal? Explain.

5. Write a four-hundred word essay defending or attacking the writer's disgust with hunting. Try to be objective in persuading the reader to agree with your arguments.

Seeking the truth objectively

Argumentation and criticism need not be hostile or defensive, but ways of making your position clear—to yourself and others. Socrates said that his truest friends were also his best critics. Argument and persuasion take place with shared interests and the search for the truth. To say that everyone's opinion is respected is not to say that everyone's opinion is of equal value. An argument must be measured by its merit.

Discuss the following arguments

1. God must exist; the Bible and the Koran say so.

2. If you don't agree with me, I'm going to hit you.

3. We haven't seen a deer all day. Therefore, no deer are in the area.

4. The philosopher from Athens is a homosexual. Therefore, his claim that the universe is made of atoms should be ignored.

5. Fish swim. John swims. Therefore, John is a fish.

6. Which is the greater sin: committing adultery or killing someone in anger?

7. Keeping the Sabbath holy means I don't have to work on Sunday.

8. Only people who are educated concerning the issues should vote.

9. Who should get available organs when there aren't enough to go around? A young mother with three children or a sixty-five-year-old alcoholic? Is it just to treat these two as equals?

10. I failed English because the teacher didn't like me.

11. "Let wives be subject to their husbands as to the Lord, because a husband is head of the wife. . . ." (Ephesians 21)

12. "If a man lies with a male as with a woman, both of them shall be put to death. . . ." (Lev. Ch. 20, 9)

13. Should we violate the law if our conscience tells us to do so?

14. Females are more emotional than males.

15. No one should get married before the age of twenty-five.

16. Poverty causes crime.

17. The full moon causes an increase in crime and violence.

18. Why do I need to take Biology 101? I'm a math major.

19. Adultery is always evil—no exceptions.

20. The grading system is unfair because of persistent student complaints.

21. All athletes should be tested for drugs.

22. Corporal punishment is wrong.

23. Rap, rock, and heavy metal music have caused immoral behavior among teenagers.

24. Condom distribution in schools will stimulate promiscuous behavior among teenagers. It's immoral.

25. Sex education in the schools doesn't work. Let's make our children concentrate on the basics: English, math, reading.

Writing assignment

Select one of the preceding ideas and write a four-hundred word essay defending your position on the matter. Be as objective as possible.

Chapter 11

Writing the Outline

There are many ways to describe an outline: a road map, a table of contents, a strategic battle plan, a skeletal framework, and others. What all of these diverse comparisons have in common may be said in one word—organization. An outline is the planned development of related ideas from which you should proceed to write your essay. Of the three types—topic, sentence, and paragraph—the topic and sentence outlines are most often used in college writing.

Parallel structure

The sentence outline is generally regarded as the easiest of the three types to write. Most students know what a sentence is and their task is therefore much simpler. A topic outline, on the other hand, requires a more subtle knowledge and handling of grammatical construction. Whichever you choose, remember that the outline must be parallel in all of its terms and subterms. Parallel structure means uniformity of construction—symmetry and balance. In a sentence outline, *all* terms must be sentences. In a topic outline, all terms must be identical in structure. Whatever structure you decide to present, for instance, gerund phrases, noun clauses, infinitive phrases, and the various other types, once you have decided upon a particular construction, do not deviate from it in the outline.

Since the outline is the skeletal framework which organizes your thoughts and the plan which you intend to follow, take extreme care in writing it. Study the following outlines for clarification.

The sentence outline

Composition Rules

Central idea: Freshman students should follow standard rules in writing their composition.

  I. Essays should be written on 8 1/2 by 11" white paper.
  - A. Hand written essays should be on lined paper.
  - B. Typed essays should be on unlined paper.

 II. Standard margins are mandatory.
  - A. The title of the essay should be spaced one inch from the top margin.
  - B. The left margin should be one and one-half inches.
  - C. The right margin should be one inch.
  - D. The bottom margin should be one inch.

III. Spacing properly aids in legibility.
  - A. Typed essays should be double spaced.
  - B. Quoted insets are double spaced and indented five spaces from the left margin.
    1. Quotations of four lines or more are inset.
    2. Quotation marks are excluded in quotations which are inset.
  - C. New paragraphs are indented five spaces.
  - D. Typographical errors are counted as errors.
  - E. Students writing in longhand should write on every other line for legibility and to permit space for the teacher's corrections.

IV. A student should follow standard rules regarding pagination.
  - A. The first page of an essay is not numbered.
  - B. Succeeding page numbers may be placed in the upper right hand corner or at the top center.

 V. A student should write his essay on only one side of the page(s).

Conclusion: A clean, neat copy, free of sloppy erasure marks and crossed out words, is a reflection of the student's attitude towards his work.

Note: In a sentence outline, all elements are sentences.

The topic outline

Writing a Process Paper

Central idea: Organizing a process paper

I. Identifying the subject
    A. Stating the process
    B. Defining the process
    C. Relating the importance of the process
    D. Listing the major steps in the process.

II. Developing the steps in the process
    A. Analyzing each step in the process
    B. Developing each step adequately
    C. Explaining each step clearly

III. Concluding the essay
    A. Completing the last step in the process
    B. Summarizing the major steps
    C. Commenting on the importance of the process

Concluding/Summarizing

Note: In this particular type of outline, all of the terms and subterms
        are gerund phrases. The writer did not disrupt the balance of
        his outline by diverting his pattern to include clauses or other
        types of phrases. Subsequently, the outline is parallel.

Balance

The mechanical structure of an outline must *always* have at least *two*
terms or divisions. By definition, division means at least two parts: naturally, there may be more. For instance, Roman numeral I must always
have a counterpart with Roman numeral II. If Roman numeral I (the
term) is divided, *A* (the subterm) must always be balanced by *B*. Note the
structure of the following.

Correct

I.
   A.
   B.
II.
   A.

Incorrect

I.
   A.
      1.
II.
   A.

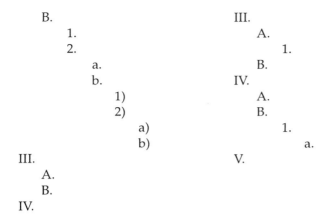

B.
   1.
   2.
     a.
     b.
      1)
      2)
       a)
       b)
III.
  A.
  B.
IV.

III.
  A.
    1.
  B.
IV.
  A.
  B.
    1.
      a.
V.

Rules to Remember in Writing the Outline

Central Idea: Formulate an outline before you begin writing an essay and remember to conform to standard English usage.

I. Do not use "outline' as your heading.
  A. Your title should refer to your material.
  B. Do not underline your title (unless it is a book title, magazine title, and so on).
  C. Do not put your title in quotes (unless it is a direct quote, essay title, and so on).

II. The central idea is the thesis of your outline and the subject of your essay.
  A. The central idea is not numbered.
  B. The central idea may be divided by capital letters or numbers.
  C. The central idea is not synonymous to the introduction.
    1. Usually an optional feature, an introduction is broader than the central idea or thesis.
      a. An introduction may define the subject.
      b. An introduction may give background information on the subject.
    2. An introduction may include the central idea.
      a. An introduction may state the scope or limits of the subject.
      b. An introduction may state the point of view of the writer.
      c. An introduction may state the plan of development of the essay.
    3. An introduction is not given a Roman numeral or capital letter.
    4. An introduction may be divided by numbers or capital letters.

III. Be sure your outline reflects parallel structure.
   A. In a sentence outline, all terms and subterms must be sentences.
       1. Do not shift person.
       2. Do not incorporate any interrogative sentences.
       3. Capitalize only the first letter of your sentences (and proper nouns according to standard usage).
   B. In a topic outline, all terms and subterms should be written in the same grammatical pattern.
       1. Capitalize the first letter of the first word in each term and subterm.
       2. Do *not* use a period after a word, phrase, or clause in the term or subterm.

IV. Be consistent in the punctuation and the arrangement of your outline.
   A. Use a period after each Roman numeral.
   B. Use a period after each capital letter.
   C. Use a period after Arabic numerals.
   D. The second and succeeding lines should begin directly under the first letter of the first word of each term and subterm.
   E. Except for unusually long outlines, page numbers are excluded.

Conclusion: The conclusion/summary is not given a Roman numeral and is treated as a separate unit comparable to the central idea.

   A. The conclusion may be divided by numbers or by capital letters.
   B. The summary may be divided by numbers or by capital letters.

Living Things

Central idea: A simplified outline of living things, concentrating on the Animal Kingdom.

   I. Plants

  II. Animals
   A. Invertebrates
   B. Vertebrates
       1. Fish
       2. Amphibians
       3. Reptiles
       4. Birds
       5. Mammals
           a. Prototheria ("primitive beasts")
           b. Eutheria ("good or true beasts")

(1) Marsupials
(2) Placental animals
    (a) Insectivora
    (b) Chiroptera
    (c) Carnivora
    (d) Artiodactyla
    (e) Perissodactyla ("beyond the regular number of digits")
    (f) Cetacea
    (g) Primates
        (i) Monkeys
        (ii) Apes
        (iii) Man

Conclusion: Specific/implied criteria for the categorizations of each animal listed

---

Guidelines in Outlining

■ Punctuate each term in a sentence outline as a sentence.
■ Do not punctuate terms in a topic outline.
■ Use capital letters to begin each term and subterm.
■ Use parallel grammatical construction.
■ Divide each term and subterm into at least two parts.
■ Begin second lines directly under first lines.
■ Do not ask questions in an outline.

The following outline was submitted by a student. What guidelines for proper outlining are violated?

Outline

Central idea: The L.C.D. calculator

A. The Radio Shack L.C.D. calculator is needed in the field of Forestry.
  I. Used in forestry, business, and for accountants.
    A. Is battery-operated.
    B. The calculator has a forty key operation.
  II. What does it do?
    A. Enters calculations
      (1) weighs only seven ounces.
      (2) economical
  III. It has an aluminum case in case of bad weather; The calculator costs only $12.95, so it is very economical.

Chapter 12

Writing the Research Paper

In the academic field of fact finding, it is generally regarded as somewhat pretentious for freshman college students to try to write what instructors audaciously assign as "research" papers. Few students on such an elemental rung of the scholastic ladder, it is widely felt, are capable of contributing anything worthwhile or important to the field of knowledge.

But the critics of such endeavors miss the point. The freshman research paper is not so much an *answer* to a complex problem or dilemma as it is an *exercise* in writing technique. The research paper is an essay which explains facts and opinions regarding a problem or a situation, evaluates those facts and opinions, and ultimately draws a logical conclusion verified by the "experts" in that particular field of interest.

Since the real purpose of a research paper deals with locating and recording facts, every college student should have rudimentary experience in library research. Sooner or later, he will have to do some type of fundamental laboratory work in his discipline. The ability to locate pertinent information as quickly as possible, to record that information correctly and completely, and to evaluate the facts objectively concerning that information is a necessary and profitable experience.

Choose a topic which is interesting

Always select a topic which you can enjoy, especially if it is in your field of study. Unless your instructor assigns a particular thesis to investigate, you should have the common sense to be willing to probe a matter of interest. If you can not find an interesting topic, remember to refer to periodicals in your field; they are more up to date than books. Also, do not neglect your advisor or instructors as resource people. Remember, if you are apathetic or indifferent regarding your topic, that negative feeling will probably be reflected in your work. Although research work and writing may not be "fun," it needn't be dreary, monotonous work—if you *like* the subject.

Define the scope of your topic

Too many students fail to set limits or boundaries on what they set out to do. Generally, their topics are too broad and have no point of view; sometimes, although more seldom, their topics are too narrow, and too little information is available in the local libraries. Vagueness must be avoided. For instance, "Stress" as a topic is nonsensical. What about stress? What is the student's point of view concerning stress? Books have been written on the subject of stress. The student offering that subject as a topic may just as well have chosen a history of the Second World War, and some students probably think *that* would be a good subject for a research paper. Avoid topics as broad as the heavens.

Similarly, some students choose topics which are too narrow, considering the availability of resource material. For instance, "Stress and its Effects upon Old English Sheep Dogs" is too narrow a focus for a research study (except for a veterinarian). Be sure that research materials and sources are sufficient and at hand for your study.

Discuss the following ideas as possible topics for a research paper:

The Life of Edgar Allen Poe

Edgar Allen Poe's Life in Baltimore's Bars

Solar Energy

Cancer

Athenian Drama

Shakespeare's Sonnets

General Custer Disobeyed Orders at the Battle of the Little Big Horn

America's Missile System

The Effect of Russian Sabotage on Cumberland, Maryland

Alcoholics Anonymous

Stress as a Factor among Policemen

The Death of Marilyn Monroe

The Watergate Tapes

Red Dye Number Two Causes Cancer

Food Additives Cause Cancer

Red Jellybeans Cause Cancer

The Effects of Alcoholism on the Family

The Effects of Alcohol on the Fetus

Abortion

The Homosexual as Underground Hero

The Life of FDR

The Advantages of Wearing Dentures

Saccharin as a Carcinogen

Saliva as a Carcinogen

Sexual Harassment of Teachers

The Advantages of Clearcutting

Bedwetting—a Psychological Problem of Infants

A Defense of Capital Punishment

The Advantages of Celibacy

State the problem being investigated

Your first statement should define immediately what problem is being investigated and your point of view, supported by facts, regarding that problem. For instance, "General Custer" may be a fitting title for your paper, but it should not be your thesis statement. "General Custer" is too broad, indefinite, and without a resolution. What is your point of view concerning Custer? The life of General Custer is certainly an interesting study, but much too broad and without focus. However, a statement such as "General Custer Disobeyed Orders at the Battle of Little Big Horn" is an excellent premise to prove (or disprove, if stated in the negative). Similarly, "Pearl Harbor" is much too broad for a proper topic, but "Japan's Attack on Pearl Harbor Was a Strategic Error" is much better concerning point of view and focus. Once again, be sure that you state definitely your attitude on the problem being investigated.

Find the sources to document your thesis

Before you commit yourself regarding a thesis, be confident that enough material is available to document your point of view. Certainly, your major resource for printed materials is the library: books, periodicals, newspapers, bulletins, documents, audio-visuals, and so on. But there are other resources to rely upon to support your thesis: the personal interview, materials published by the various governmental agencies and industries, and your personal experience. Utilize these various sources to reinforce your thesis.

Recording research information

Evaluating, judging objectively, all of your sources concerning reliability and usefulness is all important. Use primary, or first-hand sources whenever feasible. Secondary sources are, of course, more accessible, and your paper will probably rely heavily on secondary sources, depending on your thesis. Nevertheless, remember to utilize as many primary sources as possible through original documents and personal interviews. And remember that you want facts, *not* opinions.

Preparing a list of sources

In ink, record the necessary bibliographical information on 3 by 5 or 4 by 6 inch note cards, which are easier to handle and to arrange than sheets of paper. Be as complete as possible in recording data the very first time so you won't waste time going back to the library for information which you may have omitted.

Title card for a book

Zorba, Peter Edward (author's full name)

Fighting the Turks in Crete

Cumberland, Maryland: Brinks Publishing Company, 1982.

798.7 (call number of the book)

ACC (library's initials)

A title card for a book has the author's or editor's complete name, the book title (including sub-title), edition (unless a first edition), volume number (if in several volumes), city of publication, publishing company, date of publication, call number, and the name of the library.

Title card for an article from a periodical

> Zorba, Peter Edward, and Rita Psinakis
>
> "Fighting the Turks in Crete."
>
> <u>Mediterranean Journal,</u> 69 (December 1982), 33-67.

Note: In the above illustration, 69 is the volume number; 33-67 refer to the pages of the article.

A title card for an article appearing in a periodical has the author's (authors') name, the title of the article *in quotes,* the title of the periodical *underlined,* the volume number, date of publication (if the volume number is given, put the date of the publication in parentheses), and the page numbers of the entire article. No call number accompanies periodicals.

Generally, pamphlet titles are treated as book titles—underlined. The name of the organization is treated as the author. Include the necessary identifying information, especially if the work is part of a series, the city of publication, the publishing organization, and date.

Title card for a pamphlet

> U.S. Department of Health, Education, and Welfare
>
> <u>Statistics on Literacy in the Inner City</u>
>
> By the National Educational Council
>
> U.S. Dept. of HEW
>
> Washington, D.C.: Government Printing Office, 1982

Generally, pamphlet titles are treated as book titles—underlined. The name of the organization is treated as the author. Include the necessary identifying information, especially if the work is part of a series, the city of publication, the publishing organization, and date.

Title card for a personal interview

> Gringo, Eduardo Manual, Ph.D. in Latin American Studies, University of Bogota, Columbia
>
> Time: Three P.M., July 1, 1983
>
> Place: Dr. Gringo's office, 434 Sombrero Street, New York, New York

Give the complete name, title, and credentials of the person interviewed, plus the time and location where the interview took place.

Taking notes

Learn to be critical. Before you plunge into the sea of information relevant to your thesis, learn how to evaluate pertinent data. Students waste valuable time and effort painstakingly writing on note cards every word they read. *Scan* the information before you commit a word to your notes. Ask yourself if the information you are examining is important to your research; if so, then commit it to your cards. Learn how to paraphrase to same time.

Writing the summary

In academic and professional situations, summaries are vital. In the academic setting, the ability to summarize material is essential. Students are often required to prepare note cards for research papers, to write abstracts, to review books, to condense articles, or to prepare for examinations. Each of these tasks requires students to summarize the content of a larger work. Thus, a summary may be defined as a condensation of a larger work in which the main ideas are logically arranged and expressed in the writer's own words, while the essential nature of the original work (context, connotation, purpose) is maintained. If the original work is ironic in tone, the writer's summary should also reflect the tone or mood.

Types of Summaries: the paraphrase, the precis, the abstract

The *paraphrase* follows the organizational pattern of the original work and is written in the student's own words. Its major function is to clarify the meaning of the original work. Although this type of summary is usually shorter than the original work, sometimes the paraphrase may be longer than the original.

The *précis* is a short summary ranging in length from one sentence to a paragraph. Its major function is to serve as a tool for understanding and to state the work's central meaning in brief form. The précis usually appears as a part of a larger work.

One of the most popular and useful types of summary is the *abstract*, which presents the essence of the original work as though the author were summarizing it. The abstract may also be indicative, listing specific sections of a work in prose form and indicating the type of material in the work rather than informing the reader about a topic. As short as one sentence or as long as several paragraphs, the abstract usually appears at the beginning of a research report or technical paper.

Forms of summaries: descriptive, informative, or evaluative

A *descriptive* summary states the nature of the work in a general and brief way. It is used in headings to chapters and magazine articles, on the table of contents pages in magazines, in publicity for new books and pamphlets, and in annotated bibliographies.

An *informative* summary objectively presents the principal facts and conclusions in the original work in a paragraph to several pages, depending on the length of the original work.

The *evaluative* summary analyzes the accuracy, completeness, usefulness, appeal, and readability of a work. Personal comments, reactions, thoughts, and feelings may be included. Emphasizing the assessment of the original material, the evaluative summary includes sufficient information to reflect the summarizer's thorough understanding of the work. This form includes the specific main points of the original work through specific references.

Process in writing a summary

1. Read the article at least twice.

2. Underline or take notes in the margin during the second reading of the article. Circle key terms, names, or numbers that you consider important. Pay special attention to phrases, sentences, or information that the author has highlighted via quotation marks, italics, or boldface type.

3. After a second reading, write a paragraph outline of the entire article. Begin your outline by writing the thesis statement of the article. Indent below the thesis statement and write a topic sentence for each paragraph.

4. Under each topic sentence, jot down any specific details or examples that you consider essential in explaining that topic sentence.

Organizing

1. Make the thesis statement the topic sentence of your one-paragraph summary.

2. Using your outline to guide you, decide which controlling ideas are essential to support the topic sentence.

3. Use those ideas to develop the supporting sentences of your paragraph.

Revising

1. Reread the article or prose work.

2. Check for omitted words, date, or terms that should have been included.

3. Before typing or writing the final copy of the summary, be sure to document your work by including the title of the original work, its author, and any pertinent information like the title of the magazine (underlined), the date of the publication, volume number, and page number(s). This documentation may precede the actual summary as part of the heading, may be incorporated in the body of the summary as part of the first sentence, or may be provided at the end of the summary as a footnote.

(For more detailed information on writing summaries, refer to these sources: Walvoord, *Writing Strategies for All Disciplines;* Flemming, *Making Your Point: A Guide to College Writing;* Walker & McCuen, *Rhetoric Made Plain;* Gefvert, *The Confident Writer.*)

Note cards: The direct quotation, the paraphrase, and the summary

The direct quote card

If you find it important to use the author's words *exactly* as those words appear in the source, use direct quotes.

> Zamagias, <u>Flood Tides</u>   pp. 45-46
>
> ". . . the flood ravaged the downtown sections of Johnstown—
> cars floated like toys, trees spun crazily like toothpicks in the cur-
> rent. In some places, the water rose to a level of five feet. . . ."

Remember that note cards are for your use—save time. Instead of giving the complete name of the author, use his surname. Use a key word in the title of the book instead of giving the entire title and subtitle on every note card that you use. *Always* give the *exact* page numbers of the source from which you have taken a direct quote. *Always* put the quoted material in quotation marks. If you find that you do not wish to include every sentence of the author's material on the note card, use the ellipsis (three spaced periods) to signify to the reader, and to yourself, that you have omitted certain portions of the text. Make sure, however, that such deletions do not distort the author's meaning.

If you happen to find an obvious error in typography (a spelling error, transposed figures, grammatical errors), do not take it upon yourself to correct the text. Use *sic* (Latin, *thus, so*) in brackets immediately after such words or phrases to show that such an element is not your error, and that it should be read as it appears. Remember, when you use a direct quote, that you are saying to your reader, "This is exactly how I found it." The direct quote must be completely accurate.

The paraphrase note card

A paraphrase is a restatement of a text or passage in a form other than the original. When you put an author's ideas, facts, or results of research in your words instead of his exact words, you are paraphrasing. Since you are "borrowing" his ideas and data, you must still give credit to the source, although you are not using direct quotation marks. To repeat, the same rules apply to the paraphrase note cards as the direct quote card—minus the quotation marks.

```
Zamagias, Flood Tides                pp. 45-46

The Johnstown Flood was extremely severe; it destroyed the
downtown area and swept cars away; the five-foot torrent
uprooted trees.
```

Students seem reluctant to want to list their sources in paraphrasing, but such a procedure is mandatory. Ask yourself these questions: How do I know this? Where did I get this information? Give credit to the source which informs you.

The summary note card

A summary note card may be a condensation (abstract, précis) of material taken from a source, or it may be an evaluative judgment by the researcher regarding his source. The first type is a record of the main points of a source, without details or illustrations. The second type of summary is a personal evaluation which records the researcher's attitude on many aspects of a source: the writer's style, the value of data presented, the content, and so on. In short, is the source of any importance to the researcher's study of the problem?

Summary note cards are important because they remind the researcher which source is worthy of re-examination and the basic content of each source. You should not rely on memory regarding your material because, after several weeks of digging in the library, you probably have forgotten some of the sources which you have examined. A summary note card will remind you quickly.

```
Zamagias, Flood Tides                pp. 25-72

Chapter two deals with early years (15) preceding flood of
1977. Good style, but too much physical description which I
find distracting. Interesting analysis of hoodlums in a western Pa.
coal town.
```

Notecards reflect the amount of work that you have put into research. After you have completed the task of taking notes, you should be able to organize your material in preparation for the tentative outline. Notecards may be arranged in a variety of ways: alphabetically (the author's last name), numerically (numbering consecutively), topically (division), chronologically (time), or geographically (spatially). The arrangement of your notecards depends on the approach you wish to take on the subject.

Common knowledge versus esoteric knowledge

The age-old debate still continues over what a student "knows" as common knowledge versus what is known as esoteric or specialized knowledge. Examples of common knowledge as "facts" are innumerable, but every schoolboy "knows" such facts by heart. Discuss some of these aspects of "common" knowledge.

George Washington was a great general.

Abraham Lincoln freed the slaves.

The U.S. was a victim of a surprise attack by Japan on December 7, 1941.

Cigarette smoking causes cancer.

Marilyn Monroe died of an overdose of drugs.

Socrates committed suicide by drinking poison.

Now, try these on for the sake of fact finding.

George Washington was a mediocre military strategist.

Abraham Lincoln never freed a slave in his life.

The U.S. was attacked by Japan on December 7, 1941 (common knowledge), but was it a surprise?

Cigarette smoking may cause cancer of the larynx, esophagus, and lungs.

Marilyn Monroe was murdered.

Socrates was executed.

The point is important, especially in writing a research paper. What we "know" (or presume to know) and what we really "know" is difficult to prove, generally, unless we have first-hand experience of the facts. The only other path is by trusting the "experts" in the field, who, it must be noted, often disagree among themselves interpreting the facts. Take nothing for granted. Study both sides of the issue. Decide on the rational, not the emotional, side of the matter when you write your paper and draw your conclusions.

Once again, keep an open mind and ask yourself these questions: Who is my source of information? Is my source reputable? What do others say concerning this issue? How do I know that these "facts' are trustworthy? Is my information complete?

Only then will you arrive at the "truth."

Writing and rewriting the first draft

If you are dissatisfied with the first draft of your outline, simply rewrite it. Good writers are seldom pleased with their initial efforts.

After you have revised the outline, begin writing the first draft of your paper from the final outline. The most important factor in writing the first draft is getting ideas (and the facts to support those ideas) on paper in some sort of coherent fashion. Naturally, the first draft is the crude, unfinished structure. So do not exhaust yourself on punctuation, spelling, or syntactical nuances. The first draft is the place where the basic foundation of your paper is laid, with topic sentences and supporting data: quotes, paraphrases, superscript numbers in place, and so on. However, do not try to do too much in one writing session. Leave your work and rest for a few hours.

When you return to the task, start with a "clean" copy, free of erasures, crossed-out words, and typographical errors. If necessary, rewrite your material to avoid the editorial distractions of the first copy. Now shape your material, making sure your paper conforms to the detailed organization of your outline.

When you feel that your paper is organized suitably, concern yourself with style: sentence structure and variety, diction, paraphrasing, and tone. Polish your writing by correcting any errors in punctuation, subject-verb agreement, dangling modifiers, and other necessary corrections. After making the necessary mechanical improvements, stop for a few hours (or a day, time permitting) and let the ingredients marinate. Hopefully, you will return to your task with "fresh eye"—the ability to detect ways to improve your material. After a final scrutiny and revision of the material, you should be ready to type the final copy.

Documentation styles

In the world of academia, different disciplines use different formats in documenting information. For instance, the American Psychological Association (APA) recommends in-text citations, thereby excluding (generally) footnotes, endnotes. Your instructor in the social sciences (psychology, sociology) will probably utilize the APA format. Most English and humanities instructors utilize the Modern Language Association (MLA) style sheet. Some instructors in the "traditional" mode prefer endnotes; others prefer in-text citations. References in science papers may be done in a variety of ways. In history, for instance, many instructors prefer the Chicago Manual of Style, which utilizes footnotes or endnotes. The important thing to remember, regardless of which style sheet used, is to be faithful to the academic method and consistent.

Preparing the manuscript

I. If you are typing the paper, use clean type and a fresh black ribbon.
    A. Use 8 ½" by 11" white paper.
    B. The margins should be ample, at least one inch top and bottom, one inch from the right margin, and one and one half inches on the left.
    C. Except for the insets, double space throughout the paper.

II. Information on the title pages should be centered: title of the paper, your name, date, and the instructor's name.
    A. Do not underline your title.
    B. Do not put your title in quotes.
    C. D not put the title in upper case letters; this is the same as underlining.

III. The outline follows the title page.
    A. The outline's heading is the title of your term paper; do not entitle it "Outline."
    B. Double space the outline.
    C. The outline should reflect the organization and the content of the term paper.
    D. The outline is not numbered. If the outline is several pages, use small letters to number them: i,ii, iii, iv, and so on.

IV. Do not repeat the title on the first page of your research paper.
    A. Begin with the thesis of your paper one inch from the top margin.
    B. The first page is not numbered (MLA); succeeding pages are numbered in the upper right-hand corner.
    C. APA style begins numbering the title page as page 1.
    D. At the top of each page, include a header, which contains your last name and the page number: Marafino 3. (MLA)

V. Use in-text (parenthetical) citations in documenting sources.
   A. MLA citations usually require the name of the source (author) and page references.
   B. APA citations usually require the name of the source (author), date of publication, and page numbers. However, page numbers may be omitted if the entire source is cited.
   C. When referring to the author, use the last name only.
   D. Footnotes or Endnotes, which should be used sparingly, may be used to provide supplementary or explanatory notes.

VI. Use Works Cited (MLA) instead of Bibliography; use References (APA) to list works quoted or paraphrased.
   A. Do not list any sources which you have not referred to in your paper.
   B. Entries are listed alphabetically, never numbered.
   C. The first line of the entry is flush with the left margin; the second line is indented five spaces (hanging indent).
   D. Double space to avoid crowding the entries.
   E. If an author has two or more works listed, do not repeat his/her name. Generally, three hyphens followed by a period is standard.
      Zamagias, James D. *Flood Tides*. New York: Exposition Press, 1982.
      ——. *Pool Room Ballads*. New York: Exposition Press, 1969.

VII. Illustrations, graphs, charts, and tables should be placed close to pertinent material.
   A. Document all visuals by labeling them clearly, setting them off from the text.
   B. Document all illustrations with an entry in Works Cited or References.

VIII. An Appendix may be included at the end of the paper to include any supplementary material, such as additional illustrative data, maps, charts, diagrams.

IX. A Glossary may also be included to define special technical terms.

X. The research/term paper should be stapled in the upper left-hand corner.

Documentation

Always acknowledge information, ideas, words borrowed or consulted by citing your source. The following examples of in-text citations are based on the Modern Language Association and American Psychological Association styles used most frequently in academic writing. However, several other style sheets may be used, depending on your instructor's preferences; for instance, writers in the natural sciences use the Council of Biology Editors (CBE) documentation. Also, the *Chicago Manual of Style* is used in history as well as other areas of the arts and humanities.

In-text citations (MLA style)

1. You may use the author's last name (signal phrase) to introduce the material: Buckley stated that the Japanese attack on Pearl Harbor was not a "surprise." (543) [page numbers appear in parentheses.]

2. When the author is named in parentheses, include his/her last name before the page numbers in parentheses: The Japanese attack on Pearl Harbor was not a "surprise" (Buckley 543).

3. With two or three authors, cite all of the last names: Jones, Landis, and Smith reject the propaganda that the Japanese attack on Pearl Harbor was a "surprise" (543).

4. With four or more authors, use et al. [and others] or name all of the authors' last names: Schroeder et al. (1991) state that the cause of pedophilia is unknown.

5. If the author is unknown, use the full name of the organization: Harassment is no laughing matter (Professional Secretaries International 15).

6. If using authors with the same last name, include the author's first and last names in the text or in parenthetical citations: George Zamias states that shopping malls are the economic future of the nation (45–46).

7. In a multi-volume work, cite the volume number first followed by page numbers: (2: 45).

8. In a literary work, cite the page number(s) from the edition followed by a semicolon and other information in the passage. In a play, cite the act and scene: (32; sc. 2). For a novel, cite the part or chapter: (69; ch. 5). In poetry, cite the line(s): (lines 23-29). In verse plays, give the act, scene, and line numbers: (2.5.63).

9. In an anthology which reprints essays, short stories, or prose, use the author of the work. Do not cite the editor. Page numbers from the anthology should be cited.

10. In quotations from the Bible, cite chapter and verse: (John 2:23). Use an abbreviation for books with names of five or more letters: (Gen. 5.11). If the King James version of the Bible is cited, no Works Cited entry is required.

11. If an indirect source is used because the original source is not available, indicate by using the abbreviated form of "quoted in": (qtd. in Abraham 69).

12. If you wish to include material from more than one source in a sentence, cite the last names of each source: (Smith 13, Walters 17–18). If, however, two authors have the same last name, include their first names or initials: (J.D. Smith 38; H.R. Smith 17–18).

13. In a one-page article, simply list the author's name in your text; a page number is not required.

14. In citing entries from dictionaries, encyclopedias, or sources in which information is alphabetized, do not include page numbers if the entry is less than two pages; if longer, include the page numbers.

15. In citing an interview, list the interviewed subject's last name with the date of the interview: (Jones Dec. 23).

16. If tables and illustrations are used, cite the documentation directly below the material: Source: U.S. Dept. of the Treasury, *Bulletin,* (Jan. 1999): 7.

17. In citing non-print or electronic sources, provide enough information in the text or parenthetical citation for the reader to find the source in Works Cited. If the citation lacks an author, refer to the title in your text.

Electronic sources (Websites, online databases, E-mail, electronic journals)

Follow the guidelines used for print sources—refer to the author and page number(s) if possible. *Electronic sources are seldom paginated.* If no author is listed in the citation, refer to the title in the text and Works Cited.

■ Allegany College's Appalachian Room has developed a Website dealing with Cumberland's local history (Allegany College of Maryland Library).

■ The Works Cited entry would be:
Allegany College of Maryland. "Local History." 4 June 1999.
<http://www.all.org/library/mnm8.tuwm>.

Works cited

On a separate page entitled Works Cited, list all of the sources used in your research in alphabetical order. **Never** list any source that you have not cited. Each entry should include three elements with a period at the end of each section: the author's last name first, first name; title and sub-title underlined (or italicized); city of publication, publisher, and date. If several cities are listed in your source, give the first city of publication. Use the latest copyright date; if no date is given, write n.d.

Examples of book citations (MLA Style)

One author:
Zamagias, James D. *Pool Room Ballads.* New York: Exposition Press, 1969.

Two or three authors:
Brown, Dudley, Nan Putnam, and Beverly Wilcox. *Writing the College Essay.* Dubuque: Kendall Hunt, 1999.

Four or more authors:
Brown, George, et al. *The Killing of Paducah.* New York: Greene Press, 1999.

Editor's material:
Shreve, Jack, ed. Introduction. *Spanish Poetry.* By George Gonzalez. New York: Manyana Press, 1999.

Articles in reference works:
Johnes, Peter. "Alexander the Great." *Encyclopedia of Greek Kings.* 9th ed. 1999.
"Computer." *The Oxford English Dictionary.* 1990 ed.

Book of two or more volumes:
Pappas, George. *Greek Military Strategy.* 2 vols. New York: Classics Publishing, 1998.

An edited book:
Brown, James, ed. Introduction. *Kafka's Bugs.* By Gregors Samsa. New York: Metamorphosis Press, 1998.

Reprint of a book:
Diamond, James. *Turtles in the Potomac River.* 1969. Cumberland: Seafood Press, 1998.

A translated book:
Zegles, George, trans. *The Odyssey.* By Homer, 850 B.C. New York: Apollo Press, 1989.
or:
Homer. *The Odyssey.* Trans. George Zegles. New York: Apollo Press, 1989.

An anthology:
Clinton, William. "Alone in the Oval Office." *Interpretations of Linking Verbs.* Eds. Linda Tripp, et al. 5th ed. vol. 22. New York: Lewinsky Press, 1998.

Periodicals (magazines, newspapers, trade, professional journals)

An article from a daily newspaper:
Cotton, James. "The End of Welfare Cheating." *Cumberland Times.* 4 July 1998: 1-4.
(For newspapers organized by sections, include the section letter before the page number or the section number with a colon before the page number: sec. 5:9.)

Editorials:
Butterfield, Michael. "Teach our Children how to Read!" Editorial. *Cumberland Times.* 7 May 1998: A5.

Monthly magazines:
Peters, Jon. "Searching for a Party." *Playboy.* Apr. 1998: 45–56.
(Omit volume or issue numbers.)

Scholarly monthly publications (continuous pagination):
Bluefield, Roger. "Socrates and Stoicism." *Athenian Review.* 169 (1998): 12–23.

Interviews:
Pratt, Christine. Interview. "Interview with Igor Minsky." *Muscovite.* 7 Mar. 1998: 69.

Pamphlet:
State Committee on Narcotics. *Drug Offenders in Dogpatch.* Annapolis: State Printing Office, July 1998.

Personal letter:
Gringo, Jose. Letter to the author. 4 July, 1998.

Radio or television program:
The Death of Socrates. NBC. KDKA, Pittsburgh. 4 July, 1998.

Lectures:
Brown, Dudley. "F. Scott Fitzgerald." Lecture. American Literature 103. Allegany College of Maryland. 6 July 1998.

CDs, records, cassettes:
Stewart, Rod. "Do You Think I'm Sexy?" RCA, 1985.

Artwork:
Price, Robin. *Venus Rising.* Hazen Gallery, Cumberland, Maryland.

World Wide Web:
Because of the rapid growth of the Internet's databases, publications, and sites, online citations fluctuate in details. Public information varies with the electronic source. References to Websites should list the author, title of the work, and/or Web page, the publication date, access date, and the Web address in angle brackets. For example, if you wish to cite CD-ROM single edition:

"Edgar Allen Poe." *Oxford English Dictionary.* Microsoft Bookshelf 1998 CD-ROM. New York: Columbia University Press, 1995.

If you wish detailed information on citing electronic sources, the Modern Language Website will prove invaluable: *MLA Style.* Modern Language Association. April 7, 1998 <http://www.mla.org/main_stl.htm#sources>

APA documentation

APA in-text citations are placed either in text or in parentheses. Include the name(s) of the author(s), date of publication, page number(s). At the end of the paper, such in-text citations correspond to full entries in the list of references, arranged alphabetically.

1. **Author in a signal phrase.** Use the author's last name to introduce the material, with the date in parentheses after the author's name: Shreve (1999) discussed the importance of vocabulary building in college-level courses.

2. For a **direct quote,** write the page number in parentheses after the quotation: As Shreve (1999) observed, etymology plays a vital role "because word derivation is fundamental to understanding the history of language in culture" (p. 21).

3. When the **author is given in parentheses,** give the author's last name and date in parentheses at the end of the citation: A study at Allegany College dealing with remedial courses details the high percentage of freshmen needing developmental math and reading to prepare for college studies (Bracken, 1998).

4. With **two authors,** use both last names in all citations: Bracken and Putnam (1999) verified the absolute necessity of offering several sections of developmental English and reading courses.

OR: A recent study verified the absolute necessity of offering several sections of developmental English and reading courses (Bracken & Putnam, 1999).

5. With **three to five authors,** list all names for the first reference. In subsequent references, use just the first author's name and et al.: Cook, Kershaw, Wilcox, and Zamagias (1999) have conducted studies verifying the importance of Speech Communication concerning student success in the workplace.

OR: A recent study by Allegany College professors verified the importance of Speech Communication concerning student success in the workplace (Cook et al., 1999).

OR: From modern research, Cook et al. (1999) have concluded that Speech Communication is vital to student success in college and in the workplace.

6. If the name of the organization is long, spell it out the first time, followed by an abbreviation in brackets; use the abbreviated form in subsequent citations: (Professional Secretaries International [PSI], 1999). Later citations would be (PSI, 1999).

7. If the author is unknown, use the title in a signal phrase or in parentheses: A recent study proves the need for universal drug reformation in the U.S. (*A Guide to Drug Addiction and Rehabilitation,* 1999).

8. If citations include different authors with the same last name, list the authors' initials in each source: P. Stanislavsky (1999).

9. With two or more sources in the same citation, list the authors in alphabetical order: (Wilcox, 1999; Zembower, 1999). If citing works by the same author, list the sources chronologically: (Barow, 1998, 1999).

10. If naming specific parts of a source, identify the part (chap., No., p., pp., and/or Vol.) you are citing: Wilcox (1999, chap. 7) discussed the various elements of speech disorders.

11. In citing personal communications (letters, e-mail, telephone conversations, interviews), give the person's initials and last name, cite personal communication, and date: J.D. Zamagias (personal communication, July 4, 1998) verified the advantages of wearing dentures.

12. Superscript numbers[1] may be used to supplement your text; on a separate page at the conclusion of the text, list the superscript numerals under the heading of Footnotes. Double-space and indent the first line of each footnote five spaces with subsequent lines at the left margin.

Listing references (APA Style)

List all sources cited in your paper on a separate page entitled References.

1. A book with one author:
   Zamagias, J. (1969). *Pool room ballads.* New York: Exposition Press.

2. A book with two or more authors:
   Goober, P., & B. Wilcox. (1999). *Peanuts: the true aphrodisiac.* New York: Shell Press.

3. Organization as author:
   Professional Gambler's Association. (1999). *Beating the odds.* Atlantic City, NJ: Blackjack Press.

4. Unknown author:
   Turtles in the Caspian Sea. (1999). Washington, DC: National Turtle Society.

5. A book with an editor:
   Brown, G. (Ed.). (1999). *The killing of Paducah.* Cumberland, MD: Excaliber Press.

6. A selection in an edited book:
   Pappas, C. (1999). The psychological crisis of Bucephalus. In C. Boyle, C. Hoyle, & C. Toyle (Eds.). *Mammal analysis* (pp. 60–69). New York: Saddle Press.

7. A translation:
   Tallman, K. (1999). *Midgets in the ancient world* (P.T. Barnes & A.P. Cook, Trans.). New York: NY: King Press.

8. Article in a reference work:
   Brown, D. (1999). *Southern literature.* In *Appalachian encyclopedia of literature.* 9Vol. 3, pp. 69-71). New York: Cambridge Press.

9. Government document:
   U.S. Housing Bureau. (1998). *Housing statistics in the United States.* Washington, DC: U.S. Government Printing Office.

10. Article in a journal paginated by volume:
    Brown, D. (1999). Southern writers. *The Teaching of Literature, 15,* 98–101.

11. Article in a journal paginated by issue:
    Shreve, J. (1999). Teaching Spanish to community college students. *Foreign Language Quarterly, 69*(2), 69–72.

12. Article in a magazine:
    Goobers, P. (1999, July). Harvesting peanuts at night. *Georgia Magazine,* 69–72.

13. Article in a newspaper:
    Bingman, D. (1999, Dec. 20). Great books create happy times. *Cumberland Times-News,* pp. B1, C9.

14. Letter to the editor:
    Zamagias, J. (1998, April 1). As American as apple pie [Letter to the editor]. *Cumberland Times-News*, 17.

15. Unsigned article:
    Tripping the light fantastic. (1999, July). *Creative Writing*, 19.

Electronic sources (APA style)

Standard format should generally be followed by listing the author, date, and title of electronic sources.

1. CD-ROM and commercial Online Databases—basic form:
   Gregors, P. (1999). Franz Kafka and Gregors Samsa [CD-ROM]. *German Literature, 7*, 143–145. Abstract from: Berliner File: GerLIT Item: 64-12344

2. Material from an information service or database:
   Zamias, G. (1999). The role of realtors in the development of inner cities. In P. Agnew & L. Cashew (Eds.). *Improving the American landscape.* Johnstown, PA: National Institute of Realtors. (ERIC Document Reproduction Service NO. ED 227 696)

3. Software or computer program:
   RomanWay3 Release 3.7 [Computer program]. (1999). Cumberland, MD: Computer Productions, Macro Products Division.

4. Internet sources should include the author's last name first (if given); date of publication; title or subject line in quotation marks, ending with a period inside quotation marks; the address in angle brackets, and the date of access in parentheses followed by a period. After the document title, include the title of the work by underlining:
   Brown, D. (1998). Synopsis of F. Scott Fitzgerald. *Readings in Contemporary Literature.* <http://cumcenter.org/prg/prose/98-99/interlog.html> (1998, July 4).

5. NEWSBANK:
   Marafino, M. "Distance learning in the classroom." *Allegany College Quarterly* [CD-ROM], 4 July 1999: 4. CD NewsBank/NewsBank/0135590D15AAC5189EO [July 14, 1999].

6. SIRS:
   Marafino, M. (1998). "Cyberspace in the classroom." *Appalachian review* [CD-ROM]k, Dec. 1997: 7–17. Available: SIRS 1998 Family, Volume Number 9, Article 16 [April 13, 1998].

7. Gopher site: cite the URL (Uniform Resource Locator), or the word gopher, the site, and the path needed to access with slashes for menu selections:
   Bracken, J. How much does remediation cost education? *Allegany Journal*, April 1999. <gopher://nysernet.org:30/00/ABAAB/Sources/AllEJ/how-much> (1999, April 10).

8. Internet Listserv:
   DRODRIGUES (1999, July 4). Apex software. Alliance for
   Computers and Writing Listserv. [Online]. Available:
   http://english.tu. edu/acw/acw-/archive.htm[1999, July 4].

9. World-Wide Web Site:
   Gorgon, M. (1999). Greek culture, myth and reality. In *Ionic archeology
   project* [Online]. J. Pappas (Ed.). Available: http://tesia.msuppward.
   edu/ancientplaces/ionic/IonFrames.html [1999, July 4].

10. E-mail message:
    Zamagias, J.D. (jzamagias@allegany.net). (1998, December 20).
    Submit your spring grid [Personal e-mail]. (1998, January 13).

11. Film or videotape:
    Spielman, A. (Producer). (1998). *Back seat* [Film]. Johnstown: PA.

12. Television program (begin with the names of the writers; give the
    director's name in parentheses after the title of the program):
    Brown, W., Wilcox, B., & Zamias, J. (1999, June 20). Surviving on
    peanuts (G. Goobers, Executive Director). In G. Zamboni
    (Executive Producer), *D.D.T.* Cumberland: Confidential
    Broadcasting Limited.

13. Recording (cite the writer's name, date of copyright and recording date):
    Berkebile, S. (1999). Are you still here? [Recorded by G. Smith and
    the Zambonis]. On *Don't slam the door* [Cassette]. Cumberland,
    MD: Tonga Records. (1997).

Annotated bibliography

This is an example of an **annotated bibliography** for a term paper on
the West Virginia-born author Pearl S. Buck, who wrote *The Good Earth*
and won both the Pulitzer Prize and the Nobel Prize for literature.

Buck, Pearl S. *My Several Worlds.* New York: John Day, 1954. Her personal account of five decades of her life, recalling the drama and
change that have taken place in the world. Not particularly literary.

Doyle, Paul A. *Pearl S. Buck.* New York: Twayne, 1965. The only book-
length survey of her work as literature.

Janeway, Elizabeth. "The Optimistic World of Miss Buck" in *New York
Times Book Review* (May 25, 1952): 4. A sympathetic treatment of her
strengths and weaknesses as a writer.

Krebs, Albin. "Pearl Buck is Dead at 80" in *New York Times* (March 7,
1973): 1, 40. Her obituary.

Michener, James. "My Neighbor, Pearl Buck" in *Reader's Digest
Condensed Books* (Summer 1969): 477–478. A chatty, admiring enu-
meration of Buck's humanitarian endeavors.

Snow, Helen F. "An Island in Time" in *New Republic* (March 24, 1973). An obituary.

Stuckey, W.J. *The Pulitzer Prize Novels: A Critical Backward Look.* Norman: University of Oklahoma Press, 1966. Compares Buck with other Pulitzer Prize winners.

Thompson, Dody Weston, "Pearl Buck," in *American Winners of the Nobel Literary Prize.* Eds., Warren French and Walter Kid. Norman: University of Oklahoma Press, 1968. Fascinating speculation on why Buck was awarded the Nobel Prize of 1938.

NEWSBANK or BALTIMORE SUN (MLA STYLE)

Brown, Dudley. "Animal Welfare Program Labeled a Success." *Echo* 4 May 1999: 5. *CD Newsbank.* CD-ROM. Newsbank. May 1999.

SIRS (MLA STYLE)

Shreve, Jack. "What's Happening to Foreign Languages?" *Echo* 1998/ June 1999: 5–10. *SIRS.* CD-ROM. SIRS. (1999)

(If you need more information regarding your research, consult these sources: *Electronic Styles: A Handbook for Citing Electronic Information* 2nd edition, by Xia Li and Nancy Medford, NJ: Information Today, 1996; *MLA Handbook for Writers of Research Papers* 4th edition, by J. Gibaldi. New York: Modern Language Association of America, 1995; *Publication Manual of the American Psychological Society* 4th edition, Washington, DC: American Psychological Association, 1994.)

Evaluating sources

Scrutinize the sources you use in research by asking the following questions:

1. Is the source relevant to my research?

2. Is the author credible? objective? biased?

3. What is the date of the publication?

4. Who is the publisher? corporation? government agency? Interest group?

5. Is my source esoteric or simply generic?

6. For whom is the material published? general public? specialists?

7. Is the author or source cited in other publications?

8. Do I have access to the material?

Sample Research Paper (APA Style)

Condom Distribution in Schools
by Sally Berkebile
English 112
Professor Wilcox
December 7, 1999

Condom Distribution in Schools

Central Idea: As a way of controlling the spread of AIDS among young people, health professionals suggest that condoms be distributed in schools. Today, the AIDS epidemic has taken many lives. Millions of today's youths are sexually active. Educating young people in the use of condoms as a preventive measure from contracting the AIDS virus is necessary.

I. Teenagers are sexually promiscuous.
    A. Credible surveys provide startling statistics.
    B. Our culture encourages sexual activity.
    C. Teenagers are often under the influence of drugs or alcohol when engaging in sexual activity.
II. The AIDS virus is a current problem among young people.
    A. Formidable statistics on AIDS cases among young people have been compiled by health and governmental agencies.
    B. The long latency period among AIDS cases proves that most of the victims contracted the disease in their teen years.
    C. Stringent measures must be taken with utmost urgency to prevent the spread of the disease.
III. Our society needs to find solutions to control the AIDS epidemic.
    A. Promiscuity should be discouraged among teens in the media.
    B. Sexual activity should not be glamorized as romantic behavior by society.
        1. Parents should take a more visible, forceful stand against television advertisements promoting unprotected sex.
        2. School officials should offer pragmatic programs regarding "safe" sex.

IV. Condoms may be a practical solution in controlling the AIDS virus.

    A. Statistics indicate condoms are effective in preventing the spread of the virus.

    B. Condom distribution is more economical than the soaring costs of medical treatment of patients stricken with AIDS.

    C. Studies show that teenagers will use protection if condoms are made readily available by schools.

        1. Surveys provide statistics that condoms are being used when they have been made available.

        2. Information about AIDS and the proper use of condoms must be provided on a wider, more consistent basis by the schools and by public health agencies.

V. Many teenagers are still unsure how they can contract the AIDS virus.

    A. Officials in education must make "hard" choices to protect our teenagers from themselves.

    B. Condom distribution is vital in protecting our children from the horrors of the AIDS virus.

Conclusion: Studies have shown that the distribution and use of contraceptives (condoms) in our schools will save the lives of thousands of teenagers who are sexually active.

ABSTRACT

As a way of controlling the spread of AIDS among teenagers, health professionals suggest that condoms should be distributed in schools. Today, the AIDS epidemic has rapidly taken many lives, young and old. A large majority of young people are sexually active and promiscuous. Therefore, it is necessary to educate young people in the use of condoms as a preventive measure from contracting the deadly AIDS virus. To assure the health and safety of our youngsters, we must do no less.

There is no disputing the knowledge that a large majority of today's teenagers are sexually active, yes, even promiscuous . . . irresponsibly so. Many high school students are returning to the "free love" chaotic era of the 1960s. (Graham 1994) Indeed, a survey of health habits ". . . among 11,631 high schoolers, in grades nine through twelve, showed that 54% say they have had sexual intercourse." (Houston Chronicle 1992) Preventing AIDS among teenagers is going to take more than feeding adolescents the right answer, experts agree, especially when our culture (films, televisions, commercial ads) keeps encouraging you to have sex (Fain 1990).

Many teenagers engage in sexual activity when they are under the influence of alcohol and/or drugs. To cite just one example, of the students surveyed in Oregon, "nearly 14% said their last sexual encounter was coupled with drug substances that blur judgment and diminish the likelihood of safe sex" (Hochman 1993). Health officials are concerned that teenagers are impulsive. Unfortunately, sexual activity combined with drug use makes them vulnerable to a frightening virus which may destroy their lives.

AIDS is spreading rapidly among American teenagers, who account for fewer than one percent of all AIDS cases: 568 of the 146,746 cases diagnosed (Fain 1990). Nevertheless, given what we know about the long latency of the virus (approximately eight to ten years) and the number of young adults in their twenties who have contracted AIDS (one-fifth of all reported cases), it seems likely that they contracted the virus in their teens (Fain 1990). "Unless drastic measures are taken quickly, the teenage population is likely to become the epidemic's next 'hot spot,' calling it the next death march" (Fain 1990).

The long-standing debate about teenagers has been trying to discourage them from engaging in sex as a means of prevention, or in recognizing that teenagers are sexually active. A means, therefore, must be developed to protect them. Our communities must work together to provide a solution to prevent the spread of AIDS. "Progressive educators believe it is pretty tough, in the back seat of a car, to decide what to do about AIDS. It has to be done ahead of time." (Fain 1990)

Using condoms has been the only dependable weapon to control AIDS among sexually active teenagers, and the distribution of condoms is more economical than the medical costs of AIDS patients. As Berkeley (1994) stated:

A model of HIV transmission indicates that the use of condoms averted 6,000–10,000 new HIV infections per year at an approximate cost daily of about fifty cents per year for a life saved.

If condoms were made easily available, sexually active teenagers would use them for protection from AIDS and sexually transmitted diseases. Of course, information would be provided to students about the deadly virus and, also, how to use the contraceptive properly to be effective. Among sexually active students, 78% said that they had used some form of contraception, mainly condoms, during their last intercourse. (Houston Chronicle 1992) "If people would use safe sex methods, this could be the main solution for controlling the increase of AIDS" (Graham 1994). If condoms are made easily available, teenagers will use them.

Even today, with all the publicity of AIDS, many teenagers still do not know all of the causes. Interviews with Victoria Brownworth, a writer for the gay magazine The Advocate, revealed that some teenagers who have AIDS now had no idea how the disease was spread, nor that they were at risk (France 1992). If those teenagers had used condoms when engaging in sexual intercourse, perhaps they would not have to live with that dreaded disease today.

"Face the facts," Surgeon General Jocelyn Elders stated, "a growing number of teenagers are engaging in sex and suffering its harmful consequences. It is foolish, if not irresponsible, to deny that reality. If more teenagers are sexually active, why deprive them of the information they need to avoid the disease?" (as quoted in Whitehead, 1994, pp. 15–16)

To panicky parents, worried about their ability to protect their children from AIDS, comprehensive sex education, a program that provides condoms to sexually active teenagers, offers a reassuring message—the schools will teach children how to be responsible to protect themselves from AIDS (Whitehead 1994).

Many parents and religious groups believe abstinence is the only real solution in controlling the spread of AIDS. Although abstinence is a fine concept, it is not a viable, pragmatic one presently. With condom distribution, students have at least another alternative if they decide to engage in sexual activity (Fain 1990).

Local, State, and Federal governments need to take political action in schools to provide students with information. Condoms should, of course and of necessity, be provided for sexually active teenagers. "The Board of Education says the condom distribution plan will be in effect in all New York City Schools by the end of the year," says Kate Barnhart, an AIDS activist. "But we don't have time to wait. People are at risk, and we're at risk, too" (as quoted in France, 1992, p. 30).

The federal government has set national health goals for the year 2000 that call for fewer than 40% of seventeen-year-olds (11th grade) to have had sex and at least 90% of sexually active teenagers to use condoms. (Houston Chronicle 1992)

The unfortunate fact is that teenagers are going to engage in sexual promiscuity. As a community, we need to work together to protect them with all of the resources and information necessary to keep our children safe and healthy.

References

Berkeley, S. (1994). AIDS: Invest now or pay later. <u>Finance and Development, 8,</u> 49–52.

Donovan, P. (1992). Sex education in America's schools: Progress and obstacles. <u>USA Today,</u> 28–30.

Fain, J. (1990). The age of innocence, the era of AIDS. <u>Boston Globe,</u> 22–23.

France, K. (1992). AIDS explodes among teens. <u>Utne Reader,</u> 30–31.

Graham, R. (1994). Youth and sex. <http://www.albuqj.org/ 94-95/ inter.html> (1994, April 20).

Hochman, A. (1993). AIDS: teen angels. <u>Oregonian,</u> 22–23.

Survey: Teen sex rampant. (1992, Jan. 23). <u>Houston Chronicle,</u> pp. B1, C8.

Whitehead, B. (1994, October). The failure of sex education. <u>Atlantic Monthly,</u> 60–63.

Consider the following ideas as possible research paper topics

Controlling AIDS—condom distribution in public schools

Stuttering as a psychological illness

Video games' damaging effects on children

Controlling sexual harassment in the office

Saccharin—a proven carcinogen

Computers do make mistakes!

The hazards of smoking while pregnant

The advantages of wearing dentures

The shortage of nurses—cause and effect

Antietam—the real turning point in the Civil War

The threat of Pac-Man—violent adolescents

Television as villain—the declining literacy of Americans

The end of Social Security in America

Rap music—a case for cencorship

Art as a corrupting influence of youth

Affirmative action—legalized discrimination

Drinking alcohol and the fetus

The pyramids of Egypt—an engineering marvel

Red dye number two—a proven carcinogen

The case for executing child molesters

George Washington—a mediocre general

Shopping malls—the urban dilemma

The case for prohibiting firearms

Homosexuality—innate or learned?

A defense of censorship in the media

Microsoft as monopoly

Art as catharsis

Outlawing welfare

NRA as culprit: children with guns

The decline of ethics in American politics

Athletes and academics—a contradiction

"Amateur" college athletes or "professional" amateurs?

Professional athletes are over-paid.

An inquiry into the rising divorce rate in America

A study of unnecessary medical procedures

Evaluation of the Research Paper

Student's Name _____ Course and Section _____

Title of Research Paper _____

	Excellent	Good	Fair	Poor
A. Grasp of the subject				
1. Focus				
2. Organization				
B. Research				
1. Quality of material				
2. Quantity of material				
3. Adaptation of material				
4. Quotations/paraphrases				
5. Interpretation				
C. Format				
1. Appearance of manuscript				
2. Citations				
3. References				
D. Paragraphs				
1. Unity				
2. Development and coherence				
3. Transitions				
E. Grammar				
1. Sentence structure				
2. Punctuation				
3. Spelling				
F. Instructor's comments and grade				

■ Chapter 13 ■

Gathering Resource Materials

The Library

As a laboratory for research, the library offers an essential store of information. Although students generally think in terms of printed materials in connection with libraries, different types of information are available in a multitude of sources. **Periodicals** (magazines, journals, newspapers) include the more recent information in a particular field—research developments, articles about topics, and so on. **Reference books** are sources of information that may provide background information about a topic. **Dictionaries, encyclopedias, almanacs, atlases, bibliographies, directories** are examples of books that are usually included in the general collection of a library. Books that are included in the general collection usually go into more depth about a topic and can usually be checked out of the library. **Audio-visual sources** (videos, audiocassettes, CDs, CD-ROMs, slides) provide other forms of useful information.

Just as there are different types of information readily available, there are different tools to help locate such sources. The computer has made marvelous improvements in the super-highway of information today. Indeed, the **Internet** in itself is an electronic library with an infinite number of resources in scholarly research. The traditional card catalogs have met the fate of the lumbering dinosaurs—a memory.

Online catalogs provide access to information available in the library. Using these "computerized card catalogs," different vendors create their online catalogs to look differently, but the way information is retrieved is similar. Usually, there is a place for the patron (student, researcher) to type in a search, which may be one word or several words combined. Most online catalogs allow searching by subject, title, or author. Other searches may include series, call number, notes, collection, or any number of other ways that a particular library may find useful for its patrons.

The word or words typed in are searched and matched to records that provide information about an item in the library. Information usually includes the basic bibliographic information about the item: author, title, publisher, place of publication, and year of publication. Other information useful in identifying the item are call number, subject headings, collection information, location in the library, status of the item (i.e. checked out, in-library), notes, contents, or other pieces of information that may be useful.

Depending on the system being used, records or lists of records may be printed, saved on a disk, or e-mailed. Many online catalogs have the ability to be accessed by the World Wide Web. These catalogs may be restricted to be searched only by patrons of the particular library or may be available to anyone with access to the Web to search. Some catalogs have the ability to include Internet addresses as part of the record, and patrons may click on the link if the item has a World Wide Web address, which makes cataloging of Internet sites possible.

Libraries usually have many collections: general book and reference, non-print (videos, audiocassettes, music CDs, CD-ROMs, slides), periodicals, government documents, vertical files, annual reports, and other special collections. An *online catalog* is a database and may include records about any or all of these collections. By being able to search words, a patron can find items in every collection—all from the same search—if the library has included them in its online catalog.

Computer databases are also used to find information in periodicals. Researching databases may be done in several ways: CD-ROM databases may be used individually or set up in a network; index CD-ROMS give the basic bibliographic information; some may have a summary of the article available. The patron then must find if that particular library has the article available or order it through interlibrary loan. Some CD-ROM databases are full text—the complete article is included in the record. The article may then be printed or saved on a disk. CD-ROM products are usually updated on a periodical basis (monthly, quarterly).

Many libraries use the Internet to provide online access to periodical information. Libraries may subscribe to services from different vendors to give their patrons access to full-text articles. Some charge a per record fee, a per student fee, or negotiate some way for the library to pay in providing access to such information. The patron may then log on to this service and get full-text or index and summary information. These services are often updated daily so the information is current.

By using Internet or full-text CD-ROM, libraries are able to provide access to many periodicals that they can not subscribe to on a regular basis. By using CD-ROM or online access to periodicals, one is usually able to search many years of information in one search. Many CD-ROM products, as well as online services, are available on whatever topic is of interest: literature, government sources, medical information, legal information, chemistry, biology. The list is endless.

Paper indexes are another way to provide access to periodical information. They usually have information about specific topics (**Education Index, Business Periodical Index**) and give bibliographic information about the article. Many of the traditional paper indexes are available in CD-ROM or online format.

Remember that each library will have access to different databases and online catalogs depending on what the needs of its patrons are. There are thousands of choices that may be purchased by the library. The following information relates specifically to Allegany College of Maryland's library. Other libraries would have different options:

AscMe—Library Online Catalog

AscMe displays materials available: books, magazines, videos, records, and other non-print materials. Items may be accessed at the main search screen by SUBJECT, TITLE, AUTHOR, SERIES, CALL NUMBER, or NOTES.

CD-ROM Databases

Academic Abstracts—an index to magazine articles from over 800 different magazines from 1984 to the present. Citations and summaries of articles are found using KEYWORD (important words or phrases) or SUBJECT heading.

CINAHL (Cumulative Index to Nursing and Allied Health Literature)—an index to health science literature from 1982 to the present. Citations and abstracts, or full texts, of articles are found using KEYWORD (important words or phrases).

FULL-TEXT DATABASES—citations and whole articles are available.

SIRS Researcher—a database of full-text articles selected from more than 1200 magazines, newspapers, journals, and government publications. Articles are searched by SUBJECT HEADING, TITLE BROWSE (useful in narrowing a general topic to a specific idea), and KEYWORD. Articles include topics related to social issues (alcohol, drugs, crime, AIDS . . .); science developments and issues (disciplines of earth, life, physical, medical, and applied science); world affairs (historic, economic, and political).

Researcher's Almanac has three databases: **Newsline,** containing brief summaries of major news events; **Directory of Publications,** providing background information on more than 1500 publications; and **Maps of the World.**

CD Newsbank—a database of over 50,000 full-text articles covering current events from the past year selected from over 500 newspapers in the U.S. and Canada, American and international news wire services, and verbatim transcripts of major political speeches and Congressional hearings. [Articles are searched by SUBJECT WORD or PHRASE.]

Baltimore Sun—a database of full-text articles covering topics of local, state, and national concern. [Articles are searched by SUBJECT WORD or PHRASE.]

ONLINE ACCESS

SAILOR—Maryland's Online Information Network

SAILOR is an Internet-based information network providing the user access to many different topics, databases, and library catalogs through an extensive menu system. **SAILOR** is also available in a graphical interface via the Internet: http:\\www.sailor.lib.md.us.

Interlibrary Loan

Interlibrary loan provides access to materials not owned by a specific library. **Books in Other Libraries** is an index to materials which may be requested through interlibrary loan. NOTE: it may take one to three weeks to receive such materials. Articles in periodicals not in the library may be obtained in photo-duplication form only. While there is usually no charge for interlibrary loan service, in some cases a lending library requests payment for photocopying or postage.

Suggestions for library research

1. Go to the library and find three sources in your particular field of study. Of the three sources, choose a magazine article, a newspaper article, and a book.

2. Write a title card for each source. Include the author's complete name, title of the article, magazine title, page numbers, and so on, following your instructor's directions.

3. Read the article thoroughly and write a two-page outline of the article.

Suggestions for library research

1. What is the *Oxford English Dictionary?* Why is it so large? Copy three entries.

2. Cite three entries from a dictionary of slang. Include the title of the author, title, and date.

3. Cite three entries from two other specialized dictionaries. Give the author, title, and date.

4. Find *Samuel Johnson's Dictionary.* Cite three entries of words which have changed in the past 200 years and three which have not.

5. Find and examine a book on English, language, or words. Write a paragraph summarizing its purpose. Give the title, author, and date.

6. Write a paragraph explaining your choices of the best and least worthy of the dictionaries that you have examined.

7. How many men were in Stephen Crane's short story "The Open Boat"?

8. What was the song the Sirens sang to Odysseus?

9. What did Abraham Lincoln really mean in the Emancipation Proclamation?

10. What is "pornography"?

11. Discuss in an essay the problems, if any, you encountered doing the assignment, and what you may have learned in doing the research.

12. Define the following words. If there are two or more distinctly different definitions, be sure to include at least one of each. It may be necessary to consult more than one dictionary to understand each word thoroughly.

etymology	pedagogical
archaic	historical
obsolete	abbreviation
stress	slander
accent	vernacular
dialectical	pandemonium
appendix	vulgar
lexicography	philology
tyrant	democracy
synonym	antonym
homonym	onomatopoeia
gringo	nomenclator
colloquial	copyright
syntax	unabridged
italicized	nomenclature
moly	lexicon
heliocentric	geocentric
ecclesiastic	liturgical

13. Look up the word "emphasis" in a desk dictionary. How many definitions are given? What are they? What is the origin(s) of the word? What dictionary are you using? Now look up the word "emphasis" in the *Oxford English Dictionary* (OED). How many additional definitions are given? What are the differences between the desk dictionary entry and the OED entry?

14. What is the etymology of the flower called "nasturtium"?

15. From what two Greek morphemes does the word "squirrel" come? What is a "morpheme"?

16. What does "scruple" mean? Trace its etymology.

17. What did "villain" mean in Roman times?

18. Explain the etymology of "ukulele."

19. Use a dictionary to find the word-by-word translation and modern meanings for each of the following:
    sine die   per diem   post meridian   ad nauseam

20. What are the plural forms of the following English nouns? Consult a dictionary to be certain of your answers.
    | tree | man | sheep | life | deer | himself | hero |
    | shrimp | Swiss | elk | bus | goat | soprano | roof |

21. Which of the following verbs are transitive, intransitive, or both?
    smirch   smirk   sneer   sneeze   sniff

22. Give the adverb forms of the following adjectives:
    intent   greedy   obtrusive   offhand   grumpy

23. Write (a) the language of origin, (b) the etymological meaning, and (c) the modern meaning of the following words:
    alchemists   pandemonium   lunatic   cynic   robots

24. Give synonyms first and antonyms second for the following words. Consult a thesaurus.
    inflammable   contingent   emulation   formidable   epilogue

25. Using a slang thesaurus, give five synonyms of "marijuana."

26. What do the following words have in common? Be specific.
    amateur   chef   protege   fiancee   emigre   divorcee

27. What do the following words have in common? Be specific.
    alto   andante   crescendo   piano   soprano

Chapter 14

Writing the Cover Letter and the Resumé

Always enclose a letter of application (cover letter) when you send a resumé. The main purpose of a cover letter is to interest a prospective employer in you as a potential employee. Keep the following facts in mind when you prepare the cover letter and the resumé. *Be neat.*

Type your cover letter and resumé on standard size white paper (8½" by 11"). The typed copy must be "clean," free of noticeable erasure marks and typographical errors. Since the letter reflects you and your work habits, it must be neat and attractive. Make sure that the margins are not ragged, but as balanced as possible. Do not syllabicate three successive lines. Poor grammar and misspelled words are an affront to the reader, so avoid such errors by having a literate friend proofread your copy before you send it. Generally, your cover letter should be single spaced and no longer than one page. Avoid superfluous phrasing. Do not waste words—get to the point.

Address your letter to a specific person when possible. Take the time to find out who is in charge of hiring or setting up an interview. Never address the letter of application to "Whom It May Concern." Remember that the *Attention Line* usually expedites matters and appears both on the envelope and in the letter.

The first paragraph

Corporation executives say that the first twenty words are important in attracting the reader's interest. In the first paragraph, therefore, apply for a specific position and tell how you found out about the position—through the company's advertisement in the newspaper or through a friend of yours who works there.

The second paragraph

The second paragraph should elaborate briefly on your qualifications for the position and comment on the interest and contributions you can make to the employer. Refer to your resumé, citing briefly any special skills or qualifications which you consider important relative to the job. But keep it short and do not cover the same information in your resumé. Let your cover letter reflect your serious interest in the position. Avoid seeming too aggressive, familiar, or humorous. While you are anxious to be considered for the position, do not convey the impression of "begging" for the position by citing your personal problems or hardships.

The third paragraph

The third or last paragraph is generally used to request an appointment for a personal interview to discuss your qualifications at the employer's convenience. Always give your current address, zip number, area code, and telephone number. Give the time when you may be reached at home. Be sure that you are available at the time stipulated in your letter.

A necessary formal procedure in ending your letter is the *Complimentary Close*, which is placed two spaces below the body of the letter. "Sincerely" or "Sincerely yours" are commonly used and recommended. If there is no identification line, the word *Enclosure* is typed two spaces below the signature and placed even with the left margin: Enclosure: Resumé or Encl: Resumé.

Keep in mind that the letter of application has four functions:

1. To make reference to your source of information concerning the Position

2. To make a formal application for the position

3. To emphasize qualifications

4. To request an interview

The Resumé

The resumé (personal data sheet, vita) should have a minimum of four divisions: personal data, education, experience, and references. Contemporary practice, however, expands the four basic categories to six: *job objective* (an optional feature) and *other information* (special data).

Personal data include your complete name (no nicknames), complete address (with ZIP code), home and office telephone number(s), and message service. *Do not* include physical details (age, height, weight, handicap) or marital status. Unless you are applying for a "creative" position, do not use brightly colored paper or dramatic typesetting.

Under the division marked *education,* list the most advanced degree first, beginning with college and continuing through high school. List the names of the colleges which you have attended, your major(s), and the degree(s) earned with the date awarded. Include any special courses or training taken *if relevant* to the position that you are seeking. Also, include special coursework or projects and awards/honors.

Under *experience* or *work history,* begin with your current or more recent experience, listing the positions that you have held. General practice is to give the following information with each job listed: the employer's name, dates of employment, description of responsibilities, accomplishments during employment, special work-related training. Avoid listing any periods of unemployment.

Other or *additional information* is an optional feature designed to make your credentials more attractive to the prospective employer. You may list specific awards received, honors, professional organizations to which you belong, military service, volunteer work, and community activities.

Regarding *references,* list the names of at least three people who will give your prospective employer a good report concerning your work and character. Be sure that you have a person's permission before you include his/her name, together with the correct spelling of the names and the correct addresses. Do not include the names of blood relatives. If you do not list references, entitle the division of your resumé "References available upon request."

Optional Features

1. Career objective—reflects commitment to a career goal

2. Employment objective—targets your resumé to a specific position

3. Special skills—highlights special abilities and training (first aid certification, computer literacy, foreign language)

4. Activities—emphasizes community involvement and leadership

5. Interests—should be relevant to the position

6. Professional affiliations—demonstrates your commitment to the profession

7. Personal information—includes job-related information (willingness to relocate, re-train)

In preparing a resumé, keep these points in mind

∎ Use good quality bond paper; if you use photocopies, make sure that they are clean, free of smudges, and attractive. Margins must be well balanced; the spacing must give a neat appearance. Avoid a cramped, crowded layout.

- Use a letter quality printer. Use major headings and subheadings to identify and to organize the data. Make sure that the spelling and grammar are flawless. Use parallel structure in wording your resumé. Be consistent in the layout by neatly arranging headings, spacing, indentations, and underlining.
- Generally, your resumé should be one page, two at the most, but only if your work experience and credentials warrant that length. Be succinct. Avoid using "I" constantly and passive verbs. Instead of writing sentences such as, "I received a scholarship in Dental Hygiene, which I used to pay part of my tuition," use brief phrases such as, "Received a Dental Hygiene scholarship in 1982."
- Highlight academic, extracurricular, and work experiences that convey positive personal features of leadership, responsibility, and creativity. If necessary, include your complete college transcript.
- If you are presently employed, do not give your present salary on the resumé or the letter of application.
- Do not include a photograph—unless you are applying for a modeling job, acting role, or television anchor.
- Do not include political or religious affiliations—unless you know that revealing such information will benefit you.
- Do not include dangerous hobbies or pastimes such as skydiving, bull-fighting, shark-fishing, or snake-baiting.

Remember that the resumé (personal data sheet, vita) cannot guarantee you an interview with a prospective employer, much less the position that you seek. Other myths concerning the resumé are that a "good" resumé need not be changed, that one can't write a resumé without job experience, and that a professional should prepare the resumé. Select one of the following types of resumés to suit your present situation:

1 . *The Chronological Resumé*
   a. Presents your background and experience.
   b. Lists jobs in chronological order—with the most recent first.
   c. Stresses work history and advancement.
   d. Reflects a commitment to a definite career path.

2. *The Skills Resumé*
   a. Lists your qualifications under skill areas.
   b. Cites examples of your accomplishments in specific areas.
   c. Stresses skills and abilities in place of traditional experience.
   d. Associates transferable skills/abilities from unrelated job or experiences to the present employment position.
   e. Suits those returning to the work place after a long absence or lack of job experience.

3. *The Combination Resumé*
   a. Combines both work history and skill descriptions.
   b. Includes the strongest aspects of the chronological and skill resumés.
   c. Utilizes the strongest features of the chronological and skills resumés.

4. *The Targeted Resumé*
   a. Lists those skills, abilities, and experiences pertinent to a specific position.
   b. Stresses your experience and ability concerning the position.
   c. Emphasizes your qualifications and skills.
   d. Reflects job insight and understanding.

Update your resumé periodically. Remember that the resumé projects the positive image you wish to convey to a prospective employer.

Be clear, concise

As in formal composition, use clear, familiar words when addressing the reader in business letters. Never use twenty words to communicate when ten words express your message. Too often, writers try to impress the reader rather than clearly expressing themselves. Do not waste words. Replace long, unnatural words with short, familiar ones.

Clumsy, unnatural	Short, natural
At the earliest possible time	Soon
At the present writing	Now
Enclosed herein	Enclosed
In accordance with	According to
In the near future	Soon
In view of the fact that	
Because of the fact that	Because
Kindly advise me	Inform me, tell me
Permit me to say	(Ugh!)
This letter is for the purpose of requesting	Please send
With this letter I am enclosing	Enclosed
At an early date	Soon
At a later date	Later
The early part of next week	Monday, Tuesday
If this should prove to be the case	In case
First began	Began

Refer back	Refer
Repeat again	Repeat
True facts of the matter	Facts
Continue on, continue with	Continue
Just recently	Recently
Irregardless	Regardless
Cooperate together	Cooperate
Later on	Later
Past experience	Experience
Seldom ever, seldom if ever	Seldom
Quite unique	Unique
Add up	Add
Prompt and immediate	Prompt (or immediate)
Complete confidence	Confidence
First and foremost	First
First of all, last of all	First, last
Fair and equitable	Fair
Continuous and uninterrupted	Continuous
Each and every	Each
A long period of time	A long time (Try to be more specific.)
In the event that	If
It is probable that	Probably
At that point in time	At that time
Agreeable and satisfactory	Satisfactory
Exactly the same, exactly identical	Identical
Please do not hesitate to call	Please call
This is in response to your letter of July 4 in which you applied for an application for a position with our company.	Your request for a job application has been received.
Heartfelt thanks and deep appreciation	Thank you
It has always been my contention that	I believe
Ready and willing	Eager

The list of such trite phrases, redundancies, and outright errors could be multiplied easily. The important thing to remember in writing business letters or college compositions is to avoid wordy expressions, needless repetition, and unnatural, overused phrases. Conciseness provides a short, forceful, and appropriate logic that does not exhaust the reader with meaningless words.

Sample Cover Letter-Block Form

243 Utah Avenue
Cumberland, MD 21502
December 20, 1990

Board of Education
108 Washington Street
Cumberland, MD 21502

Attention: Mr. William Pangloss

Dear Mr. Pangloss:

Through Mr. Richard Thomas, a teacher at Fort Hill High School, I understand that there is an opening as a teacher's aide at Fort Hill. Please consider this letter as an application for employment for the teacher's aide position.

I plan to graduate from Allegany Community College in December of 1990 with an Associate in Arts degree in Mental Health. After two years of study at ACC, I have maintained an A average. The enclosed data sheet gives an outline of my training and experience. I was a volunteer tutor for five years before enrolling at ACC, and my experience working with learning disabled students should be of value to our local teachers and counselors.

I will be happy to furnish any additional information concerning my background or present training. I would appreciate a personal interview to discuss my qualifications concerning a position as a teacher's aid. I may be contacted at my home between eight a.m. and ten p.m. My telephone number is 724-9883. Thank you for your consideration, and I shall look forward to hearing from you.

Sincerely,

Rita Guerney
Enclosure: Resumé

Resumé

RITA GUERNEY
243 Utah Avenue
Cumberland, MD 21502
Telephone: 813-724-9883

POSITION SOUGHT: TEACHER'S AIDE or COUNSELOR'S AIDE

Education   1981-1982 Allegany Community College,
                     Cumberland, MD
                       Associate of Arts—Mental Health
                         Psychology 101, 102
                         Human Growth and Development
                         Child Psychology
                         Speech; speech therapy
                     1959 Fort Hill High School
                       Honor Society

Experience   1980-1981 Cresaptown Elementary School
                       Classroom tutor
                     1975-1980 Parks Elementary School, Cumberland
                       Volunteer tutor, teacher's aide
                     1972-1973 Grace Methodist Church, Cumberland
                       Volunteer teacher's aide, Day Care Center

Special Training   Allegany Community College
                     1982 Earned seven hours working with mentally
                       disabled
                     1982 Finan Center-volunteer work adolescents
                     1982 Finan Center-work with mentally disturbed
                       patients

References Available Upon Request

Sample Cover Letter—Modified Block

Route 3, Box 69
Friendsville, MD 21532
December 20, 1990

Director of Personnel
International Business Machines
Boca Raton, FL 45602

Attention: Mr. Robert Gibson

Dear Sir:

In the October issue of *Computer World,* I read your advertisement seeking computer programmers for work on the recently introduced Personal Computer. Please consider this letter as my application for a programming position.

Presently, I am a programmer at Micro Integration, Inc. My work here is pleasant and enjoyable, but my father, who lives in Boca Raton, is ill and I would like to find work closer to my home. The enclosed data sheet gives a brief outline of my training and experience. I have enjoyed working with computers since I first began experimenting with them in high school electronics. This fascination with computers ultimately led to my earning an Associate in Arts degree in Computer Science at Allegany Community College.

I will be happy to supply any additional information concerning my background or present employment. Although distance is an important factor, I would be pleased to fly down for a personal interview if I had at least ten days' notice. I can usually be reached at my home address before 7:30 a.m. and after 6:00 p.m. My telephone number is (301) 746-4433. Thank you for your time, and I will be looking forward to hearing from you.

Sincerely yours,

Roger R. Grungee

Enclosure: Resumé

ROGER RODNEY GRUNGEE

ADDRESS: Route 3, Box 69, Friendsville, MD 21532

POSITION SOUGHT: COMPUTER PROGRAMMER

EXPERIENCE: 1988-present: Micro Integration, Inc. Friendsville,
MD 21531. Programmer, Board Assembler,
Systems Tester, Supervisor.
1985-1987 Interstate Lumber Company,
Kingwood, WV 26501
Laborer, Construction

SKILLS: *Supervisory*   Directed a team of ten workers.
Determined work assignments based on
priorities.
Solved programming problems.

Communications Prepared written reports
Gave oral directions to workers.

Personnel   Interviewed and made recommendations
for hiring new personnel.
Prepared written performance evaluations
of workers.
Made recommendations for pay increases
and promotions.

EDUCATION: Allegany Community College
Degree: Associate in Arts, 1990
Major: Computer Science
Class Rank: Upper tenth, Magna Cum Laude
Major Subjects: Fortran   Assembler Programming
Cobol   Field Training
Calculus Electronic Design
Diploma, Friendsville High School, 1979

SPECIAL TRAINING: 1986-1987 Heath Continuing Education
Microprocessor—eighty hours
Basic Programming—forty hours

AWARDS: Outstanding First-Year Student in Computer
Programming

REFERENCES:

Mr. George Garlick, President
Micro Integration, Inc.
Friendsville, MD 21531

Mr. Peter Petroff, foreman
Interstate Lumber Company
Kingwood, WV 26501

Dr. Loo Kwan Soo, professor
Allegany Community College
Willowbrook Road, Cumberland, MD 21502

Mr. Stanley Porto, professor
Garrett Community College
Garrett County, MD 21531

21

A Concise Handbook of Grammar

■ Chapter 1 ■

Parts of Speech

Words may be classified in eight categories called parts of speech. The way a word is used determines its classification as a particular part of speech.

A. A *noun* is the name of a person, place, thing, idea, or quality.

> *George* walked to the *store* to buy *cereal.*
> *Love* is a *quality* of *virtue.*
> *"Very"* is usually an *adverb.*

There are two groups of nouns: *common and proper.* A common noun refers to one or more of a class of persons, things, or ideas.

An *abstract common noun* names intangible qualities, conditions, or ideas: love, courage, justice, death, truth, beauty, romance.

A *concrete common noun* names anything tangible: dog, suit, cloud, lake, bird.

A *collective common noun* names a group of people or objects which form a unit: staff, mob, army, union, club, committee.

A *proper noun* names a particular person, place, or thing: Monday, Halloween, Lincoln Memorial, George Smith, Negro, Kleenex.

Gender indicates a noun's sex or lack of sex: masculine, feminine, or neuter (sexless).

Number indicates singular or plural: foot, feet; cow, cows; ox, oxen; boy, boys; church, churches.

Case refers to a noun's sense relation to other words: nominative, possessive, and objective.

Exercise la

Label the nouns in the following sentences.

1. The old man bought some popcorn at the theater.

2. The U.S. Navy at Midway fought the Japanese successfully.

217

3. Pistachio the dog chewed at his collar.

4. Mr. Porter insisted that teenage love was silly.

5. The Beatles created a new fashion in music and morals.

6. Tired of cookies, the little boy wanted ice cream.

7. The teacher ordered the student to take better care of his locker.

8. The hippies chanted a protest against the terrible conflict.

9. John's wife was in the house with another man that morning.

10. Discipline was a necessity in the Spartan phalanx.

11. Basically, the dash is used for one purpose—emphasis.

12. The summary may be divided by numbers or by capital letters.

13. Page numbers are excluded in the first draft of the thesis.

14. All of us refused to shoot the Fascist pig.

15. Pete refused to pay for the furniture because several pieces were damaged by the moving men.

16. He knew that he would have to leave soon.

17. I ignored his pleading for more jelly beans at breakfast.

18. Miss Cook said that she would go to the conference tomorrow.

19. I dislike people belching at the supper table.

20. Swimming at night under a full moon is fun.

B. A *pronoun* takes the place of a noun.

Personal pronouns refer to persons and things—I, you, he, she, it—and are inflected to show person, number, and case.

In first person, the writer refers to himself—*I.*
In second person, the writer refers to the reader—*you.*
In third person, the writer refers to another—*he, she, it.*

Intensive pronouns emphasize the antecedent.

I *myself* will do the work.
Pete talked to the protesters *themselves.*

Reflexive pronouns refer back to the subject.

> You must go *yourself.*
> Sue hurt *herself.*

Demonstrative pronouns refer to the subject by pointing out the persons or things which are specified—*this, these, that, those.*

Indefinite pronouns are not specific—*all, anybody, everybody, some, none, most, such.*

Numeral pronouns represent nouns which are understood: Many dogs were hungry, but only *two* were fed.

Interrogative pronouns ask questions—*who, which, what, whoever, whichever, whatever.*

Exercise Ib

Label the pronouns in the following sentences.

1. Pete drinks too much, which causes him to be grouchy.
2. If it were not for Zorba, she would have been arrested.
3. Not all of the girls were ready for their initiation.
4. Some of the dogs ate most of their food.
5. He did not want any for himself.
6. They shouted at me as I splashed them with muddy water.
7. Whatever could be the reason for that?
8. I want to kiss that girl.
9. Doesn't anybody care about what she has done to him?
10. She is a person who communicates best at night.

C. An *adjective* modifies a noun or pronoun by answering these questions:

What kind? Which one? How many?

> The *rose* bush has *thorny* stems.
> Mr. Kelley is *an excellent* teacher.
> I want *two* pairs of *black* shoes.

Adjectives may be *inflected* to show three degrees of comparison.

The *positive degree* reflects the simplest quality: My milk is *warm*.
The *comparative degree* reflects a higher quality than the positive: My milk is the *warmer* of the two glasses. (Two objects are compared with the *er* suffix.)
The *superlative* reflects the highest degree when three or more persons or things are compared: My milk is the *warmest* of the three glasses. (The superlative degree usually ends in *est*, but many do not: best, worst, least, most.)

A *predicate adjective* modifies a noun or pronoun through a linking verb:
He is *old*. She is *pretty*.

Exercise 1c

Label the adjectives in the following sentences.

1. Pete stared at the pretty girls and their lovely earlobes.

2. Prepare for further study concerning the English test.

3. He begged his sobbing girlfriend to tell him the entire story of incestuous, sordid lust.

4. Gregory smiled with crooked teeth and slobbery lips.

5. That red-haired girl has a bountiful dispostion.

6. The American flag is red, white, and blue.

7. The grimy gringo looked at the smiling, dancing senorita.

8. I want eight of those delicious apples.

9. It was a long, monotonous, boring biology lecture.

10. In Cumberland, you will find tall buildings and various types of old, rickety houses.

11. Maria gave the dirty, disheveled wino fifteen cents and a red bingo chip for good luck.

12. His hot garlic breath stunned the pretty actress.

13. Pete Goobers was the worst player on the baseball team.

14. His test results were the better of the two student papers.

15. Rita's huge bulbous nose proved to be an erotic asset.

16. George seemed angry with Gretchen on that fateful night.

17. The Greek army fought the vicious Albanian rebels.

18. George is the new mayor of metropolitan Cumberland.

19. The large book was the new college edition.

20. The twenty-year-old contestant was exceptionally pretty.

21. This food tastes good.

22. Maria was wearing a bluish-green sweater that night.

23. An abstract noun names intangible qualities.

24. Gregors fought his way to the very top of the mountain.

25. Tired and insecure, the little boy trudged home.

26. Swimming at night under a full moon is fun.

27. Pete improved his reading speed.

28. Pancho thought Gloria was a real lady.

29. Cyrano's nose was rather large and sticky.

30. The person who said that the best things in life are free was absolutely crazy.

D. A *verb* expresses action or a state of being.

> John *smiled.*
> Pete *hit* the ball.
> I *am.*

Transitive verbs convey action to a receiver or an object:

> John *ate* the sandwich. (*Sandwich* receives the action of *ate.*)

Intransitive verbs do not convey action to a receiver or object:

> I *am shaking* with joy.
> The sun *rose.*
> Pete *laughed.*

Six tenses indicate the time of occurrence or completion of an action: present, past, future, present perfect, past perfect, and future perfect.

Verbs which join with other verbs to produce various tenses and moods are *auxiliary* or *helping verbs.*

> She *will* go. (*Will* is a helping verb.)
> It *might have* been important. (*Might have* are helping verbs.)

A *linking verb* connects a subject with a noun or adjective complement. The *Be* family verbs and those verbs dealing with the five senses are linking verbs. Other linking verbs are *appear, look, seem, remain, feel.*

> He *is* old. (*Old* is a predicate adjective.)
> He *is* the mayor. (*Mayor* is a predicate noun or predicate nominative.)
> The food *tastes* good. (*Good* is a predicate adjective.)
> I *feel* bad. (*Bad* is a predicate adjective.)

Exercise 1d

Label the verbs in the following sentences.

1. Pete smelled the flowers and grinned.
2. Diane was running home when it happened.
3. I would never have thought such a thing could happen.
4. The police raided the pool room.
5. My wife loves to play bingo.
6. Anna's anger rose swiftly.
7. He jumped into the pool and began swimming.
8. Christa was jogging with her dog along the track.
9. She appears older than she really is.
10. The papers may have been important to our cause.
11. The dog veered to the right, barked viciously, and then ran away.
12. The airplane soared high over the trees.
13. I simply love pancakes with butter dripping down the edges.
14. Paul arrived too late for the interview.
15. Garth was whispering in her ear when Bart stormed in.

16. The warring nations were uncomfortably close to expanding the conflict.

17. Paul said that he felt better as time progressed.

18. He later regretted his angry response.

19. Don't look so angry!

20. It appears that all will be well.

21. I will not jump into another dismal marriage.

22. The badly scarred drunk staggered out of the burning club.

23. George was eating the fried potatoes when Deadeye walked in.

24. The toy car was poorly constructed.

25. Blinded and hurt by the burning missiles, Pete felt the pain jab through his body.

E.   An *adverb* modifies a verb, an adjective, or another adverb, and answers the questions *where, when, how, how much,* and *why.*

Adverbs show place, time, manner, and degree.

> The dog walked *home.* (Place)
> We shall arrive *tomorrow.* (Time)
> Pete walked *slowly.* (Manner)
> The water was *very* muddy. (Degree)

Adverbs may be formed from adjectives by adding *ly,* but many adverbs do not have this ending: She is *truly* sorry.
                                                  She is *quite* sorry.

Conjunctive adverbs function as connectors, usually in compound sentences:

> *however, furthermore, nevertheless, subsequently, moreover, therefore, accordingly, thus,* and others.
> I was tired; *nevertheless,* I decided to return to the orgy.
>   (connective)
> I will, *nevertheless,* proceed to Cumberland.
>   (parenthetical)

Exercise 1e

Label the adverbs in the following sentences.

1. The badly scarred man staggered drunkenly out of the blazing bar.

2. The muddy water rose quite swiftly.

3. George arrived much too late for the test.

4. She was very sorry to see Toto leave so suddenly.

5. Maria later regretted her silly response.

6. The lovely dress was intricately woven.

7. The grimy gringo was highly respected in the bordello.

8. The jet climbed high over the mountains.

9. He arrived shortly before sailing time yesterday.

10. They sat uncomfortably close to each other.

11. The Argentinian airstrips were heavily bombed yesterday.

12. Boogers promised that he would see her promptly tomorrow.

13. The dog snarled viciously and dashed home.

14. Garth felt better.

15. Miriam spun around and laughed bitterly.

16. The train ride was somewhat tedious.

17. The commode never seemed to flush regularly.

18. Karen is the least dependable of the students.

19. Will you ever learn to study properly?

20. Taste in fashions differs considerably.

21. The dash is used primarily for emphasis.

22. He did not seem very tired.

23. Bob will, therefore, attend the meeting, perhaps tonight.

24. His critical condition was rapidly deteriorating.

25. Hand in hand, they strolled merrily off into the woods.

F. A *preposition* shows the relation of a noun or pronoun to some other word in the sentence. Some prepositions are *in, on, above, beyond, across, beneath, under, upon, of, to, by, as.*

The preposition and its object form a prepositional phrase:

John walked *with Betty to the mall.*

The object of a preposition is in the objective case: Give the money *to her.*

To whom should I give the money?

A group of two or more words may be used as a preposition: *according to, in spite of, because of, out of, as far as,* and others.

We walked *as far as* the hill.

Prepositional phrases may function as adjectives or adverbs.

The girl *with the dog* is my sister. (*With the dog* modifies the noun *girl* and functions as an adjective.)
Pete ran *along the shore.* (*Along the shore* tells where Pete ran and functions as an adverb.)

Exercise 1f

Identify the prepositional phrase and state its function as adjectival or adverbial in the following sentences.

1. The girl in the skimpy bikini is smiling at you.
2. In spite of his anger, Pete agreed to come to the party.
3. The car driven by Archie was speeding down the road to town.
4. A placement test for students is mandatory in college.
5. Her appearance at the meeting was well received.
6. A bored spouse is a danger signal in marriage.
7. He had a meeting with the hunters in Paw Paw.
8. A girl in love is a victim of mental anguish.
9. He fell off the boat into a muddy patch of debris.
10. The swarm of bees seemed to form a cloud of dust over the fields of tall corn.

11. She was without understanding.

12. According to Peterson, the old man is a drunk with a temper.

13. I would like to have a custard pie with ice cream.

14. Everyone but Pete went to the woods for a picnic in Midland.

15. The girl with the freckles walked into the living room with Pancho.

G. A *conjunction* connects words, phrases, or clauses.

Coordinate conjunctions join words or groups of words of equal rank: *and, but, or, nor, for,* sometimes *yet* and *so.*

Subordinate conjunctions introduce dependent clauses: *because, since, if, where, unless, although, as if, as well as,* and others.

Correlative conjunctions are used in pairs: *both, and; either, or; neither, nor; not only, but also.*

Exercise 1g

Identify the conjunctions in the following sentences and label each as coordinate, subordinate, or correlative.

1. I will go if you accompany me.

2. Because she was tired, Mary went to bed early.

3. Neither John nor Harry is able to attend the meeting.

4. Go and lie down for a while.

5. He arrived shortly before the boat sailed.

6. The cat growled when the dog drank the milk.

7. It alarms me when you act so foolishly.

8. Sunday was a lovely day so we went swimming.

9. Unless Joe improves, he will fail English.

10. John will never recover unless Brenda returns.

11. Birds and bats swoop and fly.

12. But she is a woman as well as a lady.

.

13. You will go over this material until you have learned it.

14. The decision will be made by either you or Gordo.

15. The girls who were sitting in the lobby laughed and joined us.

16. I love you because you're wealthy.

17. George walked home and his faithful dog followed.

18. Give me the keys or I will be angry.

19. If Pete were here now, everything would be fine.

20. I had no illusions about getting the job, so I'm not angry.

H. An *intejection* expresses emotion or surprise and has no grammatical relationship to the rest of the sentence: *oh, wow, whoopee, hey, gee, zounds,* and others.

Goodness! I didn't see you coming!
Dear me! Is that all there is?
Oh, I hope you can make it tonight.

Review of the parts of speech

Label each word as a part of speech in the following sentences.

1. The Lincoln Memorial is a beautiful piece of architecture.

2. The shark is a mile off shore.

3. She was quite excited about her new dress.

4. George said that he would meet with Jessie tonight.

5. The shimmering lights seemed to reflect a natural serenity.

6. Mary talked to whoever would listen.

7. Give me the keys or I will be angry.

8. George was tired; nevertheless, he decided to go jogging.

9. Swimming in the ocean can be dangerous.

10. She is such a pretty girl.

11. Not all of the girls were ready for their initiation.

12. Mr. Porter insisted that their argument was quite silly.

13. Billy enjoyed arguing over the most foolish ideas.

14. After you have revised the outline, begin writing the first draft.

15. The Greek language is comparatively easy to learn.

16. Freshmen students generally begin their essays well.

17. He refused to pay for the repairs on his old Chevrolet.

18. If she had remained here, I might have become angry.

19. I failed the test because I was nervous.

20. My, you are such a kind person.

21. I had no trouble with the assignment; however, I could have used a little more time.

22. There is nothing like the smell of grass after a rain.

23. Watermelons, along with grapefruit, are delicious.

24. My wife is an avid bingo player.

25. The excited puppy jumped up and down and barked at the toy.

■ Chapter 2 ■

Verbs—Transitive and Intransitive

A verb is *transitive* when its object receives the action transmitted by the verb.

> Pete Rose hit the ball. (*Ball* receives the action of *hit*.)
> He set the books on the desk. (*Books* receives the action of *set*.)
> The dog smelled the food. (*Food* is the object of *smelled*.)

A verb is *intransitive* when it has no object.

> Pete swung at the ball. (*Ball* is the object of the preposition *at*.)
> I am tired. (*Tired* is a predicate adjective because of the linking verb *am*.)
> The sun rose. (*Rose* is a finite verb and the action goes no further.)

Many verbs may be used either transitively or intransitively.

> They elected Pete mayor of Cumberland.
> Pete was elected.

Lie and lay

The verb *lie* (*lie, lay, lain*) is intransitive and means to rest or to recline.

> Go and lie down for a while. (present)
> Sue lay in her bed and refused to get up. (past)
> Pete has lain on the couch all night. (past participle)

235

The verb *lay (lay, laying, laid, laid)* means to place.

> He lays the groundwork for success. (present)
> He is laying the groundwork for success. (present participle)
> He laid the groundwork for success. (past)
> He has laid the groundwork for success. (past participle)

Sit and set

The verb *sit (sit, sitting, sat, sat)* is intransitive and means to put one-self in a sitting position.

> Come here and sit down. (present)
> Mary is sitting in the chair. (present participle)
> Mary sat in the chair. (past)
> Mary has sat in the chair. (past participle)

The verb *set (set, setting, set, set)* is transitive and means to put or to place.

> I set the books on the desk. (present)
> I am setting the books on the desk. (present participle)
> I set the books on the desk. (past)
> I have set the books on the desk. (past participle)

Note: The verb *lie* may also mean to tell a falsehood.

> She lied about paying the gas bill.
> She is lying about the gas bill.

Exercise 2a

Choose the correct form of transitive or intransitive verb in the following sentences.

1. Let's set down and talk about this problem. _____

2. Mary always left her clothes laying on the bed. _____

3. Mr. Bougars was setting in his chair. _____

4. After setting her blouse out to be cleaned, Sue left. _____

5. The teacher laid out the pencils. _____

6. The girls set around the campfire telling jokes. _____

7. Laying on the beach, Mary fell asleep. _____

8. The dog loves to lay in the sun. _____

9. The wreckage laid on the curb. _____

10. If the little boy had laid down for a while, we could have helped. _____

11. Caesar found his weapon setting against his shield. _____

12. Bernard was laying in the grass. _____

13. Porky was confident after he had lain the trap for the wolf. _____

14. After she had laid in bed for several hours, Petunia arose. _____

15. Stephen's toys were laying in the wet grass for hours. _____

16. Let's set down and talk about this. _____

17. If Sue had laid down for some rest, she wouldn't be so tired. _____

18. Don't set those boxes on the ground! _____

19. She hated to be laying in a hospital bed the night of the prom. _____

20. Lay your shirt out to be cleaned. _____

21. Petunia was laying out in the grass. _____

22. My father has always set at the head of the table for supper. _____

23. Laying in the sun for a long time is unhealthy. _____

24. The troops laid their rifles on the ground. _____

25. Pete found his slingshot setting against the chair. _____

Person, number, tense, mood, and voice

A verb is in the *first person* if its subject is the speaker.

> I see.
> I go.
> I run.

A verb is in the *second person* if its subject is the person spoken to.

> You see.
> You go.
> You run.

A verb is in the *third person* if its subject is the person or thing spoken of.

> He sees.
> She sees.
> It sees.
> They see.

Number indicates either the singular or plural nature of the subject. When a verb changes its form to agree with its subject, the verb is said to be *inflected*. Not many verbs change their form to show number.

Generally, the subject affects the verb form only when the verb is in the present tense. Add *s* or *es* to the verb when the tense is present and the subject is singular.

> Pete hopes to study geography. (singular, present)
> We hope to study geography. (plural, present)

Do not add *s* or *es* to a verb accompanied by a helping verb, regardless of the number of the subject.

> Does Sue *play* the piano?
> George *can run*.
> John *will go* the day of hunting season.

Voice shows whether the subject is acting or being acted upon.

In active voice, the subject performs the action of the verb: George hit the ball.

In *passive voice,* the subject is acted upon: The ball was hit by George.

The passive voice is formed by combining helping verbs with the past participle of the main verb.

> Pete told the employee. (active)
> The employee was told by Pete. (passive)

Mood shows the manner in which the writer conceives of the action of the verb.

The *indicative mood* is used as a statement of fact or of close relation to reality.

The history test was difficult. (a statement of fact)
Was the history test difficult? (a question about a fact)

The *imperative mood* is used to express a command or a request; the subject is usually omitted in a second-person imperative sentence.

Hand in your essays.
Hurry and get dressed!

The *subjunctive mood* expresses a possibility, hope, wish, or a condition contrary to fact.

I wish that I *were* in Paris.
Let the ballots *be counted*.
If Pete *were* here, everything would be fine.
I move that the meeting *be adjourned*.

Tense (time) indicates the time of occurrence or completion of action. There are six tenses in the indicative mood: present, past, future, present perfect, past perfect, and future perfect.

The *present tense* form refers to present time, but it may have other uses.

1. It may be used to represent action as occurring in the future:
    Classes *begin* in the early morning.
    It *is* sure *to be* a difficult test tomorrow.

2. It may be used to express a general truth.
    The truth will out.
    God is good.

3. It may be used to represent a customary or habitual action.
    Diana always talks rapidly.
    English teachers are so demanding.

4. It may be used to refer to past time as the historical present.
    Alexander the Great severed the Gordian Knot with his sword. His eyes scan the cowering Persians as they humble themselves before him, afraid to challenge his power. He is in complete mastery over the barbarians.

The *past tense* indicates that an action or condition took place or existed at some definite time in the past.

As we *studied*, the teacher *peered* over her glasses and *watched* us.

1. The *past progressive* indicates action for a continuing period in the past: They *were asking* for food to save the starving children.

2. The *past perfect* indicates an action or state as completed before a specified or implied time in the past: She *had eaten* six hamburgers before she became ill.

The *future tense* indicates action that is to be or to come.

I *shall see* John tomorrow.
She *will see* what can be done about the matter.

1 . The *future perfect* indicates action completed sometime before another event in the future: Zita *will have traveled* two thousand miles by the time she arrives in Atlantic City.

2. The *future perfect* tense is formed by using the future of the verb *have (shall have, will have)* with the past participle: I am completing my graduate work at Penn State, and in a few days I *shall have earned* my doctorate.

Verb forms

There are two types of verbs in the English language: *regular* and *irregular.*

Regular (weak) verbs form the past tense and past participle with *d, ed,* or at times *t.*

ask	asked	asked
jump	jumped	jumped
hear	heard	heard
burn	burned	burned
	(burnt)	(burnt)

Irregular (strong) verbs change vowels or forms in their past tenses and past participles: drink, drank, drunk. The principal parts of irregular verbs often cause problems. If you are unsure about a tense formation, consult a dictionary. If two forms are presented in the dictionary, the option is yours since both are acceptable: Pete *lighted* a fire; Pete *lit* a fire. If, however, the dictionary labels a form as nonstandard or obsolete, remember that it is not acceptable in formal writing.

Irregular Verb Forms—Principal Parts

Present Stem/Infinitive	*Past Tense*	*Past Participle*
arise	arose	arisen
be	was	been
bear	bore	borne, born
begin	began	begun
blow	blew	blown
break	broke	broken
bring	brought	brought
burst	burst	burst
catch	caught	caught
choose	chose	chosen
dig	dug	dug
dive	dived, dove	dived
do	did	done
draw	drew	drawn
drink	drank	drunk
eat	ate	eaten
fly	flew	flown
give	gave	given
go	went	gone
grow	grew	grown
hang	hung	hung
know	knew	known
lay	laid	laid
lead	led	led
lend	lent	lent
lie	lay	lain
ride	rode	ridden
ring	rang	rung
rise	rose	risen
run	ran	run
see	saw	seen
set	set	set
shake	shook	shaken
shine	shone, shined	shone, shined
show	showed	showed, shown

Present Step/Infinitive	Past Tense	Past Participle
shrink	shrank, shrunk	shrunk
sing	sang	sung
sink	sank, sunk	sunk
sleep	slept	slept
slide	slid	slid, slidden
speak	spoke	spoken
spin	spun	spun
spread	spread	spread
spring	sprang, sprung	sprung
steal	stole	stolen
stink	stank	stunk
swear	swore	sworn
swim	swam	swum
swing	swung	swung
take	took	taken
tear	tore	torn
thrive	thrived, throve	thrived, thriven
throw	threw	thrown
wear	wore	worn
weep	wept	wept
wring	wrung	wrung
write	wrote	written

Conjugation in grammar is the inflection of a verb in the forms corresponding to person, number, tense, mood, and voice.

Conjugation of the verb *to be*

Active voice—Present Indicative

I am	we are
you are	you are
he is	they are
she is	
it is	

Perfect Indicative

I have been	we have been
you have been	you have been
he has been	they have been
she has been	
it has been	

Past Indicative

I was	we were
you were	you were
he was	they were
she was	
it was	

Past Perfect Indicative

I had been	we had been
you had been	you had been
he had been	they had been
she had been	
it had been	

Future Indicative

I shall be	we shall be
you will be	you will be
he will be	they will be
she will be	
it will be	

Future Perfect Indicative

I shall have been	we shall have been
you will have been	you will have been
he will have been	they will have been
she will have been	
it will have been	

Conditional Indicative

I should be	we should be
you would be	you would be
he would be	they would be
she would be	
it would be	

Conditional Perfect Indicative

I should have been	we should have been
you would have been	you would have been
he would have been	they would have been
she would have been	
it would have been	

Present Subjunctive

that I (may) be	that we (may) be
that you (may) be	that you (may) be
that he (may) be	that they (may) be
that she (may) be	
that it (may) be	

Perfect Subjunctive

that I may have been	(we)
that you may have been	(you)
that he may have been	(they)
that she may have been	
that it may have been	

Imperfect Subjunctive

(if) I were	(if) we were
(if) you were	(if) you were
(if) he were	(if) they were
(if) she were	
(if) it were	

Imperfect Subjunctive

if I had been	if we had been
if you had been	if you had been
if he had been	if they had been
if she had been	
if it had been	

Future Perfect Subjunctive

I shall have been	we shall have been
you will have been	you will have been
she will have been	they will have been
it will have been	

Chapter 3

Verbals

A verbal is a non-finite verb form which *cannot* act as a predicate. Although a verbal is a word made from a verb, a verbal cannot be used *as* a verb. There are three types of verbals: the gerund, the participle, and the infinitive.

The *gerund* always ends in *ing* and is always used as a noun, functioning in every capacity as a noun: subject, direct object, predicate noun, object of a preposition, or an appositive.

> *Swimming* is good exercise. (subject)
> I enjoy *swimming*. (direct object)
> An excellent physical activity is *swimming*. (predicate noun)
> George, a lifeguard, makes his living by *swimming*. (object of the preposition *by*)
> George's occupation, *swimming*, requires endurance. (appositive)

A *participle* is a word or a phrase which is derived from a verb but acts as a modifier (verbal adjective). The two forms of the participle are the present (*ing* ending) and the past (*d, ed, n, en, t* ending). When combined with helping verbs, participles form verb phrases and may be predicates. Without the helping verbs, participles function as adjectives.

> His *swimming* suit is red. (*Swimming* is a present participle modifying *suit*.)
> He is *swimming* in the river. (When combined with a helping verb, the participle is part of the predicate.)
> The water is *running* in the sink. (*Running* is part of the verb phrase.)
> The *running* water is clear. (*Running* modifies the noun *water*.)
> The Greeks *have fought* with courage. (verb phrase)
> *Having fought* with courage, the Greeks rejoiced. (past participle modifying the subject *Greeks*)

245

Deserting the army, Pete enrolled in a bordello. (*Deserting* is a
present participle modifying the subject *Pete*.)
Pete is guilty of *deserting* the army. (*Deserting* now is a gerund,
the object of the preposition *of*.)

An *infinitive* is denoted by the preposition (infinitive marker) *to*,
which usually precedes a verb. Sometimes *to* must be implied. The infinitive may be used as a noun, an adjective, or an adverb.

Pete likes *to swim*. (*To swim* functions as a noun, the direct
object of *likes*.)
Maybelline is looking for a hat *to buy*. (*To buy* functions as an
adjective modifying *hat*.)
To avoid a scene, Porky left the room. (*To avoid* functions as an
adverb, telling why Porky left the room.)

Verbals can take subjects, objects, complements, and adverbial modifiers.

Greta showed her displeasure by *ignoring John at the party*.
(*John* is the direct object of the gerund *ignoring*, which is
modified by the prepositional phrase *at the party*. The entire
gerund phrase is the object of the preposition *by*.)
Quickly diverting his army to the river, Hannibal succeeded in
massacring the Romans at Cannae. (*Army* is the direct object
of the participle *diverting*, which is modified by the adverb
quickly. *To the river* is a prepositional phrase which modifies
army. The complete participial phrase modifies the subject
of the sentence, *Hannibal*.)
Gregors Samsa wanted *to be a cockroach*. (*Cockroach* is the complement of *to be*. The complete infinitive phrase is the object
of *wanted*.)

Note on proper usage of the gerund and the infinitive

When the subject of a gerund is a proper noun or a personal pronoun,
the possessive case is usually used.

The baby's crying annoyed me.
Karen's crying annoyed me.

If the subject is a plural noun, use the common form.

> I dislike children crying in church.
> I dislike people belching at the supper table.

If the subject of an infinitive is a pronoun, use objective case.

> I ordered *them to leave* the supper table. (*Them* is the subject of
> *to leave. The supper table* is the direct object of the infinitive.)

Do not split an infinitive.

> I would like to, if possible, see him again. (incorrect)
> I would like to see him again, if possible. (correct)
> I would like to, hopefully, see him again. (incorrect)
> Hopefully, I would like to see him again. (correct)

Exercise 3a

Identify the verbals in the following sentences and tell how each functions.

1. Nobody wants to warn Pete about his drunken ways.

2. Pancho's fighting days are over, to be sure.

3. Mary tried to call them to explain the problems concerning John.

4. Greta seems to be looking for an excuse to start trouble.

5. Willing and able, Maria left the dance with Gork.

6. I have dirty dishes to wash.

7. A broken wheel axle caused the terrifying accident.

8. Disappointed by the results, Georgia gave up the thrilling experiment.

9. Abandoned by her lover, homely Harriet walked home.

10. His check having been returned by the bank, Sam wrote another.

11. Looking stupid won't create sympathy for you.

12. Try smiling when you're depressed.

13. Nothing would help alleviate his social disease.

14. I am tired of having to be told what I should do with my life.

15. Beginning college studies after twenty years is difficult.

16. I would like to make another beginning, Sue.

17. I enjoy rolling drunks and crippled newspaper boys for extra change.

18. Whispering and sighing, Sue caressed Pete's callused hand.

19. To know her is to despise her.

20. Sky jumping is dangerous.

Exercise 3b

Identify the verbals in the following sentences.

1. The dog growled in a threatening tone.

2. Thinking is hard work.

3. My nerves are near the breaking point.

4. I would like to go swimming.

5. The reading test was easy to comprehend.

6. This course requires too much reading.

7. Maria can't stop crying over the spilt milkshake.

8. Deserted by her wretched husband, Sally decided to go out to the orgy across the street.

9. The car came to a jarring stop, the brakes screeching.

10. A student must learn to discover his own errors and to learn from them.

11. Celia went to the movies to find an escape.

12. Running water trickled into the streams.

13. I want to go home and watch television.

14. Tony earned an A in English, proving his ability to excel.

15. 1 would like to go walking with you.

16. Worn and exhausted, the horse managed to stagger home.

17. His lips quivering with desire, Gregory clutched her writhing body.

18. After painting his masterpiece, Pablo photographed the identical scene.

19. The wino standing in the doorway licked his chapped lips.

20. Anticipating defeat, Rommel decided to attack on all fronts.

Exercise 3c

Underline and label the verbals in the following sentences.

1. Hungry, the tired wolf swallowed the frozen fish.

2. Pete agreed to wash the car after reading the letter.

3. Baking bread is too time consuming.

4. John was arrested for violating the speed limit.

5. The little boy enjoyed pretending to be a bogey man.

6. Linda's low reading level was alarming.

7. Adopting a homeless animal is humane.

8. Stephen threw the burnt toast on the floor.

9. Mary sent a greeting card to cheer her depressed friend.

10. She enjoyed watching the leaping frogs.

11. Amused, the child stared at the clouds floating across the sky.

12. Mookie spent an hour studying for the test.

13. The secretary rearranged the filing system.

14. The scouts went to pitch their pup tents.

15. She hated polishing the worn furniture every day.

16. Surprised by the burglar, Sam ran to warn the police.

17. Leaving home is too sad to bear.

18. Defending her pups, the dog bit the writhing snake.

19. Karen spent the afternoon cooking supper and washing dishes.

20. Trying to smile, Sue wiped her tear-stained face.

21. Garth was trying to enter the haunted house.

22. She enjoyed slicing through the waves on her surfboard.

23. The freshmen demanded a fair grading policy.

24. After living in Magnolia for years, the Smiths moved to Paw Paw.

25. They were fighting to uphold their honor.

Chapter 4

The Sentence (Main/Independent) Clause

A sentence is a group of words which expresses a complete thought.

Go. (*You* is understood as the subject.)
Birds fly. (single subject, single verb)

The essential elements are the *subject* and the *predicate*.

The *subject* of a sentence performs an action or is that about which something is predicated.
The *predicate* consists of a verb(s) and says something about the subject.

Sentences are classified into four types

1. A *declarative* sentence asserts something: The girl is waiting.

2. An *interrogative* sentence asks a question: Is the girl waiting?

3. An *imperative* sentence expresses a command or a request: Tell the girl who is waiting to sit down.

4. An *exclamatory* sentence expresses strong feelings: What a gorgeous pair of legs Sally has!

In terms of organization, sentences may be classified as *simple, compound, complex,* and *compound-complex.*

1. A *simple sentence* consists of one main clause. (A *clause* is a group of words with a subject(s) and a verb(s): I walked.)
    In a simple sentence, either the subject or predicate or both may be compound:
    Sue and I walked.
    Sue and I walked and laughed.
    The number of modifying phrases have nothing to do in the determination of what type a sentence is: During the winter, I walked through the woods to get some of the very badly needed firewood for the hearth. (*I walked* remains as the subject and verb. In spite of all of the modifying phrases, it is a simple sentence.)

2. A *compound sentence* consists of two or more main clauses.
    Birds fly and bats swoop.
    Sue White walked; she jogged; she trotted.

3. A *complex sentence* contains one main clause and one (or more) dependent clause: I like what she said. (*What she said* is a dependent clause, the direct object of *like.*)
    What the newspapers said was false. (The entire structure here is the main clause. *What the newspapers said* is the subject of the main clause.)

4. A *compound-complex sentence* contains two or more independent clauses and one or more dependent (subordinate) clauses.
    When the books arrived (subordinate clause), the librarian noted their titles carefully, and then she began preparing labels for each. (Two independent or main clauses follow the subordinate clause.)

Exercise 4a

Determine whether the following sentences are simple, compound, complex, or compound-complex.

1. Mary was nervous until the movie started.   _____

2. My sister has written me regarding her plans for the coming year.   _____

3. To become a literate person, one must read and write with discipline.   _____

4. Study the assignment or you may be sorry. _____

5. The police realized that, when they reached the house, they had to be careful, or they would frighten the kidnappers of Porky. _____

6. My son has received an offer from a university which is interested in hiring him as a work study student. _____

7. He knew that he would have to leave soon. _____

8. What she proposed to him was absolutely ridiculous. _____

9. During the storm, the dog and cat hid under the bed in the dark upstairs room. _____

10. War, disease, and corruption have plagued mankind for centuries, and, in fact, are still serious problems. _____

11. The test was too difficult: everyone flunked. _____

12. Because of the heat from the sun, Sue Gilpin fainted. _____

13. Peter Coward, historian of note, wrote a book and lectured throughout the country. _____

14. The house on the hill overlooked the rolling meadows and the quiet village in the clearing. _____

15. Tired and exhausted from traveling, George and Mary paused to rest and to eat their sardine sandwiches. _____

16. What Cynthia sacrificed for her lover can only be measured by the tears she shed for the scoundrel. _____

17. I love you; I hate you. _____

18. The axle, the wheel, and the bearings must be cleaned, greased, and repaired. _____

19. Oedipus killed his father and married his mother! _____

20. If Richard III was not guilty of murdering the young princes, who was? _____

Exercise 4b

Determine whether the following sentences are simple, compound, complex, or compound-complex.

1. Believing her tale of deceit and treachery, I permitted my wife to deplete our savings. _____

2. Grease, food bits, and pieces of hair clogged the pipes of our sinks. _____

3. Improve your writing or suffer the consequences. _____

4. If you're having a good time drinking, you're in trouble, buddy. _____

5. What the Greeks gave humanity in cultural beauty cannot be measured in monetary value. _____

6. It pays to know people who know how to repair cars. _____

7. The dog growled and the cat arched its back. _____

8. One of our finest teachers, Mr. Peter Pietro, a graduate of Cooney State College and the holder of a Phi Beta Kappa key, leaves today for a series of shock treatments at Dogpatch General Hospital. _____

9. We will go over this material until it is second nature to you. _____

10. There shall come a time when you will be vulnerable to Cupid's arrow, my friend. _____

11. It is our responsibility to try to stop cruel behavior. _____

12. I like writing, but I find it difficult to do. _____

13. The girl with the long red hair and the thick lips is my wife. _____

14. A communist is a socialist in a hurry. _____

15. If Gork arrives soon, we shall go to see what he wants. _____

16. Maria and I saw the movie and then walked home. _____

17. I shall go but you must promise to follow me. _____

18. I shall go because you promised to follow me. _____

19. What the facts imply is obvious. _____

20. She is a girl who communicates best at night. _____

Subordinate clauses

A dependent clause has a subject and a verb which cannot "stand alone" or make a statement by itself. The three types of dependent clauses are *noun, adjective* and *adveb.*

A *noun clause* is a dependent clause which functions in the same way that a noun functions: subject, object, indirect object, and so on.

> *What Edmund did for his country* was truly patriotic. (The noun clause, *What Edmund did for his country,* serves as the subject of the entire, or main, clause.)
> I do not agree with *what she did.* (The noun clause, *what she did,* is the object of the preposition *with.*)

An *adjective clause* modifies a noun or a pronoun. The girl *who is wearing the red sweater* is my sister. (*Who is wearing the red sweater* is an adjective clause that identifies *girl.*)

The relative pronouns *which, who, whom, that,* and *whose* usually signal dependent clauses referred to as relative clauses. *That* may be used to refer to people or things.

An *adverbial clause* may be used to modify a verb, an adjective, or an adverb.

> I like English *because it is interesting.*
> Physics is more difficult *than I thought.*
> I will go to the dance *when I am ready.*

Sentence fragments

A sentence asserts something about the situation and consists of both a subject and a verb. A *sentence fragment* is a phrase or a clause that lacks a subject or a predicate or both: *If I decide to go the way I came.* Although this example has both a subject and a verb, it begins with a subordinate conjunction *if* and makes no sense by itself. When set off from the main clause on which it depends for meaning, a subordinate clause is a sentence fragment. Remember these rules: Do not set off a subordinate clause as a sentence; do not set off a verbal phrase as a sentence; do not set off a prepositional phrase as a sentence.

If the subject is implied, for instance, in a second person imperative sentence, the construction is acceptable: *Go.* (*You* is understood.)

Exercise 4c

Determine which of the following are sentences or fragments.

1. And he refused to go for a physical examination. _____

2. The disease that struck terror into the lusty loins of the sophomores—herpes simplex! _____

3. In her role of managing, editing, and writing. _____

4. Because of her happiness, Maria assuming a position as Mother Superior. _____

5. When Pete left for the army, in spite of her love for him. _____

6. Yet it was not Karen's physical deformity. _____

7. If you decide to go the distance at the meet. _____

8. Because Abe Lincoln freed the slaves. _____

9. That his country, formed upon the freedoms inherited by man. _____

10. When the moon comes over the mountain, and the stars rise. _____

11. Howard Smith, known for his eccentric ways, and one of the richest men in America. _____

12. And if you would be known as a man of virtue. _____

13. The dog barking and growling at the stranger. _____

14. Anybody can call himself whatever he wants. _____

15. And that's why Santa Claus is so fat, Gloria. _____

16. Furthermore, sentence fragments are unacceptable in writing. _____

17. What a hard luck story about old Goobers! _____

18. But Abe Lincoln freed the slaves. _____

19. Nothing like the smell of the desert after a rain. _____

20. Allegany Community College, nestled in the foothills of Appalachia, lying along the perfumed banks of the gentle Potomac River. _____

21. When the Greeks had decided to invade Persia, and the rivers ran red with blood. _____

22. I am. _____

23. Her eyes moist with tears, and the mascara streaming down her cheeks. _____

24. Go and fetch the rubbing alcohol for Daddy. _____

25. Peace on earth, good will to men. _____

26. If you decide to go to the dance with Gloria. _____

27. His army surrounded by the enemy. _____

28. Because she was angry and annoyed with Tony. _____

29. "Because" is a subordinate conjunction. _____

30. Trembling as she walked into the tavern, her lips quivering. _____

Exercise 4d

Determine which of the following are sentences or fragments. Write "S" or "Frag." in the space to the right.

1. Learning from your mistakes is important. _____

2. Vacation providing me with time to relax. _____

3. And so it goes. _____

4. An old tree toppled by the storm and as frightened as we were. _____

5. The dress that was being worn by Charo being revealing. _____

6. If you decide to go to the dance with Peter. _____

7. Across the street from us lives Mr. Pappas. _____

8. Give my condolences to her mother. _____

9. After the applause, the candidate speaking to his fans. _____

10. No, do not raise the price of milk and eggs. _____

11. Although a few good men served this country. _____

12. A development that completely puzzled us. _____

13. But he decided to continue his journey. _____

14. And I also find the concept difficult to define. _____

15. Although they are small, midgets have big hearts. _____

16. Christmas! Joy to the world! _____

17. Since the current was swift and he could not swim. _____

18. The professor, talking for hours, until he fell asleep. _____

19. Sit down and be quiet. _____

20. People who smoke cigarettes and drink. _____

Exercise 4e

Determine which of the following are sentences or fragments.

1. Since I began to work with George and received a raise. _____

2. Besides being an intelligent person and a great athlete. _____

3. Leave the car in the driveway; I will wash it later. _____

4. Which was the reason why Janet is so beautiful. _____

5. Bow thy head and pray, brother. _____

6. However long it takes to get my degree. _____

7. At last I have found an answer to my problem. _____

8. The teacher had a slight heart murmur. _____

9. And he was ill for several years before he died. _____

10. What is a sentence? _____

11. But a problem worthy of consideration. _____

12. My brother, as you can see, having come from one of the finest families in Cumberland. _____

13. The chances of her being selected as good. _____

14. In spite of the fact that the umpire called it fair. _____

15. That is absolutely ridiculous. _____

16. The whites and the yolks of the egg separate. _____

17. Because I need to pass this course. _____

18. Never lie to your mother. _____

19. Leaving the dishes in the sink, intending to wash them later. _____

20. Don't be stupid. _____

21. To support my family and needing a good job. _____

22. Wait for me. _____

23. Yet they were good parents. _____

24. What a foolish mistake! _____

25. When Pete left his station and took a ten-minute break. _____

Exercise 4f

Indicate the reason for each fragment by writing the appropriate letter in the blank. Write "S" for correct sentences.

    A. Fragment—there is no subject.
    B. Fragment—dependent clause.
    C. Fragment—verbal is used instead of a verb.
    D. Fragment—there is neither a subject nor a main verb.

1. Which is what he had intended to do. _____

2. When he left for the dance with Mary. _____

3. Wait for the doctor. _____

4. Going to the shore and having fun. _____

5. Nothing worthwhile there. _____

6. But a factor worthy of consideration. _____

7. The teacher having a slight heart murmur. _____

8. Insist on your rights. _____

9. Which Mary regretted for years. _____

10. Another foolish dream has come true for Mookie. _____

11. Having committed suicide in the prime of his life. _____

12. Add some liquid to your diet. _____

13. The odds of her being selected as slight. _____

14. A petty person, not worthy of consideration. _____

15. That is a terrible mistake. _____

16. If you decide to go to the dance, wash your face. _____

17. Jogging is good for your health. _____

18. Having a heart attack while jogging. _____

19. What is love? _____

20. Never trusting your friends as good advice. _____

Sentence strategies

Coordination: simple and compound sentences

A sentence is a group of words expressing a single idea, and two ideas that can be expressed in separate sentences often have a strong relationship between them. By increasing your knowledge and control of sentence structures, you will be able to express yourself in a variety of ways. Consider the following sentences: Jim loves his dog. The dog is big. The dog's name is Archie. Archie likes to play.

Although the preceding simple sentences are correct grammatically, the adult reader would question the maturity of the person who writes in such repetitive patterns and in such a deadly, monotonous style. Since the sentence is basic to designing effective forms for ideas, the writer must develop the ability to utilize various structures, patterns, and strategies. Sentences should be building, not stumbling, blocks.

Consider two possible revisions of the previous sentences:

Jim loves his big, playful dog, *Archie.* (appositive)
Jim loves Archie, *who is a big, playful dog.* (relative clause)

Just as a simple sentence is one independent clause, the compound sentence is formed by two or more independent clauses. Words used to join independent clauses are called *coordinating conjunctions: and, but, or, nor, for, yet, so.* "Coordinate" means of equal value or importance. Coordinate connectors join grammatical elements—subjects, verbs, objects, adverbs, phrases, clauses, and sentences:

We must hurry. We will miss the bus. (two simple sentences)
We must hurry or we will miss the bus. (coordination—compound sentence)
If we don't hurry, we will miss the bus. (subordination—complex sentence)

Coordinate conjunctions used in pairs are called correlatives:

both . . . and	whether . . . or
either . . . or	not . . . but (only)
neither . . . nor	not only . . . but (also)

And adds one thing to another.
But contrasts two things.
Or presents an alternative between two things.

Or is often used with *either; and* is often used with *both. Neither . . . nor* excludes both of the items mentioned. *Nor* is occasionally used alone.

George is *not only* charming *but also* intelligent.
not George is not only charming but is intelligent.
He wanted to buy sports equipment *either* from the Evert Corporation *or* the Spitz Company.
not He wanted either to buy sports equipment from the Evert Corporation or the Spitz Company.

Remember that coordination is correct only when the ideas are equal in importance. Faulty coordination often results from overusing *and.* Instead of using separate sentences, skillful writers combine sentence elements.

Poor: Bill had little formal education and he became a wealthy businessman.
Better: Bill had little formal education, *but* he became a wealthy businessman.
Although Bill had little formal education, he became a wealthy businessman. (subordination)
Poor: George didn't go to the conference. John didn't go to the conference.
Better: *Neither* George *nor* John went to the conference.
Poor: Tecumseh was one of the Indians' greatest leaders. Tecumseh was chief of the Shawnee nation.
Better: Tecumseh was chief of the Shawnee nation, *and* he was one of the Indians' greatest leaders. (coordination)
or: Tecumseh, *who was chief of the Shawnee nation,* was one of the Indians' greatest leaders. (subordination)
or: *Chief of the Shawnee nation,* Tecumseh was one of the Indians' greatest leaders. (appositive)

Exercise 4g

Coordinate the following sentences:

1. Bill enjoyed drinking beer. Mary enjoyed drinking ouzo.
2. John hated dancing. Mary loved to dance.
3. I did not go to the picnic. Rita did not go to the picnic.
4. The dog may go outside. The cat must stay in the house.
5. I joined the army. I wanted to defend my country.
6. Linda is the mother of two children. Linda is not married.
7. The money was not received. The water bill was not paid.
8. George washed the car. Pete cleaned the carburetor.
9. Sally said she had no money. Sally went to Atlantic City last week.
10. Garth can return to school. Garth can go to work.

Conjunctive adverbs may be used to connect independent clauses, to show a relationship between concepts, or to provide a transition from one concept to another. To join two independent clauses in a single sentence, the conjunctive adverb is often used with a semicolon:

> I was tired; *nevertheless,* I decided to continue my journey.
> (main clause semicolon conjunctive adverb comma main clause)

Conjunctive adverbs are alternate ways of expressing different concepts:

> *Time:* afterward, finally, later, meanwhile, next, soon, then, thereafter
> *Addition:* again, besides, furthermore, in addition, moreover, too
> *Reason, result, conclusion:* as a result, consequently, subsequently, surely, thus, therefore
> *Condition, qualification:* however, instead, nevertheless, otherwise, still
> *Comparison or contrast:* conversely, however, likewise, on the other hand, similarly, still
> *Illustration:* for example, for instance

Note that conjunctive adverbs may also be used parenthetically to express different concepts:

> She wasn't prepared, *however*, for the test, but she could not delay taking it. (*However* is used parenthetically.)
> She wasn't prepared for the test; *however*, she could not delay taking it. (*However* is used as a connector.)

When conjunctive adverbs do not join independent clauses, the semi-colon is not used:

> *incorrect* The little boy; however, refused to eat his spinach.
> *correct*   The little boy, however, refused to eat his spinach.

Even without the use of connectors, sentences may be joined by a semicolon if the succeeding sentence elaborates on the first sentence:

> George had to return to the market for one more item; he needed garlic for the spaghetti sauce.

Exercise 4h

Combine the following sentences using conjunctive adverbs.

1. Gregory was wounded in the battle. He continued to fight.

2. I went to the dance at eight o'clock. Sue joined me.

3. My insurance premium was not paid on time. The insurance company cancelled my policy.

4. I enjoy reading great American classics. I enjoy reading magazines like *Playboy.*

5. John is a great friend of mine. He let me borrow his car for the prom.

6. My car wouldn't start at seven A.M. I was late for my eight o'clock class.

7. I love the music of Elvis Presley. I admire the music of Richard Wagner.

8. Boris was a promiscuous man. Boris has contracted a serious social disease.

9. Mr. Jones is a demanding math teacher. The students consider him to be fair.

10. Pete was convinced Sue loved him. He bought an expensive diamond for her.

Exercise 4i

Using the coordination strategies discussed thus far, combine the following groups of sentences.

Robert E. Lee

1. Robert E. Lee was a Southerner.

2. Robert E. Lee was born in 1807.

3. Robert E. Lee died in 1870.

4. Robert E. Lee was a leader of the Confederacy.

5. Lee came from a distinguished family.

6. Lee came from a wealthy Virginia family.

7. Lee attended West Point.

8. Robert E. Lee graduated in 1829 with a perfect record.

9. In 1831 he married.

10. The woman he married was a great-granddaughter of Martha Washington.

11. Robert E. Lee acquired the estate of Arlington, Virginia.

12. The famous national military cemetery is now located at Arlington.

13. Lee could have lived a life of leisure.

14. Lee chose to remain in the United States Army.

15. Lee served in the army for the next thirty years.

16. The Civil War broke out in 1861.

17. Lee was asked by President Lincoln to command the Union Army.

18. Lee refused, with reluctance, to command the Union Army.

19. Lee decided to follow his native state of Virginia.

20. Lee had to break with the Union.

21. His decision was a heartbreaking one for Lee to make.

22. His decision was a great loss to the North.

23. A Union general said that the North lost by Lee's decision.

24. The loss was the equivalent of 50,000 men.

25. Lee fought for the South throughout the bloody war.

26. Lee was consistently outnumbered by the Yankee forces.

27. He was outnumbered in men and equipment.

28. Lee fought brilliantly.

29. Lee won battles that were almost miraculous victories.

30. Lee was a man of tact.

31. Lee was a man of unblemished moral character.

32. Lee withdrew from Richmond in the spring of 1865.

33. Richmond surrendered to Grant's troops.

34. Lee surrendered on April 9 at Appomattox Court House.

35. The Confederate troops had to surrender their weapons.

36. Grant permitted Lee's officers to keep their pistols.

37. Grant permitted Lee's officers to keep their swords.

38. The historic meeting ended.

39. Lee mounted his horse Traveler and rode off.

40. The long, bitter war was officially over.

Subordination: Complex and compound-complex sentences

A subordinate clause is a group of words with a subject(s) and a verb(s) that cannot stand by itself as a sentence. Dependent on an independent clause to complete the meaning of the sentence, subordinate clauses are classified as *noun, adjective,* and *adverb:*

Noun:	I do not know *who wrote the poem.* (object of *do know*)
	What he said was difficult to understand. (subject of the main clause)
Adjective:	People *who smoke cigarettes* are foolish. (relative clause modifying *People*)
	Ms. is a magazine *that I like to read.* (relative clause modifying *magazine*)
Adverb:	I went to bed early *because I was tired.* (answers the question *why*)
	While George was reading a book, his wife was watching television.

A sentence containing an independent clause and at least one subordinate clause is a *complex* sentence. A *compound-complex* sentence contains at least two independent clauses and at least one subordinate clause:

John played his favorite instrument, *which was the piano,*
        (main clause)   (subordinate clause)
but he also enjoyed playing the electric guitar *when his parents were*
        (main clause)   (subordinate clause)
not at home

Beginning writers often confuse subordinate clauses with sentences. A group of words that is punctuated as a sentence, but not grammatically complete, is referred to as a *sentence fragment.* Subordinate clauses cannot stand alone as sentences, and should be used to relate secondary details to the main idea of the sentence. The part of the sentence introduced by the subordinate conjunction is a *dependent clause.* Relative pronouns *(who, whom, which, that)* and subordinate conjunctions *(because,*

since, whereas, whether) may begin the subordinate clause which expresses an idea of lesser importance. The following are common subordinating
conjunctions, showing the variety of relationships that may be expressed:

Cause: because, in order that, if, since, so that
Contrast or concession: although, than, though, whereas, while
Time: after, as, as long as, before, once, since, until, when, whenever,
while
Place: where, wherever
Condition: as long as, if, provided that, unless, whether
Manner: as, as if, as though, how
Similarity: as

The preceding list may also be used as other parts of speech, depending on how they are used in the sentence. Only when they are used to
introduce a dependent clause are they referred to as subordinate conjunctions. Select the subordinate conjunction that conveys the exact
emphasis you wish to express.

Noun clauses and noun substitutes

A noun clause is a dependent clause which functions in the same way
that a noun functions: subject, object, indirect object, and so on. A noun
substitute may be classified as one of four types: infinitives (*to* plus a
verb); *-ing* nouns; *that* clauses; and *wh-* clauses.

What she said was a good idea. (The noun clause, *What she said,*
serves as the subject of the main clause.)
I liked *what the restaurant offered.* (The noun clause, *what the
restaurant offered,* is the direct object of the main clause, *I
liked.*)

The infinitive is denoted by the preposition *to,* which usually precedes a verb; sometimes, however, *to* must be implied. The infinitive may
be used as a noun, adjective, or an adverb.

I like *to run.* (*To run* functions as a noun, the direct object of like.)
To know him is *to detest* him. (*To know* is the subject of *is. To detest*
functions as a predicate nominative.)

As with infinitives, -*ing* nouns may be derived from verbs:

> The baby cried and shrieked. The theater patrons were annoyed.
> *or:* The baby's *crying* and *shrieking* annoyed the theater patrons.
> Pursuit of glory was a strange obsession with Alexander the Great.
> *or: Pursuing glory* was a strange obsession with Alexander the Great.

That clauses may also be used as noun substitutes:

> *That he had witnessed the crime* was certain.
> People have said *that they look forward to Friday.*

Noun clauses as subject:

> *Whatever he wrote* was artistic.
> *Why Bill ran from the scene* baffled the police.

Noun clauses as objects of verbs:

> The child was not sure *which toys were hers.*
> Bill didn't know *whether the dog was lost or in hiding.*

Noun clauses as objects of prepositions:

> Everything depended on *what she knew.*
> He walked to *where the concert was being held.*

Noun clauses as complements:

> The ghost was *what the boy had seen.*
> The problem was *who had kissed her.*

Noun clauses as objects of verbals:

> I heard Bill saying *that he had bought two turkeys.*
> The police were told *which gun had been used in the crime.*

Exercise 4j

Combine each set of sentences into a single sentence using at least one noun substitute.

Example: Someone purchases used clothing.
This is cheaper than buying new clothing.
Better: Purchasing used clothing is cheaper than buying new clothing.

Use -ing nouns in the following sentences:

A. A football team wins the Super Bowl. This is the crowning glory in professional football.

B. He pretended to be a student. He took part in all school activities. This helped to conceal his identity as a policeman.

C. Take the roots of Sea Holly. Grind it into powder. Add to the food. This will insure the person's love.

D. Wear the Tonka Bean around your neck. It is a powerful charm. It is found in the Guianas. It smells like the vanilla bean. The Tonka Bean may be used as a love charm or as a protective amulet.

Exercise 4k

Use infinitive phrases as noun substitutes in the following sentences.

Example: One enjoys the company of friends.
Good friends enrich one's life.
Better: To enjoy the company of good friends is to enrich one's life.

A. One lives on the farm. This means one wakes up early. This means one must go to bed early.

B. One must earn a good living. One must work hard and long hours to earn a good living. One must survive in this society.

C. One needs protection against the Evil Eye. Wear a turquoise stone. This will help protect against the Evil Eye. This will help one attain good fortune.

Exercise 4l

Use noun clauses to combine the following groups of sentences.

Example: Mary wanted the love of a good man.
This would complete her life.
Better: What Mary wanted to complete her life was the love of a good man.

A. The restaurant has a good menu. The food is excellent. I like to eat in such a place.

B. Bill saw the accident. Mary saw the crash, too. The police asked them for information.

C. The English teacher stood at the blackboard. She explained the punctuation rules to the students. The students did not understand the rules.

D. Mookie wanted to go to live in Paw Paw, West Virginia. People are nice there. Life is simple. And the hunting is good.

E. Mary didn't like Rock music until last year. She thought Rock music was too loud with stupid lyrics. Then she took a course in Music Appreciation. She knows more now.

Absolute phrases

Another effective option in sentence combining is the absolute phrase—a noun or pronoun followed by a participle—which modifies the statement as whole:

> *All things considered,* it is a good day for a picnic.
> *Her temper rising,* Sue threw the flowers on the floor.

Sometimes the participle is omitted, but it is understood: *The dinner (being) over,* we drove home.

Appositives

A word, phrase, or clause which renames, identifies, or explains a noun or a noun equivalent is known as an appositive, from the Latin *appositus,* "situated near."

> My mother, *a dancer,* is appearing on Broadway. (*A dancer* is in apposition to *mother.*)
> Mary had three things on her mind—*a big car, a soft fur, and money.* (*A big car, a soft fur, and money* are in apposition to *things.*)
> The wino's dream—that he would get a bottle of wine—was shattered. *(That he would get a bottle of wine* is in apposition to *dream.)*

Participial phrases

Derived from a verb, the participle acts as a modifier (Chapter 3, page 241). If used correctly, the participial phrase provides concise and effective writing strategies.

> The Greeks fought courageously.
> Then they rejoiced.
> Better: *Having fought courageously,* the Greeks rejoiced.
> Sue was tired after work.
> She went right to bed.
> Better: *Tired after work,* Sue went right to bed.

Exercise 4m

Using the sentence combining strategies discussed in this chapter, combine the following groups of sentences.

Tonka Wakon, My Pet

1. Tonka is an Alaskan Malamute.
2. The Malamute is a relatively young breed.
3. The Malamute has been recognized by the American Kennel Club for one hundred years.

4. This breed was bred from wolves.
5. Their background is important to their character.
6. They are strong, hardy, and massive animals.
7. They have been used for hauling freight across the frozen wastes.
8. They also make a great one-family dog.
9. They are loyal.
10. They are fierce protectors.
11. Through experience, I have found them to be highly intelligent and sensitive animals.

12. I felt my pet should have a special name.
13. I used a city in Alaska.
14. The breed originated in Alaska.
15. The rest of her name was taken from the Appaloosa horse.
16. This horse is descended from wild mustangs in the Nez Perce Indian Territory of North America, named Tonka Wakon.
17. Tonka's head measures nine inches across from ear to ear.
18. Tonka's jaw extends six inches from between the eyes to the tip of her black nose.
19. Tonka's teeth are ivory-white with a jagged appearance along the sides.
20. Tonka's eyes are medium brown, clear, and alert.

21. Tonka's ears are short and thick and stand stiffly erect.

22. Short, thick, white fur lines the inside of Tonka's ears.

23. A defined black trim outlines the edges of her ears.

24. Her neck is twenty-five inches in circumference.

25. Tonka stands thirty inches to the shoulder and thirty-two inches long from the base of the neck to the base of her seventeen-inch long tail.

26. Tonka's chest tapers back to thirty-two inches at the hind quarters.

27. Tonka's body is basically black.

28. Silver marks her shoulders.

29. Her back has a cotton-like off-white fur.

30. This fur underlies the coarse, two-inch black over-coating.

31. Her thick fur keeps her warm in even the most inclement weather.

32. Her tail flaps over her back like a plume.

33. The underside of the tail is an off-white.

34. A dab of white is at the very tip of her tail.

35. This dab of white looks as though it was dipped in white paint.

36. Tonka's legs are muscular.

37. They are white at the bottom.

38. The white trails off to nothing at the back of the upper part of the hips.

39. The hips are black.

40. A streak of light brown extends halfway down her legs.

41. Her deeply rooted claws are as thick as a lead pencil.

42. Her claws are sharp enough to dig into the ice.

43. This insures a good footing.

44. The thick fur on her stomach is a glistening greyish-white.

45. Tonka is a hefty animal.

46. She is not overweight.

47. She weighs a trim one hundred and seventy pounds.

48. She looks sweet and friendly.

49. Her temperament changes quickly when a stranger approaches.

50. This seemingly placid animal becomes a fierce opponent.

Chapter 5

Marks of Punctuation

The period

The period is usually utilized *to terminate a sentence* which asserts something (declarative): My father smoked cigars for fifty years.

A period may be used after an *imperative sentence:* Please sit down and begin reading your assignments.

A period may be used after an *indirect question:* The ravishing woman asked me if I would take her to lunch.

Use a period after a standard abbreviation:

> Mr. and Mrs. Peter J. Sellers
> Peter Panda, M.D.
> lbs. (pounds)
> pp. (pages)

Use a period before a decimal, to separate dollars and cents, and to precede cents written alone.

> 3.4 percent
> $31.17
> $ .19

Use three spaced periods (ellipsis) to show an intentional omission in the text of prose or poetry.

> The professor talked for hours about love, violence . . . until he
>   fell asleep.
> ". . . he flung the stars across the sky / And set a path for each to
>   fly . . . . "

At the end of a complete sentence, add a fourth period to show termination if the ellipsis is used.

A question mark or exclamation point may follow the ellipsis periods.

Do not use the ellipsis periods as a mere stylistic device.

Do not use a period after titles or subheadings.

Do not use a period after a quotation mark preceded by a period:

Mary whispered, "Come up to my room, later.". (incorrect)

The period (or the comma) *always* goes within quotation marks, *never under or outside* quotation marks:

Pete said, "I refuse to go with you."

The comma

Use a comma when a pause is necessary.

Generally, this rule applies but should be used with discretion. (Obviously, if someone suffers from emphysema or stuttering, the rule must be considered invalid.)

Use a comma:

To set off introductory words, phrases, and clauses:

Nevertheless, it is an option.
After the storm, we went to the dance.
When the girl smiled, we felt better.

To set off items in a series:

In grammar, a "series" means three or more items; the number of commas should be one less than the number of items in the series.

George, Pete, and Rhonda were reading their notes.
The cat purred, stretched, and jumped from the couch.
The sheriff asked us why we were speeding, where we had come from, and why we were drinking while driving.

To set off non-restrictive elements:

My father, a coal miner, is eighty years old. (appositive)
My father, who is a coal miner, is eighty years old. (non-restrictive adjective clause)
The book was written by Dr. Noreen Hayes, our department chairman. (appositive)

To join main clauses when a coordinate conjunction is present:

> He refused to pay for the furniture, *for* several pieces were
> damaged.
> *Note:* If a subordinate conjunction is used, the comma is not
> necessary unless the subordinate clause is unduly long: He
> refused to pay for the furniture *because* several pieces were
> damaged.

To separate coordinate adjectives before a noun:
Adjectives are *coordinate* when one can substitute their order logically:

> The tall, dark stranger whispered in a low, menacing voice.
> The dark, tall stranger whispered in a menacing, low voice.

To set off absolutes:

> Her eyes moist with desire, Sue looked at him helplessly.

To set off contrasting elements:

> It was a matter of pride, not greed.

To set off parenthetical (interrupting) words and phrases:

> I will, of course, attend the game.
> This plan, however, will not succeed.

To separate a person's name from a title or degree after it:

> Jon Loff, M.A.
> George Brown, M.D.

To set off items in a date or address:

> We celebrate July 4, 1776, as Independence Day.
> My address is 243 Utah Avenue, Cumberland, Maryland 21502

Use a comma in direct address in a greeting and in the closing of a letter:

> Dear Sarah,
> Sincerely yours,

> *Note:* If open punctuation is used in business correspondence,
> the comma is omitted in the salutation and complimen-
> tary close.

Use a comma after the verb of saying in dialogue:

Pete groaned, "I can't make it, Sue!"
In a trembling voice, Maria whispered, "Gee, that was good."

Avoid comma splices in formal composition and business correspondence. The joining of independent clauses with a comma in place of a coordinate conjunction reflects sloppy writing and hazy thinking. Do not commit such serious errors.

He is going, I am going. (comma splice error)

There are several ways to correct comma splices. The easiest way is simply by using the semicolon instead of the comma: He is going; I am going. *Or,* you may use coordination: He is going and I am going. *Or,* you may end one main clause with a period and begin another sentence: He is going. I am going.

Do not separate the subject from the verb with a comma:

Students who study, should pass easily. (incorrect)
Students who study should pass easily. (correct)

Avoid superfluous (unnecessary) commas:

He is a happy, and generous man. (incorrect)
He is a happy and generous man. (correct)

Pairs of subjects are not separated by commas:

George Custer, and his army were massacred by the Sioux. (incorrect)
George Custer and his army were massacred by the Sioux. (correct)

A pair of verbs should not be separated by commas:

The baby screamed, and cried over the broken toy. (incorrect)
The baby screamed and cried over the broken toy. (correct)

Do not separate a pair of direct objects with a comma:

Mary devoured the chicken, and potatoes quickly. (incorrect)
Mary devoured the chicken and potatoes quickly. (correct)

A pair of phrases should not be separated by commas:

> Rita sauntered across the parking lot, and into Pete's waiting automobile. (incorrect)
> Rita sauntered across the parking lot and into Pete's waiting automobile. (correct)

Two Common Mechanical Problems

The Comma Splice (CS)	*The Fused Sentence (FS)*
The mood was peaceful, the only light was moonlight.	The mood was peaceful the only light was moonlight.

Both the comma splice and the fused sentence occur between the two main clauses in compound or compound-complex sentences. In the case of the comma splice, *only* a comma is used to join the two clauses, to *splice* them together. In the case of the fused sentence, nothing is used between the two main clauses; therefore, they are said to be fused.

Some Solutions

1. Make two simple sentences: The mood was peaceful. The only light was moonlight.
   (This results in short, childlike sentences which may be undesirable.)
2. Make a compound sentence by adding a conjunction *or* by using a semicolon.   The mood was peaceful, for the only light was moonlight.
   The mood was peaceful; the only light was moonlight.
   (Use the semicolon sparingly, for it may confuse less-skilled readers.)
3. Make a complex sentence by subordinating one clause,   The mood was peaceful since the only light was moonlight.
   (a loose construction)
   Because the only light was moonlight, the mood was peaceful.
   (a periodic construction)
   by reducing one clause to a phrase,   The mood was peaceful with only moonlight.
   (prepositional)
   The mood was peaceful, being only moonlit.
   (participial)
   to an absolute,   The mood was peaceful, the only light moonlight.
   or an appositive when appropriate.

Note: Punctuation for *then*

> Incorrect: I took a nap, then I got up. (comma splice error)
> Remedies: I took a nap and then I got up.
>   I took a nap; then I got up.

Exercise 5a

Correct the following sentences. Explain your answers by citing the previous rules.

1. However I do consider Ginger my wife to be totally submissive.

2. Gregors refused to eat the food but drank the milk.

3. His large eyes glistening with lust Sam plunged into the dessert.

4. My sister who is a school teacher is a grouchy person.

5. The dog stretched yawned and bolted upright when he heard the noise.

6. The book was written by Renaldo Gonzalez our drinking companion.

7. The drunk wanted to know where we were going why we were in a hurry and why we refused to give him any money.

8. After the bitter altercation we left the tavern.

9. We left the tavern after the bitter altercation.

10. Babies who eat their cereal, are probably bored.

Exercise 5b

Correct the following sentences.

1. The speakers included a judge a doctor a politician and a rehabilitated addict.

2. Swimming jogging and boating are good healthful physical activities.

3. It was difficult to study when the television was blaring when the dog was barking and when the baby was bawling.

4. We delivered shoes clothes food medicine and Bibles to the savages.

5. Great cities in ancient Greece were Athens Sparta Thebes Corinth and Delos.

6. Go to the market and buy razor blades bread cakes beer a box of tissues a bag of dog food and toothpaste.

7. In spite of everything George was good in English history science and study hall.

8. With the food they had stolen from the Indians the Pilgrims survived the winter.

9. When she finished cooking the food was set on the table.

10. When Pete finished the test was scored and graded.

Exercise 5c

Insert or delete commas in the following sentences.

1. After the argument I left for the local bar to drown my sorrows.

2. She was one of the prettiest girls, I knew, but she had no personality.

3. He bought a battered rusty ten year old convertible.

4. In 1941 Japan bombed Pearl Harbor an act that shocked the world.

5. Instead of forgiving him she left the room and went to bed.

6. Poe was a morbid gloomy, writer but he must have been a fascinating man.

7. Mary come into the living room.

8. Katherine Ann Porter was born on May 15, 1890 in Indian Creek Texas.

9. The American flag is red, white and blue.

10. She was surprised not angry.

Exercise 5d

Insert or delete commas in the following sentences.

1. A purebred dog, trained and gentle and smart was what he wanted.

2. The Indians, surrounding Custer were bent on revenge.

3. She is a virtuous woman a woman of decency who deserves a better fate.

4. The storm finally over we hurried to the car, and snuggled under the blankets.

5. The piña colada was an icy sweet refreshing, concoction.

6. Paul said, that he hated teaching.

7. He journeyed from Columbus, Ohio in the spring to Cumberland, Maryland in the fall.

8. My purpose at ACC, is to pursue a career in nursing.

9. Fatso McGee, the obese fierce captain of the football team failed English.

10. The harder she tried to write her essay the more difficult it became.

Exercise 5e

Correct the punctuation in the following sentences.

1. Pete went out with his buddies his homework was done.

2. Her wrists bound; the woman was bending over the chasm.

3. Running down the smooth trunk of the elephant's tusk; a black spider searching for its mate spied a small cockroach crawling, near the tusk.

4. Betty's room was in a chaotic mess stinking socks were lying on the dresser makeup was scattered upon the floor, the bedsheets were dirty.

5. Yesterday I took my wife to the movies something I hadn't done in years.

6. I bought the jelly beans for my group of great congenial friends including Sam and Archie.

7. Goober lifted his sandwich caressed it and carried it out with him.

8. An infamous seducer of women; Casanova was a disgusting person.

9. Pistachio the puppy looked at his master waited and finally went to bed.

10. His grimy callused hands at his side Gus stood still his every muscle anticipating violence.

The semicolon

A semicolon separates parts of equal rank: Sentence; sentence.
A semicolon joins two independent clauses that are closely related:

The stew is good; the noodles are excellent.

A semicolon joins two independent clauses when the second begins with a conjunctive adverb: I had no trouble with the assignment; however, I collapsed after the exam.

A semicolon is used between items in a series when one or more of the items include commas: There were several writers at the conference: George Smith, the famous novelist; Gretta Garner, the short story writer; Peter Lovelace, the infamous poet.

Do not use a semicolon between a main clause and a dependent clause.

I love you; because you're wealthy. (incorrect)
I have no intention of going to the dance; if it starts to rain.
    (incorrect)

Do not use a semicolon between a phrase and a main clause.

To guarantee safety; George tightened the line. (incorrect)
Pete enjoyed the following; swimming at night; jogging during the day; and weightlifting. (incorrect)

Exercise 5f

Correct the following sentences.

1. I was tired, nevertheless I decided to go.

2. Purchase the following items; corn; milk; and bread.

3. These people were hired, George Jones, M.D., Mary Wishbin, R.N., Peggy Haywire, psychologist.

4. I hope you go to the party; because I'm going to be there too.

5. I hope to enjoy the sun at the beach, I also hope to go dancing at night with Tonga the jungle boy.

6. He came; however, a day late.

7. The wind was blowing the shutters began rattling the baby began crying.

8. When the storm was over; the people began to reappear.

9. George found it difficult to concentrate when the radio was on; and when his parents argued.

10. Julius Caesar came, he saw, he conquered Rome.

The colon

A colon means "as follows."
Use a colon to introduce a word, a series, or an explanation related to the previous statement: All of her thoughts centered on one objective: marriage.

There are many ways to travel: driving, flying, and sailing.

Use a colon to introduce a quotation, usually three lines or more.

The poet said: "It's better to have loved and lost
Than never to have loved at all."

Use a colon after the salutation in a business letter (except for open punctuation):

Dear Sir:
Dear Dr. Hayes:

Use a colon to separate hours from minutes when the time is shown in numerals:

5:30 a.m.
12:30 p.m.

Use a colon to separate chapter from verse when citing the Bible:

John 25:13

Do not use a colon to separate a preposition from its object.

Pete's courses consisted of: math, English, and biology. (incorrect)
Pete's courses consisted of math, English, and biology. (correct)

Do not use a colon to separate a linking verb and the subjective complement.

His favorite topics are: wine, women, and song. (incorrect)
His favorite topics are wine, women, and song. (correct)

Exercise 5g

Correct the following sentences.

1. Mary was frightened by a mysterious sound; the creaking of a shutter.
2. Pete bought: a watch, a ring, and a wallet.
3. For hours, Pete mused over one delicious thought; Georgia loved him.
4. Patton fought with this credo; never retreat.
5. Cyrano's most obvious protuberance was: his nose.
6. At 1100 a.m., Sue will be arriving.
7. The student council received money from: students and faculty.
8. He never forgot the name of his first love; Ruth.
9. The flag is: red, white, and blue.
10. To Whom It May Concern

The hyphen

Use a hyphen to syllabicate a word at the end of a line: John is performing tonight.

Use a hyphen when two or three words are used as a single unit: She was wearing a bluish-green sweater.

Use a hyphen in compounds in which the second element is capitalized: The riot was caused by a pro-Iranian mob.

Use a hyphen in compounds containing prepositional phrases: My mother-in-law is a kindly old lady.

Use a hyphen in compounds containing the prefix self: The machine had a self-starting device.

Use a hyphen when necessary to prevent confusion of similar words: The calvary re-formed ranks before charging again.

Use a hyphen in most compound adjectives and adverbs: Janus was a two-faced Roman goddess.

Use a hyphen in compound numbers from twenty-one to ninety-nine: She was forty-five years old.

The hyphen is used between the numerator and the denominator of fractions when the fraction is used as an adjective; when the fraction is used as a noun, no hyphen is necessary.

> Two thirds of the students voted.
> Pete was the winner by a two-thirds vote.

The dash

The dash (two hyphens) is used for emphasis: She had but one purpose in life—to marry a wealthy old man.

A dash may be used to set off a final appositive or summary, regardless of its form: He realized the importance of the doctor's words—cancer of the tongue.

> Teddy had one more goal in life—to be elected President.
> George could remember only one thing—Ruth loved him.

A dash may be used to set off a parenthetical element that is relevant to the sentence: His many faults—dishonesty, laziness, and deceit—cost him his beloved family.

Sometimes either a dash or a colon may be used with the same result:

> She had one fault which caused her grades to suffer:
> procrastination.
> She had one fault which caused her grades to suffer—
> procrastination.

Note: *Do not* overuse the dash in formal writing; it is effective only when used sparingly.

Exercise 5h

Supply the dash where necessary in the following sentences.

1. The union included coal miners, plumbers, janitors, all types of workers.

2. Pete's infatuation with Paula, he had seen her at the party, was the source of great misery for his wife.

3. We can never forget the greatest of the Greek philosophers Socrates.

4. He had only one purpose in life to win her hand in marriage.

5. The dash is basically used for one purpose emphasis.

Reviewing quotation marks and punctuation

1. Commas and periods always come *before* quotation marks.

2. Semicolons and colons come *after* quotation marks.

3. If the quoted material is a direct question or exclamation, the question and exclamation marks come before the final quotation marks.

4. If the quoted material is an indirect question and exclamation, the question and exclamation marks appear after the final quotation marks.

Exercise 5i

Punctuate the following lines of dialogue.

1. I am tired Mary said and I want to go home.

2. Diana told me that she was about to be engaged to Bougars.

3. She is the ugliest broad I've ever seen whispered Tom.

4. He smiled as he looked at her with worn passion whispering in her dandruff encrusted ear yeah the guy who said the best things in life are free was sure right.

5. There is no need to get angry Pete shouted because I'm leaving now.

The exclamation point

Use the exclamation point at the end of an exclamatory sentence: I was overjoyed to see her after twenty years!

Use the exclamation point after the words, phrases, or clauses that express strong feelings or emotions: Good Lord! What a disgusting performance!

The question mark

Use a question mark after a direct question: Would you like to share my potato chips?

Use a question mark inside parenthesis to indicate doubt or uncertainty about the correctness of some element: Homer, the great Greek poet, lived in the ninth century B.C. (?) and wrote *The Iliad.*

In business correspondence, a polite request is often followed by a period instead of a question mark: May we expect an immediate response concerning this matter.

Do not use the question mark after an indirect question:

Sue asked me if I would take her to the dance? (incorrect)
Sue asked me if I would take her to the dance. (correct)

Parentheses

Use parentheses to enclose words, phrases, or sentences that offer commentary or clarification:

William appeared (unfortunately) at the meeting.
Oedipus was guilty of hybris (arrogant pride).
Enclosed is a check for fifty dollars ($50.00) to settle the account.

A parenthetical sentence within another sentence does not need a capital or a period:

Cupid (the Greeks knew him as Eros) was the god of passionate love.

A comma may follow parentheses but does not precede it:

After drinking the hemlock (a form of execution in fifth-century Athens), Socrates consoled his grieving friends.

Use parentheses to enclose numerals or letters in a list: Community colleges are popular today for several reasons: (1) reasonable tuition fees, (2) geographical proximity, (3) university acceptance of credit hours, and (4) wide offerings in technical and career fields.

Exercise 5j

Use parentheses where necessary in the following sentences.

1. The escaped convict who was wanted for murdering Jimmy Jingles was captured in Cumberland.

2. The richest man in town George Goldbrick wrote out a check for one dollar $1.00 to the United Way.

3. Pete Goober inherited one thousand dollars $1000.00 from his aunt.

4. Among those attending the party were Zoe Plummer a retired nurse John Beddfellow a retired English teacher and Cyrus Marlow a retired prison warden.

5. In typing, create a dash with two hyphens—without spacing before or after.

Brackets [ ]

Brackets are used only when the writer interpolates his own clarification or interpretation of the material he is quoting.

"Tragedy [goat song] in Greece was predominantly a product of Athenian culture."

The Latin word sic [thus] should be used in quoted material where a misspelled word occurs in the text.

> "Poe was a quite fellow [sic] who wrote good horror stories."
> "Billy the Kidd [sic] was a vicious killer."

Quotation marks

Use double quotation marks to enclose material quoted and in dialogue.

> "God!" he shouted. "What I have suffered because of that woman!"
> John F. Kennedy said, "Ask not what your country can do for you, but what you can do for your country."

Use double quotes to set off words and phrases not taken on a literal level: His face was "as red as a beet."

Use quotation marks for titles of magazines and newspaper articles, essays, short stories, short poems, chapters in books, and slang expressions.

> I enjoyed reading Carl Sandburg's poem, "Chicago."
> "The Fall of the House of Usher," a short story by Poe, is exciting.
> Mary "flipped out" when she saw her English teacher in a bathing suit.

Use single quotation marks to enclose a quotation within a quotation.

> During the lecture, Dr. Smith asked, "What did Leonidas mean when he said to the Persians, 'Good, then we'll fight in the shade'?"

The period and the comma appear within quotes:

> He said, "I am tired."
> "I am tired," he said, "and I want to go home."

A colon or a semicolon appear outside quotation marks:

> General Douglas MacArthur said, "I shall return"; then he left for Australia.

Exercise 5k

Insert the dash, parentheses, or brackets where necessary in the following sentences.

1. Rousseau's illegitimate children he said there were five were deposited in an orphanage.

2. Joe Namath a quarterback at one time with the New York Jets was a great passer.

3. Oedipus which means cleft foot was guilty of *hamartia* tragic error.

4. James Fenimore Cooper's greatest novel *The Last of the Mohicans* dealt with a noble Indian chief.

5. The velour shirt costs fourteen dollars and fifty cents $14.50 and the belt seven ninety-five $7.95.

6. The Kamikaze divine wind pilots were brave, fierce fighters.

7. The Trojan War 1194-1184 B.C. was Homer's theme in *The Iliad*.

8. Fat by any standards he weighed 350 pounds George devoured cream-puffs daily.

9. The head of the department Dr. Portly Porter earned his doctorate in Assyrian Literature.

10. Gloria had only one goal in life marriage.

11. Bad breath halitosis is inexcusable.

12. The German blitzkrieg lightning war was effective in the early years of World War II.

13. The dash is used primarily to convey one element emphasis.

14. The most popular airline in Europe TWA is noted for 1 comfort 2 safety and 3 cheap fares.

15. "If you're looking for advise sic, see your neighborhood priest."

16. D.H. Lawrence's novels *Lady Chatterley's Lover, Sons and Lovers* appeal to the prurient.

17. You are a good student, Miss what is your name, by the way?

18. Pete Gordon amused himself by writing for the *Commodore* a newspaper in Paw Paw, West Virginia.

19. Charles Dickens wrote a heart-warming story about a crippled boy and a mean miser in his popular work "A Christmas Carol."

20. By the time the Trojan War ended it lasted ten years thousands of brave men had perished.

Chapter 6

The Apostrophe

The apostrophe is used to indicate the possessive case of nouns, to mark omissions in contractions, and to form certain plurals.

Use the apostrophe and s to form the possessive case of nouns.
Add an apostrophe and s to singular nouns:

the lady's hat   the man's hat   the child's toy

Add an apostrophe only in plural nouns ending in s:

the ladies' hats   the Joneses' house

Add an apostrophe and s to plural nouns not ending in s:

the children's toys   the men's horses

In joint possession, add an apostrophe and s after the last noun:

Mary and John's car is in the garage. (Mary and John own the car jointly.)

With individual ownership, add an apostrophe and s after each noun:

Mary's and John's cars are in the garage. (Each has a car in the garage.)

In compound nouns, add an apostrophe and s after the last word of the compound element:

My father-in-law's car is in the garage. (singular possessive)

An apostrophe is not used for possessive pronouns (his, hers, its, ours, yours, theirs, whose), *nor for plural nouns that are not in the possessive case:*

> Let's visit the Joneses.
> He invited the Smiths to the party.

Use an apostrophe to reflect omissions in contracted words and numerals. Place the apostrophe at the point where the omission occurs.

> It's late. (It is late.)
> I'll go. (I will go.)
> It is ten o'clock.

Use an apostrophe and an s to form the plural of lower-case letters, figures, symbols, abbreviations, and words referred to as words.

> 1980's or 1980s
> p's and q's
> the class of '76
> but's

Use the apostrophe to show omissions of letters in dialogue.

> Pete shouted, "I ain't goin' to the dance, so are you comin' or not?"

Use an apostrophe and s to form the possessive of indefinite and impersonal pronouns:

> everyone's duty
> another's problems
> someone's wallet
> everybody's right
> someone else's headache

Exercise 6a

Insert or omit the apostrophe in the following sentences.

1. The two nurses testimony proved the doctor was a scoundrel.

2. Her mother-in-laws temper was annoying.

3. Pete earned seven As and two Bs.

4. A churches steeple is inspiring.

5. She was an expert on childrens' problems.

6. The Jones's gave a party last night.

7. The dog chewed its' collar.

8. It is'nt difficult to prepare for tomorrows' exam.

9. The five churches steeples were gold.

10. He earned three weeks pay.

11. He bought a pennies' worth of candy.

12. Mr. Smiths' problem was his wifes spending habits'.

13. The soldiers helmets glistened at inspection.

14. The Smith's decided to paint their house.

15. Its no one elses business.

16. Those books' are our's.

17. I have'nt time to go to the Joneses house.

18. I cant wait 'till its' time to go home.

19. Ill love you til the rivers' run dry, darlin.

20. The American suburbs problems are many.

Exercise 6b

Correct the following sentences. Circle the incorrect words and write your corrections above the words.

1. Its' ten oclock.

2. Watch your ps and qs.

3. The attorney generals decision was firm.

4. These dollars' are hers'.

5. Ulysses travels are famous.

6. The football players' suffered from an Achilles heel.

7. Dot you'r is and cross your ts.

8. I strayed into Dr. Hayes yard.

9. Arent you callin a wrong number?

10. We eagerly awaited Bill's and John's arrival.

11. It was Pete who's degree was in mathematics'.

12. Add up the 8s in the total.

13. Several student's attended his funeral.

14. It was they're problem.

15. The IRS investigated several company's books.

16. It was an old wives tale.

17. I have the Supreme's first record.

18. The Negroes problems' are serious.

19. Those lady's hats are ridiculous.

20. Who stole Billy Adams wallet?

21. The three commander-in-chiefs made the decision.

22. There were hundreds of passerbys in the mall.

23. The class of 33 met in the cemeterys Antique Pavilion.

24. April Fools' Day is for a fools' enjoyment.

25. Lets go visit the Jones' and the Smiths'.

26. I'ld like to go to Barnabys' party.

27. Their just isnt any justice.

28. Give me a dollars' worth of dog food.

29. The Hamiltons' left their lights' on.

30. I didn't read the letters' content's.

Exercise 6c

Correct the following sentences. Circle the incorrect words and write your corrections above the words.

1. Everybodys going to the dinner at Miriams house.

2. Boris wasnt permitted to go to the reunion of the class of 85.

3. Didnt Roosevelts administration start in 34?

4. The Jones bought their new car at Prices Used Cars.

5. If you tell Pete whose going, III tell you whose paid for dinner.

6. Women have been fighting for their rights for centurys.

7. They we're fighting for what was theres.

8. Ladys should obey their husbands wishes in all thing's.

9. The mother's should take care of they're baby's needs.

10. Childrens' work improves when their happy.

11. The United State's army is proud of it's heritage.

12. Washington, D.C., has two zoos and many species'.

13. Give me a pennies' worth of candy.

14. The bank financed Rita and Steves' house.

15. I cant resist Marys' beauty, even though theres no chance for me.

16. My mother-in-laws temper is someone elses headache now.

17. Girls' and ladies hats are no longer popular today.

18 Lets' visit the Smiths house and then go to the Barnes' house.

19. Moses laws were handed down in "bibliographical" times.

20. Several hero's medals were awarded to the soldiers wives.

21. Its the parents' fault when they're childrens' problems are severe.

22. Its bad when three weeks work is wasted.

23. The actresses roles in the play were they're best work.

24. Georges profits' are greater than last years.

25. The stockholder's meetings were delayed because of several crisises.

▮ Chapter 7 ▮

Capitalization

Capitalize all proper nouns and proper adjectives.
Names of persons are capitalized:

> Leonidas, King of Sparta
> William Shakespeare
> ex-President Richard M. Nixon

Capitalize geographical, political, and racial words.

> Greece, Grecian, Greco
> Negroes, Negroid
> Empire State Building
> Maryland
> the Republican Party

Capitalize names of days of the week, months, holidays.

> Sunday
> July
> Easter
> April Fool's Day
> St. Patrick's Day

Capitalize literary titles except for unimportant words such as prepositions and conjunctions. If the preposition or conjunction is five letters or more, capitalize such words.

> *The Old Man and the Sea*
> "Stopping by Woods on a Snowy Evening"

Capitalize the word God and the pronouns referring to God.

I believe in God. Don't you believe in Him?

Capitalize historical events, laws, organizations, governmental departments and agencies.

> the Constitution of the United States
> the Federal Bureau of Investigation
> the State Department
> the Crusades
> Prohibition

Capitalize the first word of every sentence.

> Capitalize the first word of every line of poetry (usually).
> Capitalize the first word of a direct quotation.
> Capitalize the first word of the salutation and complimentary
> close in a business letter.

Capitalize titles prefixed to names of people.

> President Reagan
> Senator George Goobers
> Sir Laurence Olivier
> General Patton

Do not capitalize the names of the seasons.
Do not capitalize common nouns unless they are used as proper nouns.

> I am going to college in the spring.
> I am going to Allegany Community College in the spring.

Exercise 7a

Capitalize the necessary words in the following sentences.

1. Pete missed his class in biology lab to attend a baseball game at three rivers stadium.

2. The class was studying in history 101 how american negroes suffered during the period of slavery in the south.

3. I read the july issue of playboy magazine last night. it was a revelation.

4. He wanted to celebrate mother's day with a bottle of black velvet.

5. The ex-president of the united states appeared with his mother at carnegie hall.

6. The thirty-third meeting of alcoholics anonymous met at the holiday inn on december 5.

7. Have you read the article hollywood and cocaine in the reader's digest?

8. George bought a mercedes benz from bankrupt motors the day before easter.

9. Did you watch the Pittsburgh steelers defeat the dallas cowboys on colored television?

10. John earned an a for his term paper dealing with dramatic irony in sophocles' play oedipus tyrannus.

Exercise 7b

Provide the necessary punctuation and capitalization in the following sentences.

1. Katherine a. porter who wrote a short story entitled he was born in indian creek texas on may 15, 1890.

2. Her father garrison porter moved the family to kyle texas when his wife mary alice jones died.

3. When her grandmother died in 1910 katherine ann went to a convent school in louisiana.

4. When she was sixteen she ran away and married a rich man who she said shut me up in a big house.

5. Three years later she divorced him and made her way to chicago to find freedom.

6. At the age of twenty one she became a reporter for a chicago newspaper and managed to get a job as an actress at ten dollars a day.

7. Later she learned to sing dance and perform on stages in Chicago fort worth and austin texas.

8. A rebel but a talented literary artist miss porter won a guggenheim fellowship and traveled to europe in 1931.

9. She is best known for her short stories flowering judas and noon wine.

10. She died of a stroke on September 1980 at college park maryland.

Exercise 7c

In the following paragraph, correct the errors in punctuation, capitalization, and spelling.

1. My favorite scape goats are the kids who walk to school during a rainy

2. morning you know when the guters are gluted with streems of rain water

3. and the little buggers are walking to school along the side walk and

4. its' really pouring. When i see this situation i jump into my old

5. chevrolay and take off down the street my wheels just churnin up the

6. water especially the pudles in the pot wholes. I see the little

7. rascals jumpin away from the spray of dirty water: as their hurryin

8. to School. They see me in my car comin down the road but I deliber-

9. ately slow down to give them a false sense of Security. Just as they

10. turn their backs on me; I gun my trusty vehicle thru the pudles and

11. streems along the street sprayin their wet little legs and boddies

12. with a suden water fall of grittie rain water. They screem at me

13. as I splash by; there little fists shakin courses at me, impotent

14. oathes herled in the wind. Drenched, soaked to the skin, they must

15. return home for dry clothes or rush into the Schoolhouse, to avoid

16. me, Rotten ronnie as I crews the wet streets all mornin. Until the

17. guters are dry.

18. I simply detest Sunny days!

Exercise 7d

Correct the errors in punctuation, capitalization, and spelling in the following sentences.

1. The moulin rouge a cabaret in paris is famis for wine womin, and song.

2. The following members were present; pete peterson md. georgia gurk rn bruno brewer local alcoholic james d diggers respected international swindler and peggy pangloss renowned gossipp columist.

3. Unfortunatly billy briar has been comitted to the section eight ward at kindly harts hospitol on hawire street in Pittsburg pensylvania.

4. Dostoevsky's masterpiece as you know is notes' from the underground.

5. The crowds had gatherd the rope was thrown over a sterdy branch of the hanging tree billy the banditt gaunt and Stoic waited patiently atop the sadle.

6. General george armstrong custer perished at the battle of the little big horn a victim of the indian wars in the west.

7. With the defeet of darius alexander the great became supreeme rooler in the east.

8. Sally trembled as she walked into the last chance tavern her lips quivering.

9. His seventh army surounded by german tanks general patton devised a blitz of his own.

10. In the sherwood forest you will find snakes creeping deer leeping and boids tweetting.

▌ Chapter 8 ▌

Case of Pronouns

Case refers to the form of a pronoun—subjective, objective, possessive—which shows its relationship to other words in a sentence.

Subjective or nominative pronouns are used for subjects of verbs: I, he, she, we, they, who.

Objective pronouns receive the action of verbs and prepositions: me, him, her, us, them, whom.

1. Use the objective case when the pronoun is the direct or indirect subject of a verb: I struck *him.*
Mother fried *me* eggs.

2. Use the objective case when the pronoun is the object of a preposition: Give this to *her.*

3. Use the objective case when the pronoun precedes an infinitive: Mother asked *me* to fry the eggs.

Possessive case denotes ownership of something or a close affiliation: I love *our* dog, Champion. It is *their* turn.

1. Use the possessive case before a gerund: He hated *our* winning the game.

2. Use the objective case if the pronoun is an object and the *ing* word is used as a modifier: The police caught *us* stealing tires.

Exercise 8a

Choose the correct pronoun form in the following sentences.

1. Between you and (I, me), I think that he is angry.   _____

2. My father was the person on (who, whom) we depended.   _____

3. The problems were divided among (us, we) students. _____

4. Let's (you and I, you and me) go to the picnic. _____

5. I am taller than (she, her). _____

6. Pete warned (Sam and I, Sam and me) about the disease. _____

7. Give the money to (whoever, whomever) deserves it. _____

8. This is (she, her) speaking. _____

9. I did not like (his, him) making remarks about my homely wife. _____

10. (Those, them) dogs are covered with ticks. _____

11. I am alarmed at (Pete, Pete's) failing the course. _____

12. I wasn't sure (who, whom) was guilty of peeping through the keyhole. _____

13. I question what (their, they're) doing. _____

14. It was (we, us) who sent the money to aid the destitute winos. _____

15. Do you realize why (your, you're) writing is incorrect? _____

16. (Them, Those) students are the first midgets to enroll at ACC. _____

17. I ignored (him, his) pleading for more jelly beans at breakfast. _____

18. In spite of (who, whom) she knew at the police station, Miranda was booked for jaywalking. _____

19. All of (us, we) soldiers refused to shoot. _____

20. The players (who, whom) are tallest are in demand. _____

21. (Whoever, Whomever) assaulted the crippled newspaper boy is a scoundrel. _____

22. Pete and (he, him) were both married to Lucasta at one time. _____

23. Zita was the girl of (who, whom) we felt so proud. _____

24. Gordon knew that he was smarter than (us, we). _____

25. The coach asked us (who, whom) was ready to jog. _____

Exercise 8b

Choose the correct pronoun form.

1. (Who, Whom) do you expect for dinner? _____

2. Give the food stamps to (whoever, whomever) needs them. _____

3. Petunia was the girl (who, whom) he wanted to marry. _____

4. All of the men, Pete, Gus, and (him, he) were drafted. _____

5. Hepatitus prevented (him, his) participating in the play. _____

6. The ones competing for the prize were Pete, Gus, and (I, me). _____

7. Pablo and (her, she) have been divorced for a year. _____

8. (Who, Whom) is the fairest of them all? _____

9. I know that (us, we) Americans waste time watching television. _____

10. Gregory and (him, he) were hired to conduct the survey. _____

11. Rita promised the candy to George and (him, he). _____

12. Everyone except Karen and (I, me) knows the answers to the test. _____

13. Pete lends his car to (whoever, whomever) puts gas in the tank. _____

14. Everyone went to the meeting but Mark and (I, me). _____

15. I like reading comic books more than (he, him). _____

16. (Who, Whom) did the teacher think was cheating? _____

17. If you are wondering about the pictures, these are (they, them). _____

18. Mary likes Gregory more than (I, me). _____

19. Let's (you and I, you and me) go to the carnival. _____

20. Writing essays annoys everyone in the class, especially John and (myself, me). _____

Exercise 8c

Choose the correct pronoun form in the following.

1. Do you expect Mr. Loff and (they, them) to agree with you? _____

2. No one felt more sorrow than (I, me, myself). _____

3. These sandwiches were prepared by Boris and (she, her). _____

4. Everyone except George and (I, me, myself) went to the game. _____

5. The general and (I, me, myself) will review the troops. _____

6. The best time for Ronald and (he, him) to join is in April. _____

7. (We, Us) freshmen demand a fair grading policy. _____

8. Cheating disturbs the instructor as much as (I, me, myself). _____

9. For the Christmas holidays, the Deli is hiring George and (I, me, myself). _____

10. Did you contact the authors, Mr. Steinbeck and (she, her)? _____

11. No one studies as hard as (he, him, himself) for a test. _____

12. Only Mr. Belch and (he, him) know the route to Paw Paw. _____

13. Do you know if Plink and (I, me, myself) are going? _____

14. The girls asked two boys, Ivan and (he, him), to go. _____

15. James thinks that Wilbert is a better teacher than (he, him). _____

16. All invoices must be mailed to my clerk or (I, me, myself). _____

17. The offer was not acceptable to both Mary and (me, myself). _____

18. If you were (she, her), would you go with him? _____

19. If anyone is going, it will be (I, me). _____

20. The most gifted artist seems to be (him, he). _____

21. George wants to give you and (her, she) the money. _____

22. The money is to be divided among Bill, Sam, and (him, he). _____

23. My wife and (I, me) studied the contract. _____

24. Let's (you and me, you and I) go to the ballet. _____

25. Everyone knew the answers except Jim and (her, she). _____

◼ Chapter 9 ◼

Subject-Verb Agreement

A verb must agree in number with its subject.

1. A singular subject takes a singular verb:
    He laughs.
    She laughs.

2. A plural subject takes a plural verb:
    They laugh.
    You laugh.

3. A singular subject followed by a phrase, an appositive, or a clause with plural nouns is singular.
    A *philosopher* such as Socrates, Plato, Anaxagoras, and others *is* certainly to be admired.
    The *reason* for his impulsive change of plans *was* obvious.
    Pete, accompanied by Pork and Gork, *is* going to the dance.
    You, the mayor of Cumberland, *are expected* to attend.

4. A singular subject followed by a phrase beginning with *as well as, along with, in addition to* generally takes a singular verb.
    The mayor as well as his secretary was late for the meeting.

Note: A plural verb is often used when the additional phrase is obviously intended as a compound subject: Both the mayor, together with his attractive secretary, were late for the meeting.

5. Singular pronouns take singular verbs: *anybody, anyone, anything, each, either, everybody, everyone, everything, neither, nobody, no one, somebody.*
    Each of the girls is pretty.
    One of you is the culprit.
    Everyone is going to the orgy tonight.

6. Some nouns or pronouns may be either singular or plural, depending on the modifying phrase and the context of the sentence: *any, all, some, none, most, half, what, which.*
     Some of my money is set aside for charity.
     Some of our colleagues have earned their doctorates.
     Which (one) of the beds is reserved for me?
     Which (ones) of the beds are reserved for the hotel guards?

     None (no one, not anyone) may be either singular or plural:
     None is so blind as he who refuses to see.
     None are so blind as those who refuse to see.
     What may be either singular or plural:
     What is to be will be.
     What are feared are the crimes of men.

7. Collective nouns (plural in form but singular in meaning) take a singular verb: *class, audience, news, politics, molasses.* . . .
     The bad news is that George has herpes!
     Economics is a popular field of study.
     The committee is ready to file a petition.

8. Subjects denoting an amount, a quantity, or an extent take singular verbs when the amount is considered as a unit.
     Twenty dollars seems rather expensive for only half an hour.
     Two quarts of milk is enough for the baby.
     Two thirds of a gallon of gas is used to start the engine.
     A plural verb is used if the amount is taken as a number of individual units:
     Two dollars were given to the wino on Baltimore Street.
     There are six quarts of oil on the shelf.

9. Usage is evenly divided concerning addition:
     One and one is (are) two.
     Two times two is (are) four.
     In subtraction, a singular verb is used: one subtracted from eleven leaves ten. Ten from twenty leaves ten.

10. With two or more nouns or pronouns joined by *and,* a plural verb is generally used:
     Pete and Pork are good friends.
     The mayor and his secretary have arrived.
     Note: When the items of a compound subject denote the same person or are considered as a unit, the verb is singular: The guardian of my home and my closest friend is my dog.

11. Singular nouns joined by *and* take a singular verb when the first noun is preceded by *every* or *each*.

   Each dog and cat has received a rabies inoculation.
   Every man, woman, and child is prepared for the conflict.

12. Compound singular subjects joined by *or, nor, either—or, neither—nor* take a singular verb.

   Neither John nor Harry is able to attend the conference.
   One or the other is about to object to the decision.
   Either potato salad or cole slaw is fine.

   Note: A plural verb is standard when the verb precedes the subject in question: Are either Sally or Janice going to the meeting?

13. When a compound subject is plural, the verb is plural: No prisoners or entering refugees were tortured.

14. When parts of a compound subject differ in number and are joined by *or, nor, neither—nor, either—or,* the verb agrees with the nearer subject:

   Neither the sergeant nor the *soldiers want* to charge up the hill.
   Neither the soldiers nor the *sergeant wants* to charge up the hill.

15. Relative pronouns referring to plural antecedents take plural verbs:

   Each club has its own *cooks, who provide* tasty meals for members.

   Relative pronouns referring to singular antecedents take singular verbs: Each club has its own *cook, who provides* tasty meals for members.

   In sentences with phrases such as *one of those who* or *one of those which,* find the antecedent of the relative pronoun to determine agreement.

   My college professor in biology was one of those college *professors who were* seriously *concerned* with their students. (*Professors* is the antecedent of the relative pronoun *who;* thus, *who* is plural and takes a plural verb.)
   Sue is one of those *people who like* to study.
   I hope to get a call from *one* of my friends *who* is driving to Atlantic City.

   When *one* is preceded by *the only* or by a similar modifying word, the relative pronoun and verb are singular.

   My college professor in biology was *the only one* of my college professors *who was* seriously *concerned* with the problems of his students.

16. *A linking verb must agree with its subject, not with the predicate nominative:*
    Pete's most serious problem is his temper tantrums.
    Pete's temper tantrums are his most serious problem.

17. Words generally regarded as singular often end in *ics: physics, mathematics, economics, genetics, aesthetics, measles, news, semantics,* and others. Words regarded as plural include *jeans, trousers, suburbs, scissors,* and others.
    Economics is an interesting subject.
    The news is startling.
    Her blue jeans are rather tight about her hips.
    Joe's trousers are blue.
    Some nouns ending in *ics* that denote physical activities or qualities are usually treated as plurals: The acoustics of the auditorium are excellent.
    Note: Subject-verb determination often depends on the context:
    Statistics is a study of numbers. The statistics were easily compiled through the computer.

18. When a sentence begins with *there,* an introductory word, the subject of the sentence still determines the number of the verb.
    There *are* serious *objections* about smoking in classrooms.
    There *is* no serous *objection* to smoking in the classrooms.
    Note: It is always followed by a singular verb.

19. The title of a single work or a word, even when plural in form, is singular and takes a singular verb.
    The Capetbaggers is a popular novel by Harold Robbins.
    The Cumberland *Times* has an outstanding reputation among Maryland newspapers.

20. As a collective noun, *number* may be either singular or plural.
    The number takes a singular verb.
    A number takes a plural verb.
    The number of peasants was large. (*The number* refers to the total.)
    A number of peasants were gathering in the agora. (*A number* refers to individual units.)

Exercise 9a

Choose the correct verb in the following sentences. Write your answer in the space provided.

1. In the lagoon (swim, swims) all kinds of fish. _____

2. Twelve dollars (is, are) needed to enroll. _____

3. Both Pete and Sue (are, is) looking for Porky. _____

4. Those scissors (is, are) mine. _____

5. Here (is, are) a number of books to read. _____

6. Anyone who enrolls (is, are) welcome to attend. _____

7. The team (is, are) practicing for their game. _____

8. Drinking alcohol, in addition to smoking, (is, are) bad. _____

9. Pete's car is the only one of those cars that (have, has) a ticket. _____

10. That book of odes (is, are) by Ovid. _____

11. *Dubliners* (has, have) interested readers since the thirties. _____

12. Under the porch (was, were) valuable artifacts. _____

13. She was the only one of the students who (was, were) bored. _____

14. Neither the mayor nor the council (have, has) met all week. _____

15. Pete and I (am, is, are) going to the dance. _____

16. The clanking and banging under the hood (is, are) serious. _____

17. Each of the doctors (have, has) a patient in the ward. _____

18. Athens, not Sparta, Corinth, or Mycenae, (has, have) the largest population. _____

19. George or Samson (has, have) the deed. _____

20. Some of us (is, are) going to the convention. _____

Exercise 9b

Choose the correct verb in the following sentences. Write your answer in the space provided.

1. Watermelons, along with grapefruit, (is, are) delicious. _____

2. His only son and heir (is, are) to be hanged at dusk. _____

3. The number of smokers in Cumberland (has, have) not decreased. _____

4. The class (has, have) been given a week to file their complaints. _____

5. Neither of us (love, loves) Peter the Pure. _____

6. To a teacher, twenty dollars (seems, seem) like a huge sum. _____

7. Half of the walnuts (was, were) eaten by squirrels. _____

8. There (was, were) a dog and two puppies at my door. _____

9. Neither Sue nor Karen (feels, feel) sure about the time. _____

10. Tweezers (is, are) used to pluck one's eyebrows. _____

11. There (is, are) a few cookies and a potato chip remaining. _____

12. There (is, are) a potato chip and a few cookies remaining. _____

13. Every one of the scouts who belong to the group (is, are) hoping to camp in the woods. _____

14. Taste in fashions (differ, differs) considerably. _____

15. The grand prize (was, were) a night in Paris. _____

16. Everyone in the stadium (was, were) extremely quiet. _____

17. The dog or her puppies (are, is) responsible for the wet blanket. _____

18. Neither soldiers nor peasants (is, are) opposed to the war. _____

19. Neither of the boys (understand, understands) the answer to the problem. _____

20. Measles (is, are) a serious disease. _____

Exercise 9c

Choose the correct verb in the following sentences. Write your answer in the space provided.

1. Data (was, were) gathered about the earthquake. _____

2. The jury (is, are) returning to their places. _____

3. Gordy is one of those players who always (knows, know) when to swing. _____

4. A pack of cigars (cost, costs) one dollar today. _____

5. Archie is the only dog who (follows, follow) his master's commands. _____

6. Peanut butter and jelly sandwiches (is, are) a good snack. _____

7. Two quarts of milk (is, are) enough for the child. _____

8. Two times two (is, are) four. _____

9. Each dog and cat (has, have) received an inoculation. _____

10. (Is, Are) either Sally or Janice going to the bacchanal? _____

11. I received a letter from one of my friends who (is, are) driving to Paw Paw, West Virginia. _____

12. Sue is one of those people who (likes, like) to study. _____

13. There (is, are) no objections to smoking in the classroom. _____

14. The acoustics of the auditorium (is, are) excellent. _____

15. The number of peasants (was, were) large. _____

16. A number of students (was, were) going to the dinner. _____

17. Pete's most serious problem (is, are) his temper tantrums. _____

18. Each club has its own cooks, who (provide, provides) meals for members. _____

19. George is one of those fellows who never (care, cares) how they look. _____

20. The hero and his friends (overcome, overcomes) the villains. _____

21. A pile of *Playboy* magazines (has, have) been placed on the teacher's desk. _____

Chapter 10

Agreement of Pronoun and Antecedent

The noun for which a pronoun substitutes is called its *antecedent*. *Reference* is a term used to show the relationship between a pronoun and its antecedent. *A pronoun must agree in gender, person, and number with its antecedent, or the noun or pronoun to which it refers.*

Note: A pronoun does not necessarily agree in *case* with its antecedent because the case of a pronoun is determined by its function in the sentence or clause.

1. A singular antecedent is referred to by a singular pronoun: He is the *one who* is angry. (*One* is the singular antecedent of *who*.)

2. A plural antecedent is referred to by a plural pronoun: They are the *ones who* are angry. (*Ones* is the plural antecedent of *who*.)

3. When the antecedent is a collective noun, the pronoun may be either singular or plural, depending on the context of the sentence:
   The *team* prepared for *its* training exercises.
   The *team* prepared to have *their* pictures taken.

4. A pronoun which refers to nouns joined by *and* is usually plural:
   After *Sam and John* washed the car, *they* discovered a flat tire.

5. A singular pronoun is generally used to refer to nouns joined by *or* or *nor: Neither John nor Norman* has finished *his* test.

6. When one of two antecedents joined by *or* or *nor* is singular and one is plural, the pronoun generally agrees with the closest antecedent:

   Either Sue or her *parents* may take *their* car to the park.
   Either her parents or *Sue* may take *her* car to the park.

7. Use a singular pronoun to refer to *each, either, everyone, anyone, anybody, someone, somebody, no one, nobody.*

   Someone has left *his* dinner untouched.
   Everybody is entitled to *his* opinion.

Note: Do not use the plural pronoun *they* to refer to a singular antecedent.

8. Depending on the modifying phrase, *any, all, some, none, most,* and *more* are singular or plural.

   All of the dessert has been prepared, and *it* is delicious.
   All of the forms have been mailed, and *they* will arrive soon.

Exercise 10a

Select the correct answer in the following sentences. Write your answer in the space provided.

1. Everybody is expected to do (his, their) duty. _____

2. Neither of them had done (his, their) assignment. _____

3. Few of those who settled in Cumberland were unhappy with (his, their) decision. _____

4. Some will be unhappy because (his, their) hopes have not materialized. _____

5. Either Pete or Dusty will give Sue (his, their) jelly beans. _____

6. Several became disillusioned and refused to continue (his, their) travels. _____

7. Rita is one of those students who can be expected to do (her, their) best work. _____

8. Each of the three lawyers delivered (his, their) briefs to the judge. _____

9. Neither my parents nor my brother offered to give (his, their) help to the cause. _____

10. All of the pork (has, have) been devoured by the dogs. _____

11. When Betty and Samantha returned, (she, they) found a charred beef roast. _____

12. Everyone will give (his, their) donation to the fund. _____

13. Each of the six athletes expressed (his, their) disappointment. _____

14. Kermit, as well as Goldie and Miss Piggy, forgot to remember (his, their) lines. _____

15. A dozen of the registered nurses will receive (her, their) degrees. _____

16. None of the corn will grow to (its, their) full height. _____

17. Some of the gems will be evaluated at (its, their) market value. _____

18. Neither Odysseus nor his men expected to see (his, their) homeland again. _____

19. Our team cast (its, their) votes for a beer party. _____

20. The owner and the manager of the disco will hire (his, their) band groups this week. _____

21. Each of the four students cast (his, their) vote. _____

22. Everyone is excited about (his, their) Christmas gifts. _____

23. When everybody on the committee does (his, their) assignments, the construction can begin. _____

24. Everyone in the class was told to type copies of (his, their) work schedules. _____

25. The collection of stamps was given to a collector, who paid a huge sum for (it, them). _____

Exercise 10b

Choose the correct form in the following sentences. Write your answer in the space provided.

1. The labor union was in favor of benefits for (its, their) membership. _____

2. When Sue talked to Debbie about college, they discovered that neither of them was happy in (her, their) curriculum. _____

3. No one who has taken good care of (his, their) teeth should worry about cavities. _____

4. Every politician may have an episode in (his, their) life which may prove to be embarrassing. _____

5. The insurance company was making every effort to regain (its, their) fire losses. _____

6. On the last day of the term, neither Gordon nor Richard had turned in (his, their) term papers. _____

7. Everybody should be allowed to worship God in (his, their) own way. _____

8. Each of the students took (his, their) turn at the kissing booth. _____

9. An accident like that could happen to anybody, especially if (he, they) were careless. _____

10. Any gambler who takes such ridiculous chances should lose (his, their) money. _____

11. The church was making a sincere effort to pay off (its, their) mortgage. _____

12. Neither Sam nor Pete collected (his, their) social security checks. _____

13. The flock of sparrows was in perfect formation behind (its, their) leader. _____

14. Each of the cowards was too busy thinking of (his, their) personal safety during the fire. _____

15. The jury were instructed by the judge regarding (its, their) verdict. _____

16. Most of the scouts enjoyed (his, their) trip. _____

17. All of the employees had (his, its, their) own cars. _____

18. More of the tuna had dried on (its, their) rack. _____

19. The commentator gave the news (its, their) dramatic flair. _____

20. The chorus will sing (its, their) first song in ten minutes. _____

Exercise 10c

Choose the correct form in the following sentences. Write your answer in the space provided.

1. Either of the students may seek (his, their) teacher for clarification of the assignment. _____

2. None of the sugar could be served at (its, their) best flavor. _____

3. Both George and James became heroes in (his, their) time. _____

4. When one mails a letter, (he, they, you) should always use correct postage. _____

5. The Gringo Singers will give (its, their) first recital. _____

6. Neither Sam nor any of his friends had met (his, their) date(s) for the Christmas Dance. _____

7. Each of the two hundred freshmen submitted (his, their) application. _____

8. Gymnastics had (its, their) greatest appeal for Mary Lou. _____

9. The deer increased because (its, their) food was easily found in the woods. _____

10. The committee's final decision reflected (its, their) prejudice. _____

11. That kind of painting has (its, their) patrons. _____

12. Some of the paint left (its, their) stain on the chair. _____

13. Among all the bicycles in the area only one had (its, their) tires slashed. _____

14. Goochie was the only one of the quarterbacks who retired because of (his, their) injuries. _____

15. Has any of the cocaine been traced to (its, their) source? _____

16. None of the cowboys could return to (his, their) range. _____

17. The mob dispersed when (its, their) members were stoned. _____

18. Whoever built the computer knew what (he, they) were doing. _____

19. The scissors has/have (its, their) own case.   _____

20. Most of his students had (his, their) own opinion(s).   _____

▌Chapter 11 ▌

Dangling Modifiers

Dangling modifiers (participles, gerund phrases, elliptical clauses) refer to a word that is implied instead of clearly stated in a sentence.

Confident of her answer, it seemed to be an opportune moment.

In this type of construction, *Confident of her answer* modifies *it*.

Confident of her answer, I thought it was an opportune moment.

In the corrected version, *Confident of her answer* modifies the subject of the sentence *I*.

Drifting slowly around the bend in the road, the beautiful meadow attracted my attention. (incorrect)

The participial phrase *Drifting slowly around the bend* modifies *the beautiful meadow*.

Drifting slowly around the bend in the road, I was attracted by the beautiful meadow. (correct)
When only five years old, my father took me to see a burlesque show. (incorrect)

The dangling elliptical clause *When only five years old* modifies *my father*.

When I was only five years old, my father took me to see a burlesque show. (correct)

To correct a dangling modifier, state the subject directly *after* the modifying construction. In grammar, the logic of a sentence demands that all modifiers clearly modify the word or phrase to which they belong.

359

Exercise 11a

Correct the following sentences.

1. Happy to be back with Susie, it seemed to be a good time to ask her to marry me.

2. George always ate a big meal before sleeping, consisting of steak, potatoes, corn, and twelve slices of bread.

3. Enjoying the fresh air of the country, it seemed a fine place for our picnic.

4. When only a baby, my father and mother took me to Disneyland.

5. Upon receiving your letter, the transcript will be completed.

6. Tired and exhausted, the game was finally won by our team.

7. When writing a composition, dashes should be used with care.

8. Flying through the air gracefully, I marveled at the beauty of the eagle.

9. Staggering and swinging wildly, the canvas top provided the final stop for Pete the Pug.

10. Trickling into the streams, the oak trees provided a barrier to the muddy water guarding the city of Johnstown.

11. The report of the fire on the radio frightened everybody.

12. Having been warned several times, the teacher ordered the student out of the classroom for misbehaving.

13. Being infested with lice and ticks, Mary burned the dog's old blanket.

14. Badly burned upon his arrival at the hospital, the doctor ordered the nurses to bandage the patient's arms and legs.

15. Reaching high to place the star at the top of the tree, the chair slipped and Jim fell with a thud upon the ornaments.

16. Unable to see through the fog, the car skidded.

17. After winning the pennant for the Phillies, the manager benched Pete Rose during the Series.

18. After washing and scrubbing, the car was ready to be polished.

19. While serving with the army in Korea, Pete's daughter was born.

20. To be able to write clearly and effectively, a certain amount of practice is required.

21. In following your directions, I have given birth to twins in the enclosed envelope.

22. Please send me a letter and tell me if my wife has made an application for a wife and baby.

23. I am forwarding my marriage certificate and my two children; one is a mistake as you can see.

24. Please send me my wife's form to fill out.

25. Both of my parents are poor and I can't expect support from them since my mother has been in bed for one year, with the same doctor, and won't change.

■ Chapter 12 ■

Spelling Rules

Good spelling is as important in the business and technical fields as it is in college work. Poor spelling is not only the result of lazy and incompetent effort, but also embarrassing to both the writer and the reader. Generally, good spelling relies upon memorization. Nevertheless, a knowledge of the fundamental rules will make a difficult task easy.

1. In some words, the final *e* is dropped before adding a suffix beginning with a vowel.

come	coming	like	likable
hope	hoping	precede	preceding
choose	choosing	accommodate	accommodating
leave	leaving	achieve	achieving

2. In some words, the final *e* is kept before adding a suffix beginning with a consonant.

move	movement	manage	management
announce	announcement	care	careless
hope	hopeful	crude	crudeness

3. In forming the plural of nouns when *y* is preceded by a consonant, change the *y* to *i* and add *es.*

lady	ladies
fly	flies
sky	skies
baby	babies

4. The *y* is retained when a vowel precedes it.

play	plays
attorney	attorneys
valley	valleys
turkey	turkeys
monkey	monkeys

5. Double the final consonant when adding a syllable that begins with a vowel, and the accent is on the second syllable.

occur	occurrence
allot	allotted
transmit	transmittance
compel	compelling
permit	permitting

6. If the accent falls on the first syllable, the final consonant is not doubled.

profit	profited
differ	differed
offer	offered
suffer	suffered

7. When adding a prefix to the root word, do not double or drop letters.

prefix	*root*	
dis	appear	disappear
im	moral	immoral
un	necessary	unnecessary
mis	spell	misspell
circum	navigate	circumnavigate
ir	relevant	irrelevant
ir	resistible	irresistible

8. Avoid confusing *ie* and *ei*.
   When the sound is a long *e* ($\bar{e}$), use *ie* except after *c*.

grief	chief	achieve	priest
relief	belief	alien	siege
field	yield	friend	niece

After *c, ei* is generally used.

receive	conceive	ceiling
perceive	deceive	
conceit	receipt	

If the sound is not a long *e, ei* is generally used, particularly when the *a* sound is obvious.

eight	freight	neighbor
reign	vein	
sleigh	neigh	

Exceptions to the general rules:

caffeine	protein	either	species
counterfeit	seize	weird	forfeit

9. Some singular nouns ending in *f* or *fe* form the plural by changing the *f* or *fe* to *ves*.

knife	knives	thief	thieves
leaf	leaves	wife	wives
life	lives	calf	calves

10. Some singular nouns ending in *f* or *fe* form the plural simply by adding *s*.

chief	chiefs	belief	beliefs
roof	roofs	safe	safes
cliff	cliffs		

11. Some nouns ending in *o* take *es* to form the plural.

hero	heroes	mosquito	mosquitoes
potato	potatoes	Negro	Negroes
cargo	cargoes	veto	vetoes
tomato	tomatoes		

12. Add an *s* to form the plural in most musical terms ending in *o*.

banjo	banjos
piano	pianos
piccolo	piccolos
solo	solos

13. Add an *s* to form the plural in some words ending in *o*.

auto	autos	radio	radios
casino	casinos	ratio	ratios
Eskimo	Eskimos	zero	zeros
halo	halos		

14. In English, the only word that ends in *sede* is supersede.
Three words end in *ceed:* exceed, proceed, succeed.
Six words end in *cede:* accede, secede, intercede, recede, precede, concede.

15. Add a *k* after words ending in *c* to form the suffixes *ing, er, ed*.

panic	panicked	panicking
picnic	picnicked	picnicking
traffic	trafficked	trafficking

Commonly Misspelled Words

absence	criticism	interfere	psychology
accessible	deductible	kindergarten	pursuing
accommodate	deferred	legible	questionnaire
accumulate	dependent	leisure	receipt
achieve	desirable	liaison	receive
acquaintance	dilemma	license	recommend
acquiesce	ecstasy	lieutenant	remittance
admissible	eligible	maintenance	repetition
admittance	embarrassing	mediocre	rescind
advertisement	envelop (verb)	miscellaneous	restaurant
allotment	envelope (noun)	misspelled	rhythm
allotted	equipped	mortgage	schedule
all right	exaggerate	nickel	seize
analyze	exceed	ninety	separate
apologize	existence	ninth	sergeant
appropriate	extension	noticeable	serviceable
argument	familiar	occasion	similar
article	feasible	occurrence	siege
assistant	forcible	omit	stationary
attendance	foreign	omission	stationery
bachelor	forfeit	pageant	supersede
balloon	forty	pamphlet	surprise
believable	fulfillment	parallel	susceptible
benefit	grammar	pastime	technique
bulletin	grievance	percent	thorough
calendar	grievous	permissible	tragedy
campaign	guarantee	perseverance	transferred
ceiling	harass	personal	truly
cemetery	harassment	personnel	usable
changeable	hazardous	persuasion	usage
congratulate	illegible	pneumonia	vacuum
conscience	incidentally	prejudice	yield
conscientious	independent	privilege	
consistent	indispensable	procedure	

Chapter 13

Vocabulary Building through Prefixes and Suffixes

Etymology and Freshman Composition

I have had a great deal of success incorporating a unit on etymology into my freshman English composition classes. And by this I mean an entire, cohesive unit rather than a few desultory remarks on the subject subsumed under the "How to Use the Dictionary" section of your rhetoric. Because etymology is a field of study seldom presented in high school English programs, it comes to the college freshman as a surprise, and the proficiency he soon acquires helps him to counter the myth that freshman composition is a grueling rehash of high school English.

Too often, etymology is viewed as an adjunct field very interesting in itself—more appropriate as a hobby than an academic discipline—that figures only peripherally in the study of composition, foreign languages, and, sad to say, even in the theories of modern linguistic science itself. Some rhetorics even apologize for the inclusion of a few modest remarks on the subject ("Etymology might not help you to write better, but it's interesting").

At a time, however, when language is being inflated out of proportion and writers batter words insensitively to make their point at any cost, a knowledge of etymology can help check these abuses by honing in on specific instances (e.g., *propaganda* can be either good or bad, because in fact it is anything "propagated") and by instilling in writers a respect for the personality of the individual word. Once the processes of the history of a word are understood, the word is no longer seen as a mere tool of one's trade, an inanimate building block, but rather as a discrete and

371

individualized entity to be appreciated for its evolutionary and affective attributes as well as for its literal meaning.

The histories of words parallel the patterns of human life in some important ways—words come into being, grow, flower, and mature. Sometimes they improve with age or "meliorate" (e.g., *priest* in its most distant Greek origin meant "lead-ox") and, just as often, degenerate and acquire negative shades (e.g., *libel* was originally the innocuous Latin diminutive of *liber*, "book"). They grow reclusive and limit their meanings (e.g., *liquor*, once meaning any liquid, now refers to alcoholic liquid), or they grow expansive and spread far beyond their original confines (a *dean* no longer commands a team of ten as did his Latin antecedent *decanus*). Words enjoy their moment of popularity, begin to wane and suffer the infirmities of age, and pass into oblivion.

Some words are easily traceable four or five "generations" through four or five languages (*orange* has as ancestors French, Provencal, Spanish, Arabic and Persian; *jubilee* comes ultimately from Hebrew through the media of Greek, Latin and French). On the other hand, however, a larger number of words are foundlings (e.g., *bad, basket, buggy, job, pig*) of unknown background, or are the offspring of foundlings (e.g., *barren, bonnet, bran, giblets* and *morgue*, which are not traceable beyond French). Etymology does not claim to be an exact science.

In order to follow the "generations" of a known etymology, the student must be equipped with a basic knowledge of the major language families of Europe. Since English is a repository for words from many non-European languages as well (e.g., *boondocks* from Tagalog, *igloo* from Eskimo, *honcho* from Japanese), this discussion can easily mushroom to include many of the world's languages, and the student can, as a result, lay claim to a cosmopolitanism previously unknown to him.

The interrelatedness of languages (Latin and Sanskrit, for example, are sister-languages, and just as French, Spanish and the Romance languages are derived from the former, Bengali, Hindi and the modern Indian languages are derived from the latter) parallels the interrelatedness of words in etymology (e.g., the English and Latin cognates *heart* and *cor, cordis*, which have yielded *hearty* and *cordial*) and of ideas in composition; and still further, reflects the ever fascinating network of elements that comprise life itself.

The abbreviations of languages and language periods are one of the more bewildering aspects of etymology to the newcomer, but is an obstacle easily overcome. An inspection of the abbreviations listing in the OED or in any reputable dictionary can clarify that Gr. (or Gk.) is Greek, G. is German, and that Ger. is Germanic. The student learns that English is derived from Germanic rather than from German, and the denominations of Old English and Anglo-Saxon are (unnecessarily) one and the same.

Words are born into a language by the action of borrowing words from other languages, by derivation (using roots, suffixes and prefixes within the language), and by absolute creation.

English has long been a borrowing language, preferring to borrow words ready-made than to create words from its own resources. Even before the Norman Conquest (1066) occasioned the onslaught of French words into the English language, Anglo-Saxon was borrowing amply from the Scandinavian dialects (e.g., words as basic as *sky* and *law*). The result of all this borrowing is that English has acquired a wider range of possibilities than most languages for precise and complete expression.

When a language borrows twice from the same foreign language or language family, we have what is called a set of doublets. In the case of the same word borrowed once from Latin and once from French, English has such pairs as *fragile-frail, masculine-male* (cf. *manly*), *penitence-penance, regal-royal* (cf. *kingly*), *tint-taint*. We have triplets in the case of *place-plaza-piazza*, where English has borrowed the same word from French, Spanish and Italian. This can provide the teacher of composition with a lineup of synonyms and near-synonyms that is useful in establishing and appreciating nuances.

People and places "borrow" their names from words, and if your library facilities allow for it, students can be encouraged to research their own names, whatever ethnic background they may be. Such a project is surprisingly feasible with the proper materials.

But the process comes full circle, and the names of people and places often give their names back to things that are associated with them. The subject of words derived from names is attractively and exhaustively studied in a recent book, *O Thou Improper, Thou Uncommon Noun* by Willard R. Espy (New York: Clarkson N. Potter, 1978).

The second means by which a word is born into a language is by derivation. A discussion of derivation hinges upon the concept of the morpheme, the smallest unit of identifiable meaning into which a word can be analyzed. Sometimes a morpheme consists of a recognizable word, and sometimes it is a smaller unit (e.g., *world* consists of two morphemes, both dead today, *wer*, "man" + *eld*, "age"). Thus, *windshield* consists of two morphemes, both of which happen to be words, as do the slightly disguised *cranberry (crane + berry)* and *vicious (vice + -ious)*. Of course, not all such compounds are broken down as easily (e.g., *daisy = day's eye*), and one must be on guard for the deceptively obvious compounds such as *reindeer* (unrelated to *rein* or *rain*), *ruthless* (unrelated to *Ruth*) and *luke-warm* (unrelated to *Luke*).

Sometimes and perhaps more often than can be detected, an unfamiliar morpheme of a word is exchanged for a similar, more familiar morpheme (e.g., Anglo-Saxon *bryd-guma*, "bride-man," was converted to *bride-groom* under the influence of another word, *groom*, "stableboy").

This is called folk etymology, and demonstrates how unresistant words are to the whims of the speakers of language.

The third means by which a word is "born" we may call absolute creation, or onomatopoeia, which is perhaps analogous to, but certainly more frequent than, spontaneous generation in humans. Onomatopoeia not only accounts for the more obvious *snap, crackle* and *pop,* but also for such words as *sigh, murmur* and *rustle.* Others of the spontaneously created words were actually suggested by pre-existing words (*e.g., quiz* was suggested by Latin *quis, quid; gas* was suggested by Greek *chaos*), or are outright blends of two words, as *smog* was blended from *smoke* and *fog.*

Words "die" when they fall out of fashion or when their referents no longer serve a purpose in society (e.g., *distaff, halberd, warp* and *woof*).[1] Homonymic clash, which occurs when words sound alike and become confused in context, is cited to explain the disappearance of some words (e.g., when *cock* became generalized in speech for a part of the male anatomy, it ceased to be used for the barnyard variety, and forced into acceptance the neologism *rooster*). Yet the Western European languages seem to have a remarkably high tolerance for homonyms. In English *write, right, wright* and *rite* are all pronounced the same, as are *saint, sein, seing* and *sain* in French.

The teacher of composition can avail himself of examples from etymology to teach many of the rhetorical devices and other terms used in composition as well. Language has long been recognized as a graveyard of dead metaphors, or as Jean Paul put it, "an herbary of withered metaphors." Examples are plentiful, either from among those that are still obvious such as *ridgerunner* or *clodhopper,* or from among those that have lost touch with their original meanings (e.g., *fool* was once a bellows or a windbag, and *bulldozer* was a white man who gave Negroes a dose of the bullwhip during the Reconstruction days of the American South). The creative genius of slang in particular, it may be noted, is heavily dependent upon metaphor (cf. the synonyms for *head—bean, block, noggin,* etc.).

Hyperbole, the progression from a stronger to a weaker meaning, is operative in words such as *mortify,* which no longer implies the death dealing quality inherent in the Late Latin *mortificare,* "to kill." The opposite effect, *understatement,* where a weaker meaning develops into a stronger meaning, is seen in *decimate,* originally "to kill a group of ten," and now referring to total annihilation.[2]

The knowledge of abstract and concrete words can also be introduced to students from an etymological standpoint.

Although the naming of the more sophisticated abstract qualities occurs late in the evolution of language, abstractions tend to become concretized in their original forms (i.e., without additional morphemes, such as *charm* for *talisman, vanity* for *dressing table, fury* in *The Three Furies*) more readily than concrete words assume abstract shades. *Provision(s)* originally meant "foresight," *bounty* was "kindness," and *fruit* was "enjoyment."

Abstractions themselves are derived by composition from more basic abstractions (e.g., *devotion* is from Latin *votus*, "vow"), or less frequently, from concrete terms (e.g., *sluggishness* from *slug, facet* from *face*).

The tendency of abstract words to "go concrete" can be useful to the teacher of composition who wishes to caution students against overuse of airy generalities in favor of the more specific and predominating concrete words.

Also relevant to the study of composition is how often errors in the long run of linguistic history are accepted as correct. Language is delicate and yields easily to pressures for modification. Folk etymology, discussed previously, is one example of wrong thinking that becomes normative. Another error occasionally rendered acceptable by the persistence of usage is redundancy. *Fulfil* is actually "to fill full," *salt-cellar* is composed of *salt* + French *saliere*, "salt-cellar," and *sacrosanct* combines the Latin words *sacrum*, "sacred" + *sanctus*, "holy." Only in the case of *sacrosanct* is the redundancy perhaps justifiable as emphasis.

Grammatical ellipsis, as in

When (I was) ten, I stole an apple

has an important parallel in etymology. In Middle English *cheer* meant "face" or "demeanor," and the modern sense of "gaiety" results from an ellipsis of the phrase, *"to be of good cheer."* Very often adjectives are nominalized because their accompanying nouns have been lost in the process of usage. Thus English has *spaniel* and *pheasant*, which were originally Old French *chien espagneul*, "Spanish dog," and Greek *ornis phasianos*, "bird of the River Phasis." The desire for brevity is also seen in the clipping of individual words, where one or more syllables at either end of the word are dropped (e.g., *van* taken from *caravan, cab* from *cabriolet*).

After my students become confident using etymological research tools, they choose three words to etymologize in paragraph form. This involves expanding the abbreviated data given in the dictionaries and setting them down in a smooth-flowing narrative, as is done in Wilfred Funk's *Word Origins and Their Romantic Stories* or in the Merriam-Webster *Book of Word Histories*, which, of course, students are not permitted to use. Devising a smooth narrative from the bare facts of the case requires skill and is a main testing point of the exercise.

After completing their etymologies, the students proceed to the study of the types of writing per se. Not surprisingly, however, my students pursue their awakened interest in the lost meanings of words throughout the semester. Does the use of *score* in "to score a trench" reflect a metaphorical development of the noun *score* as we know it today, or is it a reversion to an earlier meaning? Is a corn on the foot the same as a corn in the field? Are widow's weeds and garden weeds identical in origin?

In sum, etymology can be incorporated naturally into a composition course, as indeed it should be. It gives students a depth-perception of the words they use to communicate, and works to resolve some of the mysteriousness of language that can turn them away from the study of composition. A thing that is known and understood is no longer feared, and this, if for no other reason, is the justification for a study of word history in a course that has as its goal linguistic dexterity.

Jack Shreve

Footnotes

1. These words can be resurrected metaphorically, such as in "the distaff side of the family," i.e., the weaver's (or maternal) side.

2. I am aware that the application of such rhetorical terms to etymological phenomena worked out by Leonard Bloomfield in *Language* (New York: Henry Holt, 1933), pp. 426-427, was accused of over-simplification by Robert Estrich and Hans Sperber in *Three Keys to Language* (New York: Rinehart, 1952), p. 163, but there are instances in pedagogy when oversimplification is desirable. Freshman composition students are not generally training to be professional semanticists.

Exercise

Etymologize three of the following words. Don't just copy from the etymological dictionary. Formulate your etymology into a readable paragraph. Be thorough and account for all changes in meaning. Do not use abbreviations and remember that this is not "busy work." It is a writing assignment. You may include a quotation from Chaucer, Shakespeare or another early writer of the language, but your work should be more analytical than a mere catalogue of quotations.

Example

Silly demonstrates extreme semantic degeneration in its evolution. In Anglo-Saxon (Old English), *saelig* meant "blessed," which is still the meaning that selig has in modern German. From this meaning the word progressed to "innocent," which is how Shakespeare used the word. Since innocence is sometimes seen as a pathetic condition in people, *silly* in Early Modern English became synonymous with pitiable, and later with "foolish."

Choose your words to etymologize from the following list:

abominable	mentor
accolade	moot
anecdote	narcissism
atone	ostracize
auspicious	pittance
boycott	plagiarize
chivalry	recalcitrant
danger	remorse
diatribe	sadism
dunce	sinister
epicure	stymie
farce	synchronize
galvanize	tally
homage	tantalize
humane	urbane
inexorable	zealous
limbo	zygote

Vocabulary Building Through Prefixes, Roots, and Suffixes

(Greek)	(Meaning)	(Example)
1. *a-, an-*	not, without	anarchy
2. *amphi-*	both, around	amphitheater
3. *ana-*	against, throughout	anachronism
4. *anti-*	opposing	antithesis
5. *apo-*	away, from	apology
6. *arch-, archi-*	first, chief	archbishop
7. *cata-*	away, down	catastrophe
8. *dia-*	across, apart	diameter
9. *en-, em-*	in, among	endemic
10. *epi-*	on, outside	epidermis
11. *eu-*	good, well	euphemism
12. *hemi-*	half	hemisphere
13. *hyper-*	excessive	hyperbole
14. *hypo-*	under, less than	hypodermic
15. *log-*	study	biology, syllogism
16. *macro-*	great, large	macron
17. *meta-*	change, over	metamorphosis
18. *micro-*	small	microbe
19. *mis-*	hate	misanthrope
20. *mono-*	one	monogamy
21. *para-*	beside, beyond	paraphrase
22. *peri-*	around, near	perimeter

23. *phil-*	friendly, loving	philanthropist
24. *phobia-*	fear, aversion	claustrophobia
25. *pod-*	foot	podiatry
26. *poly-*	many, several	polygamy
27. *pro-*	before	prognosis
28. *syn-, sym-, syl-,* *sys-*	together	sympathy, systematic

(*Latin*)	(*Meaning*)	(*Example*)
1. *ab-, a-, abs-*	from, away	abdicate, abstain
2. *ad-, ac-, af-, ag,* *al-, an-, ap-, ar-,* *as-*	to, toward	advocate, accede, affiliate, aggression assimilate
3. *ambi-*	around, both	ambidextrous
4. *ante-, anti-*	before, previous	antecedent, anticipate
5. *bi-*	two, twice	bilateral
6. *circum-*	around	circumscribe
7. *com-, co-, col-,* *con-, cor-*	with, together	compose, confer, collect, control
8. *contra-*	against	contradict, contrast
9. *de-*	away, from, down	destroy, deduct
10. *demi-*	half	demigod
11. *dis-, di-, dif-*	away, down, opposing	dissent, digress
12. *ex-, e-, ef-*	away, from	excise, emit, effect
13. *ex-*	former, previous	ex-convict
14. *extra-, extro-*	outside	extrovert
15. *in-, il-, im-, ir-*	in, into; not	induce, illuminate, immigrate, irreverent
16. *infra-*	below	infrared, infrastructure
17. *inter-*	between	interrupt, interfere
18. *intra-*	within	intramural
19. *intro-*	inward	introvert, introduce
20. *non-*	not	nonentity
21. *ob-, oc-, of-, op-*	over, against, toward	obstruct, offend, opposite
22. *omni-*	everywhere	omnipotent, omnibus
23. *ped-*	foot	pedestrian, biped
24. *per-*	through	permeate
25. *post-*	after, following	postpone, postscript
26. *pre-*	before	prevent, precede
27. *re-*	back, again	return, revoke
28. *retro-*	back, backward	retroactive
29. *rupt-*	break	rupture
30. *se-*	away, aside	seclude, secede

31. *semi-*	half	semiconscious
32. *sub-, suc-, suf-,*	under, beneath	submarine, succinct,
sug-, sum-, sup-,		suggest, summon
sus-		susceptible
33. *super-*	over, extra	supervise, superscript
34. *trans-*	across, beyond	transmit, transpose
35. *ultra-*	beyond	ultrasonic
36. *vice-*	in place of	vice-chairman
37. *viv-*	alive	vivid, vivacious
38. *vor-*	greedy	voracious

Prefixes Denoting Number

Latin:			**Greek:**	
semi-	half	semicircle	*hemi-*	hemisphere
uni-	one	unicycle	*mono-*	monocycle
bi-	two	biweekly	*di-*	dimeter
tri-	three	triangle	*tri-*	tricycle
quadr-	four	quartet	*tetra-*	tetrameter
quinque-	five	quinquennial	*penta-*	pentagon
quint-		quintet	*pente-*	pentecost
sex-	six	sextet	*hexa-*	hexagon
sept-	seven	septet	*hepta-*	heptameter
oct-	eight	octogenarian	*octa-, octo-*	octopus
nona-	nine	nonagenarian	*ennea-*	ennead
dec-	ten	decimal	*deca-*	decalogue
duodec-	twelve	duodenum, duodecimal	*dodeca-*	Dodecanese dodecahedron
cent-	hundred	centipede, centenarian	*hecto-*	hectogram
milli-	thousand	millipede	*chili-, kilo-*	chiliad, kilogram

Greek Root Words

anthrop-	man	misanthrope
arch-	chief, ancient	monarch, archaeology
aster-	star	asterisk
auto-	self	automobile
bibli-	book	Bible, bibliography
bio-	life	biology
chrom-	color	chromosome
chron-	time	anachronism
cosm-	world, universe	macrocosm
crac-, crat-	rule	democracy, theocratic

crypt-	secret	cryptic
cycl-	wheel, circle	bicycle
dem-, demos-	people	democracy
derm-	skin	epidermis
dox-	belief	orthodox
erg-	power	energy
gen-	race	eugenics
geo-	earth	geography
graph-	writing	bibliography
heli-	sun	helium
hem-	blood	hemorrhage
homo-	similar	homosexual
hydr-	water	dehydrate
iatr-	cure	geriatrics
lith-	rock	monolithic
log-	study of	zoology, biology, logorrhea
mega-	large	megaphone
metr-	measure	geometry
micr-	small	micrometer
mon-	one	monotony
morph-	shape	amorphous
necr-	dead	necromancy
nes-	island	Polynesia, Indonesia
orth-	correct	orthodontist
pan-	all	panacea
path-	feeling	sympathy
ped-	child	pediatrics
phil-	like, love	bibliophile
phon-	sound	phonetics, phonics
phot-	light	photograph
pod-	foot	podiatrist
poly-	many	polygamy, polyp
proto-	first	prototype
psych-	soul	psychology
pyr-	fire	pyromaniac
soph-	wise	philosopher
tac-, tax-	arrangement	syntax
techn-	skill, craft	technician
tele-	distant	telegraph
the-	god	atheist
therm-	heat	thermometer
zo-	animal	zoology, zodiac

Latin Root Words

ac-, acr-	sharp	acute, acrimonious
agr-	field	agriculture
ali-	other	alibi, alien
alter-	change	alternate
am-, amic-	friend, love	amicable, amity
annu-, enni-	year	anniversary, annual
aqu-	water	aqueduct
art-	skill, craft	artificial
aud-, audit-	hear	audience
aur-	gold	aureole
bell-	war	belligerent
ben-, bene-	good	benefit
brev-	short	abbreviate
cap-, capt-, cept-	seize	capture, intercept
capit-	head	decapitate, captain
carn-	flesh	carnal, carnivorous
ced-, cede-, cess-	go, yield	precede, secede
cid-, cis-	cut, kill	homicide, incisive
cit-	impel, summon	citation, excite
clam-	shout	exclaim, proclaim
clar-	clear	clarity
cogn-	know	recognize
corp-	body	corpse
cred-	belief	credulous, incredible
cruc-	cross	crucifix
culp-	blame	culprit
dent-	tooth	dentist
dic-, dict-	speak, word	predict, dictionary
doc-, doct-	teach	indoctrinate, docile
duc-, duct-	lead	conduct, induction
equ-	equal	equity, equitable
err-	wander	aberration
fer(ous)-	bear, produce	coniferous, vociferous
fid-	faith	confidant(e), fidelity
fin-	end, limit	infinite, finality
firm-	strong	confirm, affirmation
flect-, flex-	bend	flexible, genuflect
flor-	flower	florid, floral
frag-, fract-	break	fragment, refract
grav-	weight	gravity
ject-	hurl, throw	eject, project
junct-	join	adjunct, juncture
jur-	swear	perjury

leg-	law	legislate
liter-	letter	literature, literal
loqu-, locut-	speak	elocution, interlocutor
luc-	light	translucent
magn-	large	magnify, magnificent
mal-	bad	malady, malicious
man-, manu-	hand	manual, manufacture
mar-	sea	marine
mater-	mother	maternal
medi-	middle	mediocre, median
merg-, mers-	plunge	submerge, immerse
min-	little	minute, minus
mor-	custom	morality
mort-	death	mortician, mortal
multi-	many	multiply, multitude
nomin-	name	nominate
ocul-	eye	binocular
omni-	all	omnipotent
orn-	decorate	ornament
pater-, patr-	father	paternal, patriotism
pel-	drive	impel, compel
pend-, pens-	hang	suspend, suspense
port-	carry	transport, portable
prim-	first	primal, primitive
quir-, quis-	ask	inquiry, inquisitive
rupt-	break	rupture, interrupt
sanct-	holy, sacred	sanctity, sanctuary
scrib-, script-	write	manuscript, description
sequ-	follow	sequel, sequence
sol-	alone	solitary
solv-, solu-	loosen	solve, solution
spec-, spic-	sight	spectacle, aspect
strict-, string-	draw tightly	restrict, constriction
struct-	build	construction
suad-, suas-	advise	dissuade, persuasion
tang-, tact-	touch	tangible, tactile
tend-, tens-, tent-	stretch	extend, distend, intensive
tenu-	thin	tenuous
terr-	land	territory
test-	witness	testify
tors-, tort-	twist	distort, torture
tract-	pull	extract, detract
umbr-	shade	umbrella
und-	wave	undulate

urb-	city	urban, suburban
vac-	empty	vacuum, vacant
verb-	word	verbal, verbose
ver-	true	verisimilitude, verify
vest-	dress	vestal, vestments
vict-	conquer	victor, invincible
vid-, vis-	see	visual, video
vit-	life	vitamin, vital
vulg-	common	vulgar

■ Chapter 14 ■

Sentence Diagramming

Although the practice of diagramming sentences has apparently fallen into a state of limbo in American high schools and colleges, it is a useful visual tool which enables students to understand the connection of sentence parts and sentence patterns. Diagramming is an exercise in the logic of grammatical construction.

A horizontal line provides the basic foundation in the diagram. Vertical lines divide the horizontal line to separate the basic parts of the sentence:

Space allowed for art (ms. 346)

Simple sentence: Subject-verb-direct object pattern

Peter and Sam hit the ball.

Space allowed for art (ms. 346)

A simple sentence with a compound subject (Peter and Sam) and a direct object (ball).

Note: *And,* a coordinate conjunction combining the compound subject, is placed on a dotted line.

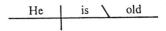

A simple sentence with a subjective complement
Subject-linking verb-predicate adjective pattern
Note the slanted line after the linking verb (is) to indicate the complementary nature of the adjective (old).
Subject-linking verb-predicate noun or nominative:

Remember that prepositional phrases act as adjectival or adverbial modifiers:

The pretty girl kissed the ugly boy with the red pimples.

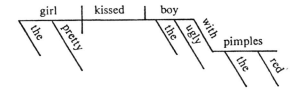

Miriam walked slowly over the plush carpet.

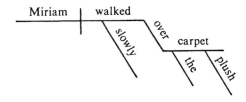

Simple sentence
Subject-verb pattern
The following is a simple sentence with a compound subject and a compound predicate:

Birds and bats swoop and fly.

The indirect object is an implied prepositional phrase.

Mother fried me eggs.

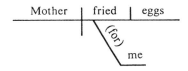

Simple sentence
Subject-verb-indirect object-direct object pattern
Note: in such a construction, the indirect object always precedes the direct object.

An appositive is placed in parentheses beside the subject.

My wife Sally is a lovely woman.

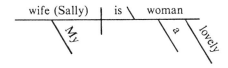

Simple sentence
Subject-verb-predicate noun pattern

In the second person imperative, the subject is understood and placed in parentheses:

Give me the eggs.

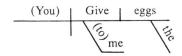

Simple sentence
(S)-verb-indirect object-direct object pattern

The interrogative sentence:

Where did she go?

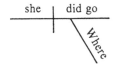

Simple sentence
Subject-verb pattern

The objective complement is separated from the direct object by a line slanting to the right.

The peasants elected Pablo mayor of Caramba.

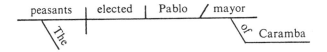

Simple sentence
Subject-verb-direct objective complement

The compound sentence:

Birds fly and bats swoop.

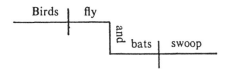

Or

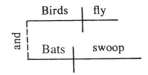

Give me the keys or I will be angry.

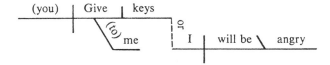

(S)-verb-indirect object-direct object pattern in the first main clause; Subject-linking verb-predicate adjective pattern exemplified in the second main clause.

The complex sentence:

Mary talked to whoever would listen.

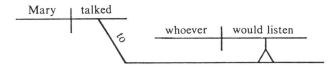

The noun clause, *whoever would listen*, is the object of the preposition *to*. Usually, the dependent clause is placed on a "ladder" to illustrate its dependency.

What Peter wanted was illegal and obnoxious.

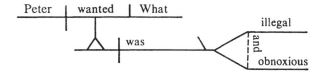

The noun clause, *What Peter wanted*, is the subject of the main clause.

The compound-complex sentence:

The girls who were waiting in the lobby laughed, and they joined us at the bar.

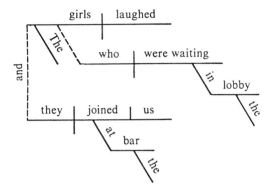

Diagramming verbals: the gerund.

Swimming is fun.

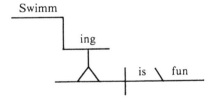

A gerund as the subject of a sentence

Swimming in the ocean can be dangerous.

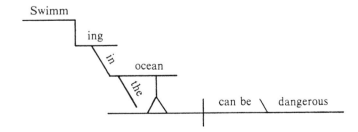

A gerund phrase as the subject of a sentence

I enjoy jogging.

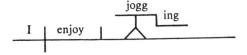

Gerund as direct object

The participle

Whispering softly, Peter caressed her trembling arms.

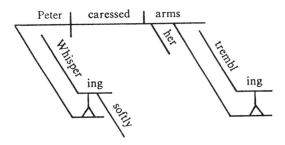

The infinitive

I have dishes to wash.

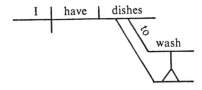

The infinitive *to wash* functions as an adjective modifying *dishes*.

Peter likes to go swimming at night.

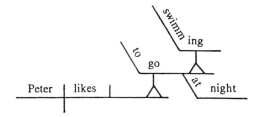

To go functions as a noun, the direct object of the verb *likes*. The gerund phrase, *swimming at night*, is the direct object of the infinitive *to go*.

Note: Remember that many colleges vary in diagramming styles, some being more artistic than others. Nevertheless, the basic procedures are similar.

_____■ Review ■_____

Exercise R1

Label the following elements as participial (par.), absolute (abs.), relative clause (rel.), or appositive (app.).

1. My favorite teacher, *Mrs. Smith,* has just received her master's degree.

2. The internal revenue service is investigating George Wilson, *a free-lance photographer from Gomorrah.*

3. *Her cheeks streaked with tears,* Betty ran out of the boudoir.

4. Jim went out the third-floor window, *screaming her name.*

5. *His homework finished,* Peter sighed, belched, and lit a cigar.

6. *Tired,* Paula went out to see a movie.

7. *Her wet hair wrapped around her head,* Paula finally went to bed.

8. *Crying for no apparent reason,* the baby finally threw up its milk.

9. *Searching for its breakfast,* the black insect spied a small fly *crawling over a flower.*

10. Going home for the holidays is fun, *not a bother.*

11. A merchant *borrowing money at ten percent interest* makes money on the cash *that he borrows.*

12. When the Persians were routed, the Greeks came down from the *rolling* hills.

13. They could hear nothing but echoes—*weary voices sighing across the tempest-tossed boats on the shimmering bay.*

14. There is a little dog *standing by the bushes.*

15. The valley was in chaos—dying men *lying on the earth,* weapons *scattered on the bloody grass,* horses *neighing with fear.*

16. *Her anger soaring,* Mary whipped the glistening horses into a *frenzied* rush along the road *that stretched north of the valley.*

17. Peter was a man *who had no scruples.*

393

18. Peter, *a man who had no scruples,* stole ten cents from his son's piggy-bank.

19. *Her lipstick smeared,* Zita stifled a sob and walked home.

20. In spite of her *bulging* eyes and buck teeth, Brenda is a pretty girl, *all things considered.*

Exercise R2

Punctuate the following sentences.

1. Samson lifted her body, caressed it and carried Luna out to sea.

2. I will nevertheless go on to fight this battle regardless of what you say.

3. A seducer of women Casanova was a magnetic person; handsome bold and clever.

4. I think you are nice, however, I am disappointed in your behavior at times.

5. The following items will be needed to prepare supper; potatoes, beans; salad; garlic and salt.

6. George Gingivities Ph.D. will be coming to the dance with Mary Halitosis his wife.

7. In 1839, Jesse moved his family to Cumberland Maryland on the banks of the silver Potomac.

8. Slowly surely inevitably Goobers prepared himself for his life's work; slumming.

9. "Hello Bill Do you have to work.

10. The following people applied for the position, Peter Peterson Ph.D. Mary Marietta R.N. Jody Johnson C.P.A. and Wilber Witless contractor.

Exercise R 3

Identify the underlined clauses as noun, adjective, or adverbial.

1. It was a time *when all men were concerned.* _____

2. *What she had to offer* was worth the effort. _____

3. Mother said *that she would come on Monday.* _____

4. I have a cousin *whose father is a doctor.* _____

5. I do not like *what she said.* _____

Exercise R4

Identify the following sentences as simple, compound, complex, compound complex.

1. It was a time when all men were concerned about the future. _____

2. What she had to offer was important, but rather expensive. _____

3. Mother said that she will come on Monday, but for us not to wait. _____

4. I have a cousin whose father is a doctor. _____

5. Rising with the morning tide, Peter laughed aloud, hoping to enjoy the bitter-sweet fruit of Laura's burning lips, lips of desire and eternal damnation. _____

Exercise R5

Correct the misspelled words in the following.

1. chiming	_____		6. receive	_____
2. biting	_____		7. valleys	_____
3. slopeing	_____		8. immediately	_____
4. seperate	_____		9. wierd	_____
5. grammer	_____		10. advertise	_____

Exercise R6

Answer the following questions on plurals and possessives.

1. the plural of Negro _____

2. the plural of potato _____

3. San Diego has two (zoo) _____

4. Give me ten cents worth of candy. _____

5. All the reflex of the patient must be studied. _____

6. The employees bargained for two weeks paid vacation. _____

7. The ladys hats were on sale. _____

8. The Smiths house is on fire. _____

9. Six attorney generals came to the conference. _____

10. I love Keats poetry. _____

Exercise R7

Determine whether the following prepositional phrases are adjectival or adverbial.

1. Are any of those students your friends? _____

2. Most of the movie was enjoyable. _____

3. Tommy was injured during the game. _____

4. The small dog swam to the raft. _____

5. Do they have cause for complaint? _____

Exercise R8

Using the key below, identify the part of the sentence that the participle modifies.

A—subject   D—predicate nominative
B—direct object   E—indirect object
C—object of the preposition

1. Dr. Hall spoke to the students gathered at the pool. _____

2. Give the boy washing the car more soap. _____

3. That is my girl combing her long, golden locks. _____

4. You will find your brother sitting at the bar. _____

5. Finding the assignment tedious, we went for a ride. _____

Exercise R9

Using the key given, identify how the gerunds are used.

A—subject   C—object of the preposition
B—direct object   D—predicate nominative

1. Giving speeches made George very nervous. _____

2. We found our dog after searching for hours. _____

3. Jody does his carousing after midnight. _____

4. Miriam's favorite hobby is watching soap operas. _____

5. Gambling at casinos is often expensive. _____

Exercise R10

Using the key given, identify the use of the infinitive.

A—noun   B—adjective   C—adverb

1. To avoid an accident, Peter walked home. _____

2. Margo has learned to drive carefully. _____

3. Mother has loads of clothes to iron. _____

4. Goobers used a ladder to paint the ceiling. _____

5. Politicians are men to watch. _____

Exercise R11

Using the key given, determine if the following are correct or incorrect.

A—fragment   B—fused   C—comma splice   D—correct

1. When the battle is over, and the men come home. _____

2. He did not know anyone at the party, he was lonely. _____

3. And I intend to remain at home. _____

4. Rome survived Hannibal, it still stands. _____

5. Deciding to go with Jack to the party. _____

6. When did she buy the new car? _____

7. The body is willing the mind is not. _____

8. Tired, exhausted, Richard sitting on the curb. _____

9. Athens fascinated the tourists. _____

10. Go. _____

11. Brut is a man's cologne I like it. _____

12. I am. _____

13. But she is quite unhappy. _____

14. Only a liar telling you that. _____

15. I panicked I called the doctor. _____

16. Meanwhile, I was getting some weird stares. _____

17. The jury came in, and it was hot in the courtroom. _____

18. Bill Snopes, cursing and spitting, watching them. _____

19. Declaring that he had returned all that his father
    had given him, and that he would have no father
    but God. _____

20. If you say so. _____

Exercise R12

The following sentences contain problems in grammar, usage, and diction. If there is an error, select the underlined part that must be changed by writing the letter in the space to the right.

1. Mary gave the money to one of the girls <u>who</u> <u>was</u>
                                                          a   b
   trying to work <u>her</u> way <u>through</u> college. <u>No error.</u> _____
                   c   d   e

2. <u>Between</u> you and <u>I,</u> the little boy <u>should</u> never <u>have been</u>
        a   b   c   d
   permitted to drink the beer. <u>No error.</u> _____
                               e

3. The employer <u>would like</u> to talk to <u>anyone</u> <u>who</u>
                             a   b   c
   <u>are going</u> to the business conference. <u>No error.</u> _____
     d   e

4. <u>Give</u> this food to <u>whoever</u> you feel <u>needs</u> to eat <u>it.</u>
     a   b   c   d
   <u>No error.</u> _____
     e

5. <u>In spite of</u> the danger, Mr. Pangloss <u>decided</u> against
        a   b
   <u>them</u> <u>going</u> to the site. <u>No error.</u> _____
      c   d   e

6. Linda <u>or</u> you <u>has</u> been selected <u>to give</u> the graduation
           a   b   c
   speech <u>on</u> commencement day. <u>No error.</u> _____
         d   e

7. Fifteen dollars <u>are</u> needed <u>to buy</u> the food <u>that</u> <u>will feed</u>
               a   b   c   d
   the dogs and the cats. <u>No error.</u>   _____
                         e

8. After <u>signing</u> the invoice, Pete <u>asked</u> for <u>who</u> the order
           a   b   c
   <u>was to be</u> delivered. <u>No error.</u>   _____
     d   e

9. Mary <u>decided</u> that she <u>either wants</u> to go now or <u>to wait</u>
           a   b   c
   <u>until</u> tomorrow. <u>No error.</u>   _____
     d   e

10. <u>If</u> she <u>was</u> <u>ill</u>, I <u>would call</u> the doctor. <u>No error.</u>   _____
     a   b   c   d   e

11. The student <u>could</u> <u>best</u> describe the old man <u>as a</u> sort
                 a   b   c
   of <u>a</u> bum. <u>No error.</u>   _____
     d   e

12. Richard <u>hadn't</u> hardly <u>time</u> to <u>complete</u> <u>his</u> essay.
            a   b   c   d
   <u>No error.</u>   _____
     e

13. Mary would not <u>have come</u> home <u>anyways,</u> <u>even</u> if we
                   a   b   c
   had wanted her <u>to do so.</u> <u>No error.</u>   _____
                d   e

14. Rita Grinch <u>was</u> the <u>most unique</u> person <u>that</u> I have
                a   b   c
   <u>ever</u> known. <u>No error.</u>   _____
     d   e

15. Pete Rose <u>played</u> more <u>than</u> <u>any</u> <u>other</u> player on the
              a   b   c   d
   team. <u>No error.</u>   _____
       e

16. <u>There</u> is no doubt <u>that</u> Betsy was the <u>more lovelier</u>
      a   b   c
    <u>than</u> the other girl. <u>No error.</u>   _____
      d   e

17. <u>As soon as</u> Ringo <u>completed</u> the song, <u>his</u> mother <u>has</u>
        a   b   c   d
    a stroke. <u>No error.</u>   _____
             e

18. <u>One</u> must convince <u>yourself</u> not to give <u>in to</u> the
      a   b   c
    pressure of drugs by <u>one's</u> peers. <u>No error.</u>   _____
                 d   e

19. A bag of cornflakes <u>were</u> <u>always</u> on the table <u>when</u>
                     a   b   c
    we <u>ate</u> our breakfast. <u>No error.</u>   _____
        d   e

20. The faculty <u>members</u> <u>taught</u> in <u>their</u> present building
               a   b   c
    <u>every</u> year for ten years. <u>No error.</u>   _____
      d   e

21. The <u>stunt</u> man <u>performed</u> his tricks <u>bravely</u> and
        a   b   c
    <u>with great speed.</u> <u>No error.</u>   _____
        d   e

22. A team of teachers <u>have</u> been <u>given</u> the document,
                      a   b
    which <u>is</u> to be <u>studied.</u> <u>No error.</u>   _____
      c   d   e

23. <u>Either</u> Janet or <u>I</u> <u>are going</u> to the conference to <u>discuss</u>
      a   b c   d
    the issues. <u>No error.</u>   _____
            e

24. I thought the girl <u>who</u> <u>cheated</u> on the test <u>was</u> <u>she.</u>
                      a   b   c   d
    <u>No error.</u>   _____
      e

25. Sue is <u>as angry</u> or <u>more</u> angry <u>than</u> her <u>sister.</u> <u>No error.</u> _____
             a   b   c   d   e

26. <u>Be</u> sure <u>and</u> study for the test <u>before</u> you <u>go</u> to the
    a   b   c   d
party. <u>No error.</u>   _____
       e

27. The <u>amorous</u> young man <u>asked</u> his girl, "Why not,
         a   b   c
Sue"? <u>No error.</u>   _____
   d   e

28. <u>Were</u> not happy <u>signing</u> this <u>piece</u> of paper, <u>nor</u> are
    a   b   c   d
we happy with the turn of events. <u>No error.</u>   _____
                            e

29. Mary told her father <u>that</u> she <u>neither</u> likes reading <u>nor</u>
                      a   b   c
writing. <u>No error.</u>   _____
   d   e

30. The doctor <u>assured</u> <u>Mary's</u> mother <u>that</u> everything
              a   b   c
would be <u>alright</u>. <u>No error.</u>   _____
         d   e

31. If I <u>was</u> <u>rich,</u> <u>I</u> <u>would</u> be a happy man. <u>No error.</u>   _____
      a   b   c   d   e

32. <u>Neither</u> of the girls <u>were</u> <u>going</u> to drive <u>home</u>. <u>No error.</u> _____
    a   b   c   d   e

33. <u>You're</u> studies <u>are</u> more important <u>than</u> <u>your</u> social life.
    a   b   c   d
<u>No error.</u>   _____
   e

34. George <u>or</u> John <u>has</u> been selected <u>to go</u> to the convention
         a   b   c
to represent <u>us</u>. <u>No error.</u>   _____
          d   e

35. My wife <u>admitted</u> that she <u>is</u> not <u>as</u> bright as <u>me.</u>
          a   b   c   d
<u>No error.</u>
   e

36. <u>Tired,</u> I <u>went</u> home, my dog <u>followed</u> me. <u>No error.</u>
    a   b   c   d   e

37. Boris is <u>as angry</u> or <u>more</u> angry <u>than</u> <u>his</u> father. <u>No error.</u> _____
   a   b   c   d   e

38. I <u>would</u> love <u>to go</u> swimming, <u>dancing,</u> and <u>to the game.</u>
   a   b   c   d
   <u>No error.</u> _____
   e

39. Be <u>sure</u> <u>and</u> feed the dog <u>before</u> you <u>go</u> to the dance.
   a   b   c   d
   <u>No error.</u> _____
   e

40. If the policeman <u>would of</u> been there, the accident
   a
   <u>would</u> not <u>have</u> <u>occurred</u>. <u>No error.</u> _____
   b   c   d   e

41. Mary <u>is</u> the <u>prettiest</u> of the <u>two</u> contestants <u>whom</u> we
   a   b   c   d
   have seen. <u>No error.</u> _____
   e

42. The policeman <u>displayed</u> great bravery, therefore, he
   a   b   c
   <u>was given</u> a citation. <u>No error.</u> _____
   d   e

43. <u>When</u> the girls <u>arrived</u> at the party, the band had
   a   b   c
   <u>already</u> left. <u>No error.</u> _____
   d   e

44. The <u>Smith's</u> house <u>is</u> the <u>prettiest</u> house in the
   a   b   c
   <u>neighborhood</u>. <u>No error.</u> _____
   d   e

45. Sally and <u>myself</u> <u>belong</u> to the <u>most</u> <u>exclusive</u> club in
   a   b   c   d
   the city. <u>No error.</u> _____
   e

46. Mary, give <u>this</u> food to <u>whomever</u> <u>needs</u> it. <u>No error.</u>
   a   b   c   d   e

47. There is a number of people who complain about
    a   b   c
almost everything. No error.   _____
   d   e

48. Regis was usually generous, courteous, and liked to be
                a   b   c
kind to his children. No error.   _____
            d   e

49. After entering the office, the typewriter was found by
    a   b   c
the secretary. No error.   _____
    d   e

50. Our teacher told us to refer back to the glossary.
    a   b   c   d
No error.   _____
   e

_____■ Glossary of Grammatical Terms ■_____

Absolute phrase An absolute phrase is usually a noun or pronoun followed by a participle. An absolute phrase modifies the statement as a whole: *The weather being good,* they decided to eat outdoors. *All things considered,* it is a good day for a picnic. An absolute phrase with a subject is called a nominative absolute: He watched her every movement, *his eyes searching every contour of her body.* The participle is sometimes omitted, but it is understood: *the dinner (being) over, we drove home.*

Abstract noun An abstract noun denotes a quality: love, beauty, glory, despair.

Accusative A seldom used word for objective case in English.

Active voice The form which states that the subject performs the action.

Adjective A part of speech which modifies a noun or pronoun.

Adjective clause A subordinate clause which modifies a noun or pronoun: I direct your attention to the girl *who is wearing only a smile.*

Adverb A part of speech which modifies a verb, an adjective, or another adverb.

Adverbial clause A subordinate clause used to modify a verb, an adjective, or an adverb:
> I followed her down the street *because she is pretty.*
> This is easier *than I thought.*
> Peter smiled more often *than the others did.*

Agreement Agreement is the correlation between a pronoun and the noun to which it refers, or a verb and its subject: We *are* (not *is*) going to the dance. Everybody should enjoy *his* (not *their*) bounties in life.

Alliteration The repetition of an initial consonant sound in two or more words:
> Silent Susie *sp*un a *sp*ool of *s*ilken *s*atin.

Antecedent The noun or pronoun to which a pronoun refers: The *boy* lost *his* gloves. (*Boy* is the antecedent of *his*.)

Appositive A word, phrase, or clause which renames identifies, or explains a noun or noun equivalent: My father, *a coal miner,* is eighty years old. (*A coal miner* is in apposition to *father.*)
> Peter had three things on his mind—*wine, women, and song.* (*Wine, women, and song* are in apposition to things.)
> Porky's goal in life—*that he would marry Petunia*—was shattered. (*That he would marry Petunia* is in apposition to *goal.*)

Articles Adjectives. The indefinite articles are *a* and *an.*
> The definite article is *the.*

Assonance The similarity of sound in a series of words or syllables stressing vowels: sigh—cry; die—lie; try—buy.

Auxiliary verbs (helping verbs) Auxiliary verbs are used to help another verb in producing tenses and moods:
> I *will* return.
> I *would* appreciate some dinner.
> I *shall be* returning.
> I *might have* been a better person.

Bibliography Literally, a "list of books," but the word has been converted incorrectly to include all other types of sources—periodicals, personal interviews, and so on.

Case Case refers to the forms that nouns or pronouns have to show their relation to other words in the sentence: nominative, possessive, objective.

Clause A group of words with a subject(s) and a predicate(s).
An independent clause is also called a main clause or a sentence.
A dependent clause has a subject and a verb which cannot "stand alone" or make a statement by itself.
The three types of dependent clause are noun, adjective, and adverb.

Collective noun A noun which denotes a group considered as a unit: team, faculty, mob, jury, staff.

Colloquial Informal or spoken English which is unacceptable in formal writing.

Common noun A common noun denotes a member of a general group. In contrast with proper nouns, common nouns are written in lower case letters: dog, year, street, girl.

Comparative degree/comparison The form of an adjective or adverb to indicate degree in quantity, quality, or manner between two elements. To form the comparative degree, add *er* to the root form (sweet, sweet*er*); use *more* (famous, *more* famous); or substitute words (good, *better*).

Complement To complete. A word or group of words that complete the meaning and structure of the predicate. A predicate (subjective) complement may be a noun a pronoun or an adjective which follows a linking verb and describes or renames the subject: He is *old*. (*Old* is a predicate adjective or subjective complement.)
Pete is the *mayor*. (*Mayor* is the predicate nominative/noun which identifies or renames the subject *Pete*.)
An objective complement is a noun or adjective which follows a direct object and completes the meaning of the sentence: The citizens of Dogpatch elected Elmer *mayor*.

Complex sentence One independent clause (sentence) and at least one dependent (subordinate) clause:
I laughed when she showed me her engagement ring.
What Pete did was foolish.

Compound sentence Two or more independent clauses. If a subordinate clause is in the structure, the form is *not* compound: I love Sue, but she detests me.
I came; I saw; I conquered.

Compound complex sentence Two or more independent clauses, and one or more dependent clauses:
Although I love Winnie, I know that I shall never have her, but I can still hope. What he said was foolish, but I agree with him.

Concrete noun A noun that names anything tangible or something that is capable of being perceived by the senses: dog, water, tea, song, rock.

Conjugation Inflectional changes in the form of a verb to show tense, mood, voice, number, and person.

Conjunction A part of speech that connects words, phrases, or clauses. There are three types of conjunctions:
Coordinate—*and, but, or, nor, for,* sometimes *yet* and *so*
Subordinate—*because, as, since, although.* . . .
Correlative—*both, and; either, or; neither, nor; not only, but also*

Conjunctive adverb A type of adverb that may also be used as a conjunction to coordinate main clauses: *however, therefore, consequently, hence, thus, moreover, furthermore, nevertheless. . . .*

Coordinate conjunction Of equal value or importance: *and, but, or, nor, for, yet, so*

Correlative conjunction Coordinate conjunctions used in pairs (see conjunction).

Declarative sentence A main clause which states a fact, a possibility, or a condition.

Declension The inflectional changes in the form of a noun or pronoun to indicate case, number, and person.

Demonstrative pronoun A pronoun which identifies, points to, or calls attention to: *this, that, these, those.*

Dependent clause A subordinate clause which does not express a complete thought in itself. The three types are noun, adjective, and adverb.

Direct object That which receives the action of a transitive verb: I hit the *ball*. (*Ball* is the direct object of the verb *hit.*)

Direct quote The exact words as written or spoken:
Paul said, "Give me the quarter you owe me, Joe."

Elliptical clause The deletion of a word or words from a sentence, usually understood from other words in the context of the sentnece:
When only six years old, I went to the circus.
When (I was) only six years old, I went to the circus.

Exclamatory sentence A sentence expressing strong feeling or emotion:
We finally made it!

Expletive A word that merely introduces a sentence or clause: *there, it.*
There she goes
It is snowing.
An expletive is not the subject of the sentence it introduces.
There she goes. (*She* is the subject. *There* is an adverb.)

Finite verb Full verbs in sentences and clauses:
I *came.* She *laughed.*

Gender The labeling of nouns or pronouns according to sex: masculine, feminine, neuter, and common (either sex).

Genitive a rarely used word which means possessive case.

Gerund A verbal noun that always ends in *ing:*
Swimming is fun.
I enjoy *swimming.*

Homonym A word with the same pronunciation as another word but with a different meaning: *boy, buoy; steal, steel; four, fore; dear, deer.*

Idiomatic The dialect of a region or class; the characteristic style of a writer. Idiomatic expressions are generally acceptable or standard in writing, but there are exceptions:
She caught my eye.

Imperative sentence Expresses a command or a request:
Go to the blackboard.

Indefinite pronoun A pronoun that refers to no distinct person, place, or thing:
someone, everybody, each, none, everything, nothing.

Independent clause (main clause, sentence) A complete sentence.

Indicative The mood of a verb which expresses a fact: ACC is an institution of higher learning.

Indirect object A noun or a pronoun which always precedes the direct object of a verb. Before an indirect object, the prepositions *to* and *for* are understood.
Mother fried *me* eggs (*Me* is the indirect object of *fried*.)
Mother fried eggs *for* me.

Indirect question The restatement of a direct question—without quotation marks.
Pete asked, "Who is going to the dance?" (Direct quote)
Pete asked who was going to the dance. (Indirect question)

Infinitive A non-finite verb form preceded by *to*. Usually, but not always, *to* is the infinitive marker. The infinitive may serve as the subject, as a complement, or as a modifier.
To earn money is not always easy. (subject)
We expected *to be called* for our reservations. (complement)
I bought a book *to read*. (adjective modifying *book*)
To avoid Karen, Pete left the dance early. (adverb)

Inflection A change in the form of a word to show its change in meaning or use.

Intensive pronoun A pronoun generally used immediately after its antecedent for more emphasis:
I *myself* shall slay the dragon.

Interjection A part of speech expressing surprise or emotion. It has no grammatical relationship to the rest of the sentence:
Wow! What a lovely girl!

Interrogative sentence A main clause which asks a question and is followed by a question mark.

Intransitive verb A verb without a direct object:
She laughed at him.
Peter sighed.

Irregular verbs Verbs which do not follow a set pattern in the formation of their principal parts, which are usually formed by changes in vowels: *drive, drove; lose, lost; shrink, shrank.*

Linking verbs (copulative verbs) A verb that joins its subject to a predicate noun or a predicate adjective: the "Be family" verbs and the verbs dealing with the five senses—*look, seem, sound, appear, become. . . .*

Modify To describe or limit.

Mood The manner in which a statement is expressed: indicative, subjunctive, and imperative.

Nominative The form of nouns or pronouns as subjects or predicate complements.

Non-finite (verbals) Non-finite verb forms cannot serve as predicates: gerunds, participles, infinitives.

Non-restrictive (interpolated) elements Single words, phrases, or clauses ordinarily set apart from the rest of the sentence by commas. Parenthetical (interrupting) elements should be set apart by appropriate punctuation.
George is, unfortunately, a friend of mine.
I intend to go to the dance, whether you agree or not.
The dog, following his master's example, ran to the tree.
We arrived, however, too late to take the test.
My cousin, a coal miner, lives on Bituminous Street, which intersects Anthracite Avenue.

Noun The name of a person, place, thing, or concept. Nouns are used as subjects, objects, or complements.

Noun clause A dependent clause which functions as a noun:
What the Greeks gave humanity cannot be measured in monetary terms.

Number The formation of noun, pronoun, or verb to show singular or plural construction.

Object That which receives the action of a verb; also, the noun or pronoun after a preposition.
Peter kissed Sue. (*Sue* is the direct object of the verb *kissed*.)
who, whom, which, that. . . .

Object(ive) complement A word used after a direct object to complete the meaning of the sentence:
I shall try to make my meaning *clear.*

Onomatopoeia A word which imitates the sound associated with the object or action involved: *whoosh, zoom, buzz, grr, rff, meow. . . .*

Participle A verb form used either as part of the predicate or as an adjective.
The present participle ends in *ing;* the past participle ends in *d, ed, n, en, t.*
I am going to the dance. The present participle *going* is part of the predicate.)
I have lost my favorite frog. (The past participle *lost* is part of the predicate.)
Her swimming suit is red. (*Swimming* is a present participle used to modify *suit.*)
Tired, I walked home. (*Tired* is a past participle modifying *I.*)

Passive voice The form of a verb which denotes that the subject is acted upon. In forming the passive voice, some form of the helping verb *to be* is used with the past participle:
The young woman *was* followed by the stranger.

Person The form of pronouns and verbs to denote the speaker, the person spoken to, or the person spoken about.

First person	I, we	laugh.
Second person	You	laugh.
Third person	He, she	laughs.
	It	laughs.
	They	laugh.

Phrase A group of words without a subject and verb.

Possessive case The form of nouns or pronouns indicating ownership:
The lady's hat is red.
The ladies' hats are red.

Predicate A verb or verb phrase which tells what the subject does, or what is being done to the subject—an action, condition, or state of being.

Predicate adjective
An adjective used after a linking verb:
He is *confident.*
She looks *bad.*
I feel *good.*

Predicate noun (nominative)
A noun or pronoun used after a linking verb:
Joyce is a *secretary.*
It is *I.*

Preposition A connecting word that relates a noun or a pronoun to another part in a sentence: *in, to, across, under, above, beneath, beyond, between, from, through.* . . .

Pronoun A word which is used in place of a noun: *I, you, he, she, it, they.* . . .

Proper noun The name of a specific person, place, or thing; proper nouns are capitalized: Walt Whitman Bridge, George Brett, Catholic, Easter, Tuesday, English, History 101. . . .

Reflexive pronoun A joining of *self* or *selves* with a form of personal pronoun, generally following a verb or preposition: *myself, himself, ouselves, themselves.*
I asked *myself* what I was doing in a nudist colony.
She often argued with *herself.*

Regular verbs The most common verbs formed by adding *d, ed,* or *t* to form the past tense and past participle: *ask, asked, asked; love, loved, loved.*

Relative pronoun A pronoun which connects an adjective clause to its antecedent: *who, whom, which, that.* . . .

Restrictive A phrase or dependent clause that limits or identifies. Internal punctuation is incorrect in setting off a restrictive modifier.
My sister is the girl *who is sitting closest to the window.*
(restrictive adjective clause)
My sister is the girl *sitting closest to the window.*
(restrictive participial phrase)
You will find his car *parked next to the fire hydrant.*
(restrictive participial phrase)
The book *with the torn edges* is my dictionary
(restrictive prepositional phrase)

Sentence (main clause, independent clause) A group of words that express a complete thought.

Sentence fragment A group of words that do not express a complete thought.

Simple sentence One main clause with a subject (simple or compound) and a predicate (simple or compound):
Birds fly.
Birds and bats swoop and fly.

Squinting construction A modifier (adjective or adverb) which, due to its ambiguous position in a sentence, can alter the meaning of the sentence.
I love *only* Joan.
Only I love Joan.
I *only* love Joan.
I love Joan *only.*
Each of the above sentences has a different meaning because of the placement of *only.*

Subject A person, place, thing, or idea about which a statement or assertion is made.

Subjunctive mood A verb form denoting a possibility, hope, wish, desire, or a condition contrary to fact:
I *wish* I *were* in Athens.
If she had remained, I *might have become* angry.

Subordinate clause Another term to denote dependent clause.

Subordinate conjunction Conjunctions which link dependent and independent clauses: *because, when, although, if, until.* . . .

Superlative degree Denotes the form an adjective or an adverb takes in comparing three or more objects:
>This is the *hottest* day of the year.
>This watch is the *least* expensive of the three.

Most adjectives form the superlative by adding *est* and *st.*

Synonym A word which means the same as another word, or a word which approximates the meaning of another word: *love, ardor; infatuation, passion.*

Syntax Logical word order; sentence structure.

Tense The time of action.

Tone A manner of writing that conveys the writer's attitude toward the subject, particularly concerning diction, style, and spirit.

Transitive verb A verb followed by a direct object:
>I hate spinach. (*Spinach* receives the action of *hate.*)

Verb Expresses action or a state of being:
>I *am.* (state of being)
>I *hate* eggs. (action)

Verbals Non-finite verb forms which cannot act as predicates: gerunds, participles, and infinitives.

Voice (active and passive) The quality of a verb which denotes whether the subject acts or is acted upon.

▬▮ Common Problems in Usage ▮▬

Words and phrases that are commonly misused in writing are frequently corruptions of form, confusions of meaning, or colloquialisms. The following list analyzes the most common errors in freshman writing. When in doubt concerning correct usage, consult a dictionary.

A/an
Use the article *a* when the next word begins with a consonant.
Use *an* when the next word begins with a vowel.
    A cow   *An* added incentive
    A dog   *An* unusual incident
Exception: if the consonant is silent, use *an*—*an* hour, a usual problem

Accept/except
Accept meant "to receive."
Except means "to leave out."

Advice/advise
Advice is a noun meaning "counsel."
Advise is a verb meaning "to recommend."

Affect/effect
Affect is usually a verb meaning "to influence."
Effect, as a verb, means "to accomplish."
Effect, as a noun, means "result."

Aggravate/irritate
Aggravate means "to make worse."
Irritate means "to cause discomfort."

A lot/alot/allot
A lot is a colloquial expression and should be avoided in written English; furthermore, it is two words, although frequently misspelled as "alot."
Allot means "to apportion."

All ready/already
All ready means "prepared" and refers to people or things.
Already means "by this time."

All right/alright
All right means that everything is acceptable or in order.
Alright is not acceptable in standard English usage.

All together/altogether
All together means as a "complete group and refers to people or things."
Altogether means "entirely."

Allusion/illusion
Allusion is an indirect reference or implication.
Illusion is a "false perception."

Almost/most/mostly
Almost means "nearly."
Most means "a majority."

Mostly means "primarily."
Note: Do not use *most all* in writing.

Among/between
Among is used in reference to three or more people or items.
Between is used in reference to two people or items.

And etc.
Redundant and not acceptable in standard composition.
Avoid *etc.* generally—except in technical writing.

Anyone/any one
Anyone is a pronoun similar to everybody, everyone.
Any one means "one of many."

As
Do not use *as* to mean *because* or *since:* I failed the test *as* I was tired. (incorrect) I failed the test *because* I was tired. (correct)

As far as
Without being followed by a verb, this phrase is clumsy.
As far as politics, I am a complete cynic. (incorrect)
As far as politics is concerned, I am a complete cynic. (correct)

Avocation/vocation
Avocation means a hobby or a diversion.
Vocation refers to one's business or livelihood.

Auto
A colloquial abbreviation for automobile.

Awful
An adjective which means "extremely bad" or unpleasant.

Awhile/a while
Awhile is an adverb which means for a short time; it is not preceded by *for,* although the noun *while* may be. Either of the following is correct: Stay awhile; stay for a while; stay a while. But it is incorrect to write "Stay for awhile."
A while is, obviously, two words and means "for a short time."

Because
A subordinate conjunction which should not be used to introduce a noun clause:
Because she loved him was why she married him. (incorrect)
She married him because she loved him. (correct)

Beside/besides
Beside means "next to."
Besides means "in addition to."

Bust/busted
Slang. Use *burst. Bursted* is archaic.

Can/may
Can implies the physical ability to perform a function.
May implies gaining permission to perform a function.

Cannot help but
Colloquial. In formal composition, *cannot help* is followed by a gerund.
I cannot help but think of you. (incorrect)
I cannot help thinking of you. (correct)

Can't hardly
Double negative. The correct form is *can hardly*.

Childish/childlike
Childish refers to the negative qualities of a child.
Childlike refers to the positive or finer qualities of a child.

Could of
Substandard. *Could have* is the correct form.

Credible/creditable
Credible means "believable."
Creditable means "praiseworthy."

Cute
A slang expression which should not be used in formal writing.

Data/datum
Data is the plural form for the singular Latin *datum*.

Differ from/differ with
Differ from means to be unlike someone or something in comparison.
Differ with means "to disagree."

Disinterested/uninterested
Disinterested means to be impartial, not swayed by selfish motives.
Uninterested means without regard or interest in a matter.

Elude/allude
Elude means "to escape."
Allude means to make an indirect reference or implication.

Emigrant/immigrant
An *emigrant* is someone who moves *out* of an area.
An *immigrant* is someone who moves *into* an area.

Equally with/equally as
Equally with is standard usage.
Equally as is incorrect.

Farther/further
Farther refers to geographic distance.
Further refers to degree *in addition to*.
I can walk no farther.
I can offer you no further extensions on your bill.

Gotten
The past participle of *get*. Both *got* and *gotten* are correct forms.

Gym
A colloquial abbreviation for *gymnasium*.

Had ought/hadn't ought
Neither form is standard in formal writing.

Hanged/hung
Hanged is tranditionally used in reference to executions.
Hung is the past tense and past participle of *hang*, which means to suspend
or to fasten from above with no support from below.
Big Nose Smith was *hanged* by the posse. (not hung)
My mother *hung* the drapes.
We will *hang the room* with curtains. (to furnish or decorate)

Hardly/scarcely/but

These words are negatives and should not be combined with a negative.

I couldn't hardly write my essay. (double negative)

I could hardly write my essay. (correct)

Height/Heighth

Height refers to elevation, the highest point, or stature.

Heighth is a misspelling.

Hisself

Incorrect for *himself.*

Incredible/incredulous

Incredible means unbelievable.

Incredulous means disbelieving, skeptical.

Ingenious/ingenuous

Ingenious means clever.

Ingenuous means innocent, artless, without sophistication.

Irregardless

Redundent for *regardless.*

Is because/is when/is where

Incorrect. Do not use an adverb clause as a predicate nominative.

its/it's/its'

Its is a possessive pronoun: The cat ate its food.

It's is a contraction for *it is:* It's my money.

Its' is incorrect usage.

Lead/led

As a noun, *lead* has multiple meanings and pronunciations.

They mined for *lead.* The runner has a giant *lead.* He will *lead* us.

Led is the past tense of *lead;* I know that she *led* in the primaries.

Leave/let

Leave means to depart.

Let means to permit.

Lend/loan

Lend is a verb: Lend me your pencil.

Loan is a noun: The bank refused my loan.

Liable/libel

Liable means legally obligated or "likely to have."

Libel is a malicious written or printed statement.

Like/as

Look at the words that follow *like* or *as* before deciding which to use. Generally, if the words form a clause, use *as.* If the words do not comprise a clause, use *like.* As a subordinate conjunction, *like* is overused and is referred to as colloquial. Nevertheless, do not avoid *like* as a necessary preposition.

Loath/loathe

Loath is usually an adjective meaning "unwilling."

Loathe is a verb meaning disgust or hatred for something.

Loose/lose

Loose means unconfined, unbound, free.

Lose means to misplace or be deprived of something.

Mad/angry
> *Mad* is a colloquial expression when it is used to mean angry or furious.

May be/maybe
> *May be* is a verb form meaning a possibility or likelihood.
> *Maybe* is an adverb meaning "perhaps."

Moral/morale
> As an adjective, *moral* means "ethical" or "honorable."
> As a noun, *moral* means "lesson."
> *Morale* means a mental condition regarding courage, a willingness to
> endure.

More/most/almost
> *More* is used in a comparison between two things.
> *Most* is superlative of *many* and is used for any number over two.
> *Most* should never be used in place of *almost.*
>> Most all of my friends are going. (incorrect)
>> Almost all of my friends are going. (correct)

Ms.
> Now acceptable as a title for a married or unmarried woman.

Nice
> An overused word with several meanings. Avoid using such vague words.

Not hardly
> A double negative. The proper form is *hardly*, meaning barely or not at all.

Of
> Not standard when used for *have* after helping verbs.
> *Would of, might of* are incorrect. The correct form is *would have, might have.*

Off of
> Redundant. The boy fell off of the boat. (incorrect)
> The boy fell off the boat. (correct)

Often times
> Superfluous for *often.*

Passed/past
> *Passed* is a verb, the past participle of *pass.*
> *Past* may be used as a noun or as an adjective.

Pass out
> A slang expression meaning to faint or to become unconscious.

Pep/peppy
> Slang for vigor or energetic.

Phone
> Colloquial for *telephone.*

Plenty
> Colloquial for "very."

Practicable/practical
> *Practicable* means that which can be put into practice, usable, useful.
> *Practical* means obtained through practice or action.

Pretty
> Overused as an adjective and as an adverb.

Principal/principle
As an adjective, *principal* means main or foremost.
As a noun, *principal* may mean a sum or money or the leading person.
Principle is always a noun meaning code, moral, doctrine, rule.

Quite/quiet
Quite is an adverb meaning completely, really, truly
Quite a is colloquial in phrases stating *more than a* or to a great extent: quite
a handsome man, quite a few, quite cold. Avoid overusing *quite.*
Quiet means silence.

Raise/rise
Raise is a transitive verb requiring an object.
Rise is an intransitive verb that requires no object.
    Raise the *Titanic.*
    Will you please rise when a lady walks into the room?

Real/Really
Real is an adjective meaning actual, in fact.
Really is an adverb meaning actually.
    I was real tired. (incorrect)
    I was really tired. (correct)

Refer back
Back is superfluous. Use *refer.*

Seeing as how
Incorrect. Us *since* or *because.*

Seldom ever/seldom if ever
Incorrect. Use *seldom,* meaning infrequently.

Set/sit
Set is generally a transitive verb meaning "to put" or "to place."
Sit is generally an intransitive verb meaning to place onseself in a sitting
position:
    Will you please sit down?
    He set the books on the desk.
Note: *Set* may be used intransitively: The moon set behind the hills.

Stationary/stationery
Stationary means rigid, unmoving.
Stationery means paper for writing purposes.

Than/then
Than is usually a conjunction used to introduce the second element in a
comparison.
Then is usually an adverb meaning soon afterward or next in time.

There/their/they're
There is an adverb.
Their is a possessive pronoun.
They're is a contraction for "they are."

Thusly
Archaic. Use *thus.*

To/too/two
To is a preposition and should be followed by an object.
Too is an adverb meaning "also" or excessively.
Two is the number.

Try and
   A colloquial expression for *try to.*

Very
   Overused. Find a more concrete word to intensify adjectives and adverbs.

Where at
   Redundant for *where.*

Whether or not
   Redundant. Use *whether* or *if.*

Who's/whose
   Who's is a contraction for *who is* or *who has:* Who's going to the dance?
   Whose is a possessive pronoun: Whose watch was stolen?

A List of Correction Symbols

Agr/pn — faulty pronoun-noun agreement

Agr/sv — faulty subject-verb agreement

apos — use the apostrophe for the possessive case

awk — awkward usage

Coh — coherence weak

C S — comma splice error

Dangl — dangling modifier

Frag — fragment

M M — misplaced modifier

Num — improper use of the Arabic number

Paral — parallel structure faulty

Pred — incorrect usage of the predicate

Ref — faulty reference

Rep — needless repetition

Sp — misspelled word

Trite — worn out expression

Wordy — too wordy; be concise

W W — wrong word

[ ] — delete

⊂ — close up the space

♂ — take out

⊙ — insert a period

⟨,⟩ — insert a comma

⟨;⟩ — insert a semicolon

⟨'⟩ — insert an apostrophe

(cap) — use a capital letter

∧ — insert item in the margin

¶ — start a new paragraph

no ¶ — no new paragraph

(tr) — transpose

(lc) — use lower case letter

▄ Index ▪